THE POWER TO CHANGE: ISSUES FOR THE INNOVATIVE EDUCATOR

*Edited by Carmen M. Culver and
Gary J. Hoban*

The concern for change in our schools, and for the processes effecting change, is paramount among American educators. A demand for the improvement of education on the one hand, and a welter of schemes for bringing it about on the other, leave the educator with two central questions: What changes should be made? and, How are such changes to be brought about? It is these basic questions which this volume attempts to examine through a collection of original articles, each with a different perspective, based on the work of the Research Division of the Institute for Development of Educational Activities, Inc. (|I|D|E|A|).

During a five-year period, |I|D|E|A| worked with the staffs of eighteen representative schools in southern California—elementary through junior high —to encourage them to attempt significant innovations relevant to their specific programs as well as to provide them with ways in which they might solve their own educational problems.

The contributors to this volume, each of whom actively participated in the projects, take the single school as the point of departure, the logical unit in which to develop improved schooling, examining the phenomenon of change from three basic points of reference: principal leadership, teacher power, and accountability. The range of articles includes discussions of research findings concerning the principal as a

|I|D|E|A| REPORTS ON SCHOOLING
JOHN I. GOODLAD *General Editor and Director*

EARLY SCHOOLING SERIES
assisted by Jerrold M. Novotney

SERIES ON EDUCATIONAL CHANGE
assisted by Kenneth A. Tye

THE POWER TO CHANGE: ISSUES FOR THE INNOVATIVE EDUCATOR

edited by
Carmen M. Culver
and Gary J. Hoban

Foreword by
Samuel G. Sava
Executive Director
|I|D|E|A|

A CHARLES F. KETTERING FOUNDATION PROGRAM

McGRAW-HILL BOOK COMPANY
New York   St. Louis   San Francisco   Düsseldorf   London
Mexico   Sydney   Toronto

Library of Congress Cataloging in Publication Data
Culver, Carmen M.
    The power to change.
    (|I|D|E|A| reports on schooling. Early schooling
series)
    "A Charles F. Kettering Foundation Program."
    Bibliography: p.
    1. School management and organization—United States—
Addresses, essays, lectures. I. Hoban, Gary J., joint
author. II. Title. III. Series: Institute for
Development of Educational Activities. Early schooling
series.
LB2805.C84   372.1'2   73-17118
ISBN 0-07-014890-2

|I|D|E|A| is the service mark for the Institute for Development of Educational Activities, Inc., an incorporated affiliate of the Charles F. Kettering Foundation.

|I|D|E|A| was established in 1965 to encourage constructive change in elementary and secondary schools. It serves as the primary operant for the Foundation's missions and programs in education.

As an institution committed to stimulating constructive changes for the benefit of mankind, the Kettering Foundation believes strongly in the potential of education to help bring about such changes.

Robert G. Chollar

President and
Chief Executive Officer
Charles F. Kettering Foundation

ACKNOWLEDGMENTS

Acknowledgments for permission to reprint selections from copyrighted material are as follows:

Patrick W. Carlton and Harold I. Goodwin, eds., *The Collective Dilemma: Negotiations in Education.* Copyright 1969 by Patrick W. Carlton and Harold I. Goodwin. Used by permission of Charles A. Jones Publishing Company.

Peter Coleman and Herbert A. Wallin, "A Rationale for Differentiated Staffing." Copyright 1971 by Peter Coleman and Herbert A. Wallin. Used by permission of Ontario Institute for Studies in Education

change agent, various techniques and studies geared toward encouraging teachers to become change agents and to share or to take over completely decision-making responsibility in the school, and the relationship of the accountability movement to innovation in education — to present change in the school as an organization, in the working relationships of principals and teachers.

|I|D|E|A| did not tell the schools what to change or what changes to bring about; rather, it attempted to help the schools establish a climate in which change would be possible, and it studied the processes by which such change took place.

Dr. Carmen M. Culver has been a teacher at the college level and has served as a consultant in various aspects of education. She is presently working on the evaluation of an Experimental Schools Project.

Dr. Gary J. Hoban is the Editorial Coordinator for the San Diego County, California, Department of Education. He has been a teacher and department chairman at the secondary school level.

em Help or Hinder?" Copyright
itional Education Association for

nge. Copyright 1968 by Lillian K.
pment of Educational Activities,

ity Boundaries." Copyright 1972
r and McGraw-Hill Publications

nsions of Teacher Leadership in
ne Gordon and Leta McKinney

a, A Proposal by Thomas White
. Used by permission of Instruc-

ight 1972 by Hulda Grobman.
cations Company.

yright 1971 by Roger T. Lennon.
Development in Education.

nterstate Project Conference on
1972 by Myron Lieberman. Used

ountability: Review of Literature
ht 1972 by the North Carolina
n of the North Carolina Depart-

d Effecting Change in Education.
. Used by permission of Citation

ional Manpower: From Aides to
L. Olivero and Edward G. Buffie.

opyright 1964 by Judson Shaplin
Row, Publishers, Incorporated.

Jacket design by John L. Horton

McGRAW-HILL BOOK COMPANY
1221 Avenue of the Americas
New York, N.Y. 10020

CONTENTS

FOREWORD

THE POWER TO CHANGE

This volume is part of a series reporting on the five-year Study of Educational Change and School Improvement conducted by the Research Division of the Institute for Development of Educational Activities, Inc. (|I|D|E|A|). |I|D|E|A| was established by the Charles F. Kettering Foundation in 1965 as its educational affiliate and given the specific mission of accelerating the pace of change in education. Before advocating yet another collection of "innovations" based on the best insights then available, we decided to begin by examining the total context in which change was to take place. Under the direction of Dr. John I. Goodlad, |I|D|E|A|'s Research Division selected 18 schools from 18 Southern California districts, the "League of Cooperating Schools," to participate in the design and testing of a new strategy for educational improvement. The several volumes now being published by McGraw-Hill report on the variety of human and organizational influences that operated within this new social system of schools.

The schools of the League were not committed to implementing specific innovations. Goodlad and his associates proceeded from the assumption that the individual school is the key unit for constructive educational change. Unless a critical mass of persons in each school seeks to identify pressing problems and reaches for appropriate solutions, not much is likely to happen. Therefore, they encouraged a free process of dialogue, decision making, action, and evaluation (DDAE) through which the faculty and other responsible persons might become increasingly responsive to their problems and possible ways of dealing with them. Over time, a kind of self-renewing ability developed.

This entire process was reinforced by membership in the League. Change is, at best, a difficult, lonely process. The League served as a mechanism for supporting change and reducing this loneliness. In effect, the League of Cooperating Schools became a new social system, encouraging change and innovation.

But there is no point in seeking to describe the full strategy or to report the research findings here. This is done in several of the volumes produced from the work of the Research Division and the cooperating schools. The present volume deals with an array of factors likely to strengthen or weaken the ability of the individual school to change. It was written with the intention of providing useful ideas to those who would seek to make the individual school an interesting, dynamic place for teachers and students alike.

All the authors were employed, at some time or other, by the Research Division of |I|D|E|A|. Several were among the three dozen or more research assistants who completed doctoral dissertations at UCLA during their period of employment. On behalf of |I|D|E|A| and the Charles F. Kettering Foundation, I wish to express gratitude to the school board members, school administrators, teachers, children, and parents who helped to make the studies and this volume possible.

Samuel G. Sava
Executive Director
|I|D|E|A|

THE POWER TO CHANGE: ISSUES FOR
THE INNOVATIVE EDUCATOR

INTRODUCTION

The concern for change in our schools, and for the processes which effect change, is paramount among American educators. A demand for the improvement of education on the one hand, and a welter of schemes for bringing it about on the other, leave the educator with two central questions: What changes should be made? and, How are such changes to be brought about?

It is in response to these questions that *The Power to Change* has been written. The authors of the several chapters comprising the book were members of the Research Division of the Institute for Development of Educational Activities, Inc. (|I|D|E|A|), an affiliate of the Charles F. Kettering Foundation.

During a period of five years, |I|D|E|A|'s Research Division studied the single school as the theatre for change, the logical unit in which to develop improved schooling. This is to say that the single school was seen as an organic whole, made up of parents and pupils, a professional team of teachers with a designated leader, and the necessary accouterments such as buildings, equipment, and materials. Although recognizing the existence of guidelines and aims determined by superordinate levels of control such as district, county, and state boards of education, |I|D|E|A| espoused the notion from the beginning of its studies that the power to change lies within the single school.

Thus, in discussing the questions of what changes should be made and how they are to be brought about, each writer in this volume takes the single school as his point of departure. Each brings to these questions his own unique perspective, however, as each played a different role in the study of the single school. An understanding of these varying perspectives is aided by a brief explanation of the two major projects with which |I|D|E|A|'s Research Division was involved, the Study of Educational Change and School Improvement (SECSI), and the Elementary School Appraisal Study (ESAS).

THE STUDY OF EDUCATIONAL CHANGE
AND SCHOOL IMPROVEMENT

This project had as its basic purpose to study the process of change as it took place in elementary schools which were attempting to improve in a variety of ways. That is, the SECSI staff did not tell the schools what changes to bring about; rather, it attempted to help the schools establish a climate in which change would be possible, and it studied the processes by which such changes took place.[1]

Three major assumptions guided the study. The first of these has been mentioned—the single school, with what John I. Goodlad has termed its "organismic wholeness," is the most strategic unit in which to develop improved schooling. Secondly, it was assumed that the principal can and should be the key agent for change in his school; that is, SECSI saw the proper role of the principal to be that of a leader—a person who maintains open communication with his staff and engages the staff in a cooperative approach to dealing with the problems and making the decisions necessary to bring about change in the school.

To say that the potential for change lies within the single school is not to say, however, that the principal and his staff can always bring about that change unaided. On the contrary, despite the cry for school improvement, the school is faced with many countervailing forces that inhibit the very changes which might bring about such improvement. SECSI saw the major force tending to inhibit change as the bureaucratic nature of school districts, with all the vested interests, gatekeeping, and power manipulation therein. For this reason, the Study took as its final assumption that some mechanism must be employed to assist the individual school to set improvement norms for itself, to gain support and rewards for abiding by these norms, and to enjoy some type of affiliation with schools having similar norms. Rather than searching for support for the school within the school's own district, SECSI created a new social system, with its own set of expectations and norms, designed to encourage innovative behavior. This new system was brought about by banding together eighteen elementary schools into what was called the League of Cooperating Schools.

These schools, each from a different Southern California district, were selected as a representative sample of American elementary schools. Thus, in the League consortium there were both old and new buildings, schools organized for nongrading and others organized for self-contained classrooms, new teachers and experienced teachers, principals skilled in leadership and others who knew very little about leadership, all-white suburban children and minority ghetto children. In short, the League was envisioned as a microcosm of schools and educational problems of the United States, so that most principals and teachers in the country would be able to identify with at least one of them.

The strategies used by the SECSI staff were designed to help the League schools to bring about changes which the schools themselves wished to effect and to increase the importance of the League as a reference group for its members. Initially, SECSI provided help to the schools in a variety of ways. Sessions designed to help each school staff develop skills of communication, decision making, and problem solving were offered, along with reading materials, films, expert consultants, and the like to provide information about possible innovations. As time went on, however, there was a gradual movement toward increased involvement of principals and teachers in planning and carrying out their own innovations, as well as in carrying out their own intra-League activities.

The League, then, helped to provide support to each of its members as they searched for their own ways of improving their schools. To study the *process* of change as it took place in each school, SECSI developed a communications model, know as the *Dialogue, Decision making, Action,* and *Evaluation* model, or *DDAE.* Although no League school was making the same kinds of substantive change as any other school, all were undergoing the change process. Thus, all the school staffs had in common the fact that they were engaging in dialogue concerning changes, were arriving at decisions, taking some sort of action to implement these decisions and evaluating both the process and results. The DDAE model therefore provided SECSI with a means for studying the process undergone by each school, regardless of the kinds of change each was attempting. This model, as well as other aspects of the SECSI Study and the League project, is discussed in various chapters in this volume.

THE ELEMENTARY SCHOOL APPRAISAL STUDY

ESAS was a second major project undertaken by |I|D|E|A|'s Research Division. The staff of this study shared with that of SECSI the assumption that the single school is the logical unit for change. Shared also was the notion that it is the school staff itself which must engender and carry through its own attempts to change. In addition, as in the SECSI study, it was recognized that in order to deal effectively with its own problems, the typical school staff needs to develop skills of decision making and problem solving. However, in contrast to SECSI, which had created the League as a mechanism for helping to promote such skills, the ESAS approach lay in the development of an extensive self-help program. This program, which is designed for implementation by the single school without the aid of consultants, consists of a package of materials and activities whose purpose is to help the staff to become both more systematic and more collaborative in its approach to problems which the school encounters.[2]

THE POWER TO CHANGE

As the foregoing description of these two projects implies, the contributors to this volume do not answer the question of what changes should be made in the school by espousing particular pedagogical techniques or specific educational programs for children. They speak instead of changes to be made in the school as an organization, in the working relationships of principals and teachers. Their answers to the question of how such changes can be brought about vary as they discuss the functions of principal leadership, describe principals and teachers who experienced change, examine the role of teachers, and explore an issue to which the concerns about change in the school are intimately tied—accountability.

Principal Leadership

That the principal should take responsibility for the leadership of his school may seem to be an obvious assumption, and yet, as Jerrold Novotney points out in "The Integration of Education and Leadership," the true leader is a rare commodity in our schools. Out of an ignorance of the nature and the functions of leadership and a preoccupation with the management and maintenance of the schools, we have trained principals to be not leaders, but administrators. What, then, is a leader? Novotney answers this question through an examination of the efforts of the many researchers who have sought to define the dimensions of leadership.

What is the difference between a leader and an administrator? Kenneth Tye explores this distinction in "The Elementary School Principal: Key to Educational Change." He points out that although it is the business of the principal as administrator to follow established policy and see that his staff does likewise, the role of the principal as leader is to organize himself and his school for planned change, to create in the school an atmosphere in which the processes of decision making and problem solving necessary for bringing about change can be shared with the staff. The principal is the key because it is he who creates the climate in which productive change becomes possible.

In Chapter 3, "The Power of the Principal," Ann Lieberman examines further the assumption of the principal as key by exploring the question of whether or not the behavior and attitudes of the principal influence the behavior and attitudes of the teachers in his school. That is, if the principal is in fact the most significant leader in the school, then it would be reasonable to assume that his influence would be evident among those whom he leads. Lieberman tested this question by asking more than 700 teachers in thirty-one elementary schools to describe their principals in terms of a variety of leadership characteristics. Next she questioned the teachers to determine how their perceptions of their principals seemed to influence morale and teachers' attitudes toward their profession. Finally, she asked pupils to rate the teachers themselves in the same terms in which teachers had rated their principals, in order to discover the extent to which teacher behavior and attitudes mirrored those of their principals.

Lieberman found much to substantiate the assumption that the principal can be the key agent for change in the school when he plays the role of leader (as Novotney and Tye have defined leadership); that is, she found that when the principal shares decision making with his staff and when he involves himself and the teachers in organizing the school to deal with its problems, the teachers respond with higher morale and greater professionalism. Under such leadership, then, teachers become more willing to engage in the processes of bringing about fruitful change in the school.

Principals and Teachers in Transition

As we have seen, to study the processes involved in bringing about change in the school was a major objective of SECSI. "Rational" change models would have it that change is brought about by the institution of prescribed steps: goals are selected, means for achieving these goals are implemented, and progress is assessed. Not so, say

Ann Lieberman and David A. Shiman in "The Stages of Change in Elementary School Settings." They present a number of case studies to illustrate a very different pattern of change, one in which actions precede the setting of goals. In observing League schools, these authors saw that school staffs passed through definable stages of dialogue, experimentation with an innovation, and subsequent questioning of the value of that innovation before they were ready to establish new goals for change. In this chapter, Lieberman and Shiman also examine a number of schools in which the change pattern was never completed and conclude that to succeed, changes in the school must be supported by those most intimately involved—not just the principal, but the teachers and the parents as well. They also conclude that district support aids the adoption of innovations in the school. Thus, although a temporary system such as the League of Cooperating Schools can be instrumental in providing the impetus for change, change is most successfully effected when *all* levels of the individual school's own system support its efforts.

Although a temporary system, the League nevertheless did function as a mechanism for providing support to its member schools. "Working Together: The Peer Group Strategy" describes the gradual emergence of the League as a social system. The authors of this chapter focus upon SECSI's efforts to create and implement strategies for strengthening the League and discuss the dawning realization that if the SECSI staff expected teachers and principals to behave in new ways, it, too, must adopt new behaviors. If the League was to develop as a decision-making body whose members valued one another as sources of information and support in their efforts to adopt productive innovations, then the SECSI group must abandon the traditional interventionist role of "telling the schools what to do." Just as the principal and teachers of each school, and the collective staffs of all the League schools, had to learn to work together, so the SECSI staff had to learn to work together with them.

The Role of Teachers

Although it may fall to the principal to maintain leadership of the school, teachers have their own role in the change effort, for without their support and active involvement no meaningful change can be brought about; and as Culver, Shiman, and Lieberman report in "Working Together," teachers can exercise powerful peer leadership in their own right. Roger Rasmussen and Adrianne Bank explore this point further in "Mobilizing Group Resources for School Problem Solving." The authors maintain that feelings of vulnerability to criticism both from within and without the school, a sense of powerlessness in the face of tight district control and student rebellion, and the problems of time, space, and money have impeded the development of group resources within the school. So, too, has the fact that many school staffs lack the group skills necessary for effective task-oriented collaboration. Drawing upon their experiences with the ESAS study, the authors describe the many ways in which the use of teacher groups can strengthen the school and suggest a variety of steps to be taken in removing the impediments to the development of such resources.

Although Rasmussen and Bank point to teachers' feelings of vulnerability and powerlessness as a source of problems, Samuel Christie maintains that, quite the contrary, it is the growth of teacher power which potentially imperils the school. In Chapter 7, "Beyond Teacher Militancy: Implications for Change Within the School," Christie traces the recent history of teacher strikes and resultant negotiations at local and national levels to illustrate the point. Indeed, as Christie points out, the conflict between teachers and administrators can tear the school apart, as in some cases it has. The problem of trust between teachers and administrators is real, and to the extent that the problem is denied it does have the potential for destroying the school. But this need not be the case. Christie advocates changes in the organizational structure of the school as an answer to the conflict. Agreeing with Tye and Lieberman that the principal still has the power to influence the climate of the school, Christie calls upon the principal to abandon his traditional authoritarian role in favor of accepting conflict as legitimate and engaging his staff in open dialogue, cooperative decision making, and the taking of actions which can bring meaningful change to the school. He also calls upon teachers to accept with an openness of their own the responsibility of sharing with the principal the task of building better schools.

Gary Hoban is less optimistic in his view of the outcomes of teacher militancy. In "The School Without a Principal," Hoban argues that recent conflicts, in concert with a number of other factors, have only heightened an awareness that teachers and principals are in two different camps. The teachers, says Hoban, view the principal as an authoritarian figure and thus eye him with suspicion. The principal, meanwhile, has been socialized to administrative norms, with concerns and problems which are different from those of the teachers. Furthermore, the principal who would share decision making with his teachers is in a difficult position, for it is he alone who will be held accountable for those decisions. Hoban, then, suggests that the conflict between teachers and principals creates a gap too wide to be bridged, even by the schemes of organizational development and cooperative functioning advanced by other writers in this book. He calls instead for a total restructuring of the school, in which the principal would work himself out of a job, as his previous duties became absorbed by a differentiated staff of teachers.

The Question of Accountability

Although the issues of decision making and the locus of power within the school may remain open, it is becoming increasingly clear that there is another issue with which all schools, regardless of their organizational structure, must be prepared to deal. This is the question of accountability, a topic which looms large in education today. In "Accountability: Fact, Fiction, or Farce?" Jerrold Novotney discusses the major elements of this complex issue. He notes that the confusion and controversy about accountability are evidenced by the many definitions and the multiplicity of suggestions for implementation which a host of educational associations, governmental agencies, and individual educators have advanced.

The single school, then, is confronted with demands, and in some cases with legislation, calling for accountability; yet the question of for what it is to be held accountable has not been fully answered, the procedures for carrying out the necessary processes have not been defined, nor have the skills for engaging in those processes been specified.

Concern with the viability of the single school in the face of these difficulties informs the final chapters of The Power to Change. In "Toward a Definition of Teacher Accountability," Kenneth Tye focuses upon the need for a clear statement of the school's obligations as a basis for its accountability. He delineates the responsibilities of the various levels of the educational system, pointing out that principals and teachers can legitimately be held accountable for schooling only to the extent that they are given the wherewithal to do their jobs. For example, while the school may be held responsible for the implementation of effective educational programs, it must have the cooperation of the society in setting the goals on which these programs are based.

One way in which the school can exercise its power with regard to the accountability issue is to develop the expertise necessary to determine goals and evaluate its own performance in attaining them. In "An Institutional Evaluation System," Irene Frieze discusses the importance of involving the community served by the school in the establishment of goals and describes a number of techniques whereby these goals can be determined. She then explores methods which the school can employ to assess the effectiveness of new programs instituted to meet determined goals and explains how the use of these methods can result in a continuous process of ongoing evaluation in the school.

Yet another way in which the single school can meet the challenge of accountability is to arm itself with information concerning its functioning as an organization. Through the use of instruments as described by Bette Overman in "Criteria for a Good School," the school can gather the data it needs to direct its own self-renewal and thus become less vulnerable to directives from without. The CRITERIA instrument which Overman describes grew out of the desire of the League schools for a reliable means of determining what changes should be made in their operations. Prepared by League teachers and principals in concert with the SECSI staff, the instrument deals with the processes of dialogue, decision making, action, and evaluation (DDAE) described earlier, as well as with the climate and effectiveness of staff meetings and the role of the principal and the teachers. Overman describes the CRITERIA instrument in detail and provides instructions for its use.

Like most public school principals today, League principals were alert to the accountability controversy. Working with Richard Williams, of |I|D|E|A| and UCLA, they engaged in a systematic review of various proposals for accountability, seeking a scheme that could be implemented in their schools. They wanted a plan which, while comprehensive and workable, did not limit the freedom of their schools to be innovative. When the search proved to be a vain one, the League principals derived their own model, which Williams describes in "A Plan for an Accountable School District." The principals based their plan upon the assumptions that no one school organization or program will be appropriate for all children, that parents differ in their preferences for educational programs and should be allowed to choose from among several alternative schooling models, and that school districts will prosper from the existence of a variety of schooling plans. Noting that parental disapproval of various innovations has resulted in bland, "homogenized" programs which will offend no one, but which no one finds totally satisfactory either, the principals reasoned that the provision of alternative pedagogical models within a district would free each school to develop fully its own program while providing parents with a choice. The chapter outlines the responsibilities of each level of the educational system in the plan.

This last chapter brings together in several ways the notions concerning change which are presented throughout the book. It demonstrates the viability of the single school by noting that each of the districts containing a League school was able to tolerate, and in many cases benefit from, that school's uniqueness. It emphasizes the need for principals and teachers to work together cooperatively to bring about productive changes in the school, and it acknowledges that when the school recognizes its own organic quality, it does indeed have the power to change.

The chapters which compose *The Power to Change* provide a variety of answers to the questions of what changes should be made in the school and how these changes are to be brought about. These are not the only answers, nor have the writers of this volume abandoned the search. The reader wishing to join in the pursuit will find ample provision in Lillian Drag's Bibliography on the Process of Change, which completes this book.

Carmen M. Culver

NOTES

1 The story of the SECSI study is told in Mary M. Bentzen and Associates, *Changing Schools: The Magic Feather Principle*, McGraw-Hill, New York, in press.

2 Samuel G. Christie, Adrianne Bank, Carmen M. Culver, Gretchen McCann, and Roger Rasmussen, *The Problem Solving School*, Institute for Development of Educational Activities, Dayton, 1972.

CHAPTER 1

THE INTEGRATION OF EDUCATION AND LEADERSHIP

Jerrold M. Novotney

During the period that |I|D|E|A| was conducting its studies of school improvement and elementary school evaluation, Jerrold Novotney served as assistant director of the Research Division and special assistant to the dean of the UCLA Graduate School of Education. In this chapter, Dr. Novotney reviews the general aspects of leadership and their relationship to effective group processes. In particular, he identifies the essential qualities needed by leaders and the activities engaged in by leaders as they strive to bring about innovation in the schools. Novotney's comments thus set the stage for other chapters in this volume which provide a variety of responses to the question of the locus of power for bringing about change in the individual school.

Everybody has thought and written about leadership: military men, journalists, politicians, novelists, dramatists, poets, feminists, financiers, physical scientists—everyone, for indeed leadership as a ubiquitous aspect of interpersonal behavior, is the concern of every man and woman.[1]

Educators are conspicuously absent from the above listing. This may or may not have been by design, but it serves to underline a problem. For the most part, educators have been so preoccupied with administering our schools that they have given little attention to our leadership needs. Teachers and administrators have been trained, but we have not made an attempt to train leaders. The result is that the American educational scene faces a critical shortage of leaders capable of helping teaching personnel and concerned citizens to focus their efforts on the better education of children, of leaders who are aware of the traditions of the past and who have an imaginative grasp of the future. We have not trained leaders because, as our present training programs suggest, a large segment of the educational community does not understand the nature of leadership or its functions.

No one will argue that understanding alone will guarantee fruitful activity, but it is certainly a step in the right direction. I shall attempt here to bring to the foreground some relevant facts about leaders, leadership, and groups as culled from various behavioral science sources, plus some additional thoughts that fall out of my own conceptualization. The hope is that some people within the educational community may be helped not only to understand but also to apply this knowledge in their own leadership activities and to explore seriously the creation of new programs in educational leadership training.

LEADERS AND LEADERSHIP

Man is by nature a social being and as a consequence seeks out the companionship of others. The fulfillment that cannot be found in self is sought through group association. Nevertheless, because human beings vary so much in physical and intellectual endowment, in every gathering of men, regardless of size, certain individuals seem to come forth spontaneously to influence others. When one examines the power structure among members of such groups, it is customary to speak of the individual possessing the most power or influence as "the leader." In some groups, he is called "the boss" or "the supervisor"; the remaining members are his followers or his subordinates. Because of his perceived dominance, members—consciously or not—look to the leader for guidance and direction.

From earliest times leadership has been an integral link in the relationship of one human being to another. In a democratic society, such as ours, leadership boils down to being a process concerned with stimulating and aiding groups to articulate common goals and to devise voluntary means for moving toward them. This, however, is no simple task. The process may call upon a leader to provide facts and ideas to help his group intelligently define and reach objectives. If his attempts are successful, his leadership contributes to the realization of his people's creative capacities and ultimately increases their desire to expend energy purposefully. The more complex society has become, the greater has grown the need for human fulfillment and consequently for competent leadership.[2]

As a process, leadership is dynamic. In whatever kind of group a leader operates, he faces similar tasks and has need of the same basic orientation and understanding of his role as well as insight into the potentialities of the group he is leading. He must be able to recognize the problems that the group confronts for what they are. He must judge whether their solution falls within group capabilities or outside its range. Group members in turn look to the leader for recognition as individuals and for treatment in accord with their own self-concept. It falls to the leader to mold the group into a solidarity that will bring about not only the desired ends of the group as a whole, but of the individuals as separate entities as well.[3]

Over the past fifty years, the importance of leadership has been gradually recognized—particularly in business and government. In the search for an explanation of the phenomenon of leadership and for better ways of identifying potential leaders, many studies have been carried out. Generally, these have been of three kinds: (1) those concerned with the traits of the leader; (2) those concerned with the situation in which leadership acts take place; and (3) those concerned with the forces bearing upon leaders. Although these studies leave many questions unanswered, their findings have created a more than adequate data bank which can help delineate the parameters of good leadership.

Studies of the physical, intellectual, and personality traits of leaders and followers have generated lists of traits seeming to make for good leadership. The problem is, however, that the lists are far from identical. Only 5 percent of the traits listed in over 106 such studies have appeared in four or more studies.[4] Other observations indicate that personal qualities common to leaders in varying situations exist not only in leaders but also in persons who never actually seek out or achieve leadership status. The conclusion seems to be that although leaders do possess patterns of traits, there is no justification for saying that traits or personal qualities *alone* account for, much less explain, leadership.

These findings tended to discourage researchers from seeking the answer to leadership in traits alone. Instead, they began to look at leadership as a function of the social situation, particularly as that situation interacts with individual personalities. From such interaction, there seem to arise what are commonly called leader "attributes." Researchers have abstracted from a total interactional situation those leadership qualities which are defined by a particular social role. This does not mean that there cannot be potential leaders. It does seem to indicate, however, that their potential cannot be directly known or forecast outside of the particular social situation that calls it into being.[5] Again, the solutions arrived at do not seem to be completely satisfying.

Since many variables apparently enter into the production of leaders, another tack has been to look at the forces which influence leaders as they emerge. This approach is in a sense an amalgamation of the two just mentioned but deals more directly with group processes. It recognizes that motivation by personal drives is important but that people sometimes find themselves in leadership positions as a result of group needs of which they may or may not be aware. The conclusion drawn is that the internal drives in combination with the external forces cause leaders to emerge in order to perform any of four major functions: a symbolic function, a decision-making function, a dispensing function, and a plan-initiating function. The pressure within the group for such leadership acts arises from the group's need to deal with problems connected with achieving goals or achieving greater cohesion as a group. This point will be treated in greater detail as we proceed. Suffice it to say, however, that this approach has failed also to produce definitive answers to the leadership query.

Even though individual studies have taken various routes, common to much that has been done are the conclusions that (1) although a leader often possesses characteristics which seem to have a causal relationship to his peculiar status position within the group structure, possession of these qualities alone does not guarantee leadership activity; (2) leaders come forth to dominate a group partially because the nature of the situation within which individuals are attempting to operate appears to demand it; and (3) external forces and personal drives interact and coalesce under group pressure and are either limited or freed by group influences to cause an individual to take up a leadership role and perform the leadership acts the group needs to function.

Perhaps the most important finding of all leadership research has been that leadership is multifaceted; it encompasses not only the concepts of leader and follower, but all aspects of group life and group management. This means that we cannot talk about a leader or about leadership without also talking about the group that is led.[6]

THE GROUP

Human culture with all its aberrations and variations is still a group culture. We tend to live in groups, we belong to groups, we work in groups, we play in groups. The solutions to most of our problems are found in group living. Many of us find security and satisfying experiences among other people like ourselves. In groups, we can divide our labor and thereby increase our skills, the efficiency of our production, and the supply of our goods.

Americans in particular accept group activity without question. We consider it normal and efficient to solve a problem by first appointing a committee and then calling a meeting. Our democratic orientation (backed by research, I might add) leads us to believe that collective cogitation will produce superior results. In such a cultural setting, the origin of most groups can be traced to a felt need. Groups congregate as a result of tensions which demand action.

Group life, however, is not always successful. In too many instances, failures can be traced to a lack of understanding of group organization, group production, and group processes.[7] To be effective, groups must be able to reconcile the competitive and cooperative forces of group life. A competitive spirit containing elements of self-assertion and degrees of emotion is an integral part of group interaction. However, even though the objectives of that assertion and emotion may be the achievement of group goals, successful group living demands acceptance of individual differences and an allegiance to the group-set standards of service and fair play. The common cause must serve to motivate the group to rise above controversies and individual striving for success.[8]

As a group forms, it must develop some kind of inner structure, be it ever so frail or immature. The early stages of group life may see prolonged periods of internal trial and conflict. The group may possibly become impotent and die. On the other hand, group members may discover and follow productive practices which cause the group to grow rapidly to maturity. Three elements play a significant part in the maturation process: a common group task, the individual, and the interpersonal relationships among members.

If a group of people are to work as a unit, there must be a center of involvement. This will be supplied by the task to be done or the problem to be solved or even the common experience to be enjoyed. Such a central focus serves as a basis for generation of group objectives. Of equal importance are the personal needs each individual brings to the group. Individuals usually join a group because in it or through its leader they anticipate finding the means to satisfy particular needs of their own. Resignation usually follows the perception that a particular group has ceased to offer such means.[9] These needs may include a need to belong, a need for social recognition, for participation, or simply a need for the emotional support that a group can give. The individual may also bring certain problems for which he is seeking solution. He may simply need someone to listen to him. But regardless of kind, personal needs must find legitimate expression and satisfaction. These elements, without a doubt, make for a complex situation, but their satisfactory integration is essential if the group is to function well.[10]

Groups generally expend their energy on two kinds of work. The first job is to solve the problem with which the group is concerned; the second is to build, strengthen, regulate, and perpetuate the group as a group. These have been referred to as the "problem-solving" and the "process" functions in group life. The attainment of the second, the creation of trust and cohesion among members, will radically affect the accomplishment of the first. A feeling of being accepted and of accepting must be generated by members as they work, think, and feel together, if they are to struggle successfully with a real problem.[11]

A leader truly distinguishes himself when he manages to create a climate in which such acceptance is possible. Here again the complexity of the leadership role is demonstrated. Group climate is really the sum total of group member feelings, attitudes, and perceptions. The creation of the most advantageous climate involves setting the stage so that circumstances will facilitate constructive interaction among group members in a communicative atmosphere. To achieve such an end requires that a leader be aware of and responsive to member feelings, attitudes, and perceptions. This, in turn, assumes he has some diagnostic skills which enable him to determine how each member reacts to a given situation. Underlying the leader's effectiveness is the creation of a two-way flow of influence from leader to others and from others to leader. Such a process must aim at, and to a large degree result in, group interactions which generate group thought, group initiative, group responsibility, and ultimately, group action.[12]

Three types of group climate have been identified and labeled: (1) anarchy—every person does just as he pleases, with the expectation that everyone else will be so tolerant and considerate that no one will be in another's way; (2) autocracy—everyone is forced to do what the leader desires; (3) democracy—the middle-of-the-road approach. Whereas anarchy provides no leadership as such, and autocracy provides almost negative leadership, democracy seeks to provide positive leadership. To the American mentality, the democratic atmosphere would seem generally to be most desirable. But it would be incorrect to assume that there is no place, even in democracy, for independent activity or external control. Most group atmospheres tend to be a combination of the three, rather than the pure form of any one.[13]

Clearly, group climate has a vital effect on group accomplishment. Where the atmosphere is one of tension, where the members are afraid to say what they think, communication barriers are erected which tend to isolate group members from one another and to immobilize group activity. Research findings emphasize that an atmosphere of trust and security is absolutely necessary for reaching group goals. Mutual confidence and respect are essential; each member must feel free to express himself openly on any vital issue. If each can be motivated to listen with a genuine desire to understand another's point of view, even though it may differ from his own and that of the majority, real progress can be made in establishing operating norms that lead to personal satisfaction and ultimate levels of group productivity.

LEADERS AND GROUPS

Leaders simplify or complicate group life. Sometimes they make groups uncomfortable by their passivity; at other times they cause irritation by their assertiveness. Nevertheless, regardless of whether or not members are completely satisfied, the leader has a role which he must maintain. In his hands lies the key to the whole pattern of group operation, and he often controls the "group temperature." Members of a group react to a leader's behavior. They do not necessarily react in the same way, but all will react.[14] In careful and accurate reading of the subtle indications of group reaction, a leader finds his most important task. He must be able to diagnose group process ills by arranging his random observations into a meaningful pattern. He will foresee difficulties. He will be able to prescribe workable remedies.

A good leader, therefore, is unavoidably concerned with both the accomplishment of group tasks and the process orientation. Simply stated, he must be aware of both the ends and the means of group activity. When a leader has been chosen by a group of people who already have a goal or objective in mind, the leader's task is usually not too complicated. When appointment has come from an outside source or from self-election, however, the leadership task becomes considerably more complex. In either case, group members must perceive the leader to be working toward acceptable goals (whether or not he actually is) in a way which will satisfy the needs of the group. This may take some doing, but it is absolutely necessary if the leader is to get the group to move forward. Whether a leader has been chosen because of his ability, because there simply is no one else, or even because at the moment he appears to be the lesser of two evils, the task facing him will remain the same.[15]

Ultimately, a leader's major concern is to increase group maturity. The maturity spoken of here is closely related to accurate self-evaluation. Groups must be helped to evaluate the actual and potential contributions of members in the light of whether or not these contributions help in getting the job done well. This assessment, in turn, requires an understanding by the group of its common goals and purposes. Thus the leader must help the group to distinguish accurately between its long-range and its short-range objectives. It falls to the leader to help the group get accurate and pertinent information in order that it may diagnose its own position, locate barriers within its operation, and determine the resources available to it. The principal means of accomplishing such data collection is through active participation of group members. In fact, as group maturity develops, leader-centered activities should decrease. In a mature group, leadership will not inhere continuously in any one person. Typically, a mature group will delegate different leadership functions to subgroups so that leadership is exercised by a team or by those recognized as resource persons rather than by any one individual.[16]

LEADERSHIP ESSENTIALS

As can be gathered from what has already been said, the way in which the leader is perceived by his followers is more important than the way in which he actually behaves. A leader must be perceived as symbolizing the values and purposes of the group or organization he leads. The group must see some relationship or some obvious tie between themselves and the one designated to lead. If group members perceive a leader to be too different from themselves, they will feel that he cannot represent them properly, that communication with him will be too difficult. This does not imply that a leader cannot be better than the group members, but rather that he must be better in a way that is perceived as acceptable.

Effective leaders exhibit the ability to identify with an organization and its purposes. This means that a leader must be what psychologists call emotionally involved in a group—it is a part of him.[17] Dedication of this kind results in his giving the attention and help that are so necessary to attainment of the objectives sought by the participants in any group activity. The danger in such situations, however, is that personal interests may become mixed with devotion to the organization. Where this occurs, the result is generally traumatic. A leader cannot afford to build himself at the expense of the group. Generally, members will be quick to perceive that the leader is taking advantage of them. Morale tends to plummet, and group relationships deteriorate. Eventually, the only needs being met are those of the leader, and in the absence of coercive force, followers will tend to pursue other avenues to satisfy their needs.

A leader must be a person of foresight. Concern for the future of the group is vital. The average member is usually concerned with the here and now. The leader's plans, on the other hand, must include the long-range perspective of how the group will continue to meet the needs of its members or how to overcome future difficulties that may keep the group from achieving its purposes. In short, a leader must be alert to anticipate events and alternatives. He will be able to take steps to overcome forces which threaten the security or the effectiveness of the group or, possibly, even to use these forces to the advantage of the total group movement.[18] Seeing a situation in much broader perspective than the average group member, leaders are able to make interpretations that help to encourage others and to involve them more deeply in group activity.

Leaders, more than others, seem to have an innate drive to get things done. A certain anxiety arises from an unfinished job or an unmet goal that goads them on to the completion of a task or the solution of a problem. But the effective leader does not permit his drive for accomplishment to block delegation of authority. He knows that where power is most widely shared and distributed, the greatest advances will be made. Sharing of power promotes deeper member involvement and an opportunity to enhance member ego strength. This, in turn, results in greater commitment to the group and its task.

Leaders characteristically differ from other people in their willingness to assume responsibility, to take initiative, to plan and to carry through the tasks that need to be done, but a willingness to accept responsibility suggests an acceptance of the possibility of failure as well as the possibility of success. For this, one must be willing to give up a measure of personal freedom and if necessary invest considerable personal energy. To lead may actually require a good deal more time and energy than to follow. Leadership frequently turns out to require considerably more than what one expected.

Most leaders are able to tolerate a greater degree of tension than others. Tension is tiring, and organizational tensions frequently are accompanied by frustration and hostility. Together, these are the greatest threats with which a leader is faced. The ability to maintain a positive spirit and to stand firm in the face of hostility is generally not a natural skill; it must be cultivated. The same is true for tolerance of isolation. As an individual steps out from the crowd to lead, he immediately becomes more visible. Attack is easier not only from the forces he confronts but also from those he is trying to lead. Because he has in a sense come to occupy the pinnacle, like it or not he is apart from the group. Such a position can be devastatingly lonely at times.

Communication skills are closely correlated with successful leadership and are basic to its interpretative function. The objectives of any group are not always succinctly stated and require articulation so that members will easily see in which direction the group must move. Although goals and means may have been arrived at through group decision making, their effective articulation is the leader's responsibility. In addition, a leader must often spell out clearly the means to be utilized for the achievement of goals so that unity of action may occur.

In summary, several generalizations about leadership are possible. Leaders are more deeply involved in a group or organization than the other members. Leaders are more concerned with power and seek to create a productive climate for group work. They symbolize or represent the values that the group holds important. They seem to have greater ability to tolerate tensions. They are superior in their ability to communicate. Their drive for accomplishment serves the common group goals. They are able to assume responsibility to plan and carry out tasks and to delegate and share authority where appropriate.[19]

TRAINING FOR EDUCATIONAL LEADERSHIP

Most people in positions of power in education today have learned what they know about being leaders from watching other educators in action or simply from their own experience. The problem is that when a leader learns by trial and error, he easily can misinterpret his own experience or learn the wrong lessons from those whom he observes. He may acquire skills, information, and possibly even tricks or gadget know-how, but he rarely acquires enough insight into what he is confronting to permit him to manipulate the variables successfully. Knowing the mathematical intricacies of the state formula for allocating funds or the subtleties of Supreme Court decisions may be important for some, but it is hardly of aid to the local school superintendent or principal who today—either by choice or necessity—spends the greatest portion of his time dealing with "people problems" of one kind or another. This is not to say that knowledge of school finance and school law are of no consequence, but it *is* to say that the time spent in traditional training programs on these kinds of things has not produced in proportion to the investment. Unfortunately, most graduate schools turn out relatively competent technicians rather than well-rounded educators prepared to provide innovative leadership.

Part of the problem also lies in the process by which we have traditionally selected individuals to fill positions of importance in our school systems. Underlying our methods of employee advancement has been the assumption that to be a "good" principal, an individual has to have been a "good" teacher, or to be a "good" superintendent one had to be a "good" principal. Few have questioned this assumption, largely perhaps because we have done little to analyze and clearly delineate the knowledge and skills needed today by school personnel not only to survive but to render true leadership. Yet, question it we must. There is nothing in educational research literature that clearly correlates teaching experience with innovative leadership or even with highly successful administration. If history shows us anything, it points to the fact that classroom expertise salted with traditionally required graduate courses and seasoned by years of experience fails to generate consistently good educational leadership. We may be far better off to let the proficient teacher remain in the classroom and reward him adequately for what he does well. Our leadership recruitment would perhaps be more satisfactorily accomplished in the world of sociology, psychology, or business.

Given our present situation, however, if leadership is indeed a multidimensional phenomenon involving individual personality characteristics, job demands, role definitions, the satisfaction of personal needs, and the organizational context in which leadership is expected to occur, then close scrutiny must be given to these factors as they relate to the educational world.

As far back as thirty years ago, a psychologist, Fritz Roethlisberger, talked of industry as both an economic enterprise and an intricate social complex. Hardly anyone has yet to clearly determine the nature of the educational "beast." Most certainly, it has its economic side. It is perhaps the largest financial undertaking currently under way in our country, and any board member, superintendent, or even legislator will testify that education is a heavily charged political entity. The immensity of its social impact is difficult to quantify. Few would suggest that the present system should be totally eradicated. With all of this, the strange thing is that we really know so little about what schools in fact do or about what it takes to supply leadership to guide the system's destiny through these fast-changing times. What is desperately needed is a thorough study of the school and the system of which it is a part on a national scale. In the absence of such a study, however, we must assume that the principles of leadership talked about earlier are equally operative in and applicable to the school and its setting. Thus, a curriculum of educational leadership training would seek to train people (1) to understand leadership theory and its relationship to the educational enterprise, (2) to test the applicability of leadership and group research findings in the environs of the school and classroom, (3) to synthesize new leadership techniques to suit the idiosyncrasies of the educational complex, (4) to analyze ongoing educational undertakings for the purpose of bettering their leadership structure, and (5) to lead in the introduction of educational change where necessary.

These objectives imply a rationale for a new kind of training which would embody at least three broad categories of knowledge: one concerned with human interaction, another with organizational operation, and the last with education as an idiosyncratic entity. Carried further, the following framework emerges to map out necessary areas of knowledge upon which specific educational experiences might be built.[20]

1   Human interaction
   a   Intrapersonal: the knowledge concerned with individual awareness and assessment of self
   b   Group: the knowledge of how human beings mold and regulate group life
   c   Organization: the knowledge associated with the interaction of individuals and groups in institutional arrangements
   d   Community: the knowledge of social group interaction in a communal arrangement
   e   Culture: the knowledge of human interaction as it affects and is affected by cultural patterns

2 Organizational operation
   a Problem solving: the knowledge embodied in the theoretical foundations of problem solving and decision making
   b Change topography: the knowledge of all aspects of change theory and research findings
   c Process implementation: the knowledge of theory which contributes to the delineation and facilitation of administrative processes
3 The idiosyncratic dimension
   a School organization: the school as unit, the district, state, and federal involvement
   b Curriculum: theory behind its development, research and evaluation
   c Guidance: personnel policies and problems, plus the theories underlying various approaches
   d Educational research: pertinent problems to be confronted and attacked
   e School plant: philosophies guiding the match of physical settings to instructional programs
   f Major issues: an examination of the present in relation to future needs and projections.

A curriculum built upon such a framework, fleshed out under the auspices of the educational community and implemented in our training institutions, would go a long way toward meeting our current need for leadership. Given a careful selection process to identify individuals with innate ability and demonstrated commitment to the improvement of education, we could within a relatively short time look forward to a new generation of dynamic and resourceful educational leaders.

NOTES

1 Luigi Petrullo and Bernard M. Bass, *Leadership and Interpersonal Behavior,* Holt, Rinehart and Winston, New York, 1961.
2 Gordon McCloskey, *Education and Public Understanding,* Harper & Row, New York, 1959, p. 251.
3 Lawrence K. Frank, *How To Be a Modern Leader,* Association Press, New York, 1954, p. 15.
4 R. M. Stogdill, "Personal Factors Associated with Leadership: A Survey of the Literature," *Journal of Psychology,* vol. 25, 1948.
5 Paul Hare, Edgar Borgatta, and Robert Bales, *Small Groups: Studies in Social Interaction,* Knopf, New York, 1955, p. 89.

6 C. G. Browne and Thomas Cohn, *The Study of Leadership*, Interstate, Danville, Ill., 1958.

7 Malcolm Knowles and Hulda Knowles, *How To Develop Better Leaders*, Association Press, New York, 1955, p. 1.

8 Hare, Borgatta, and Bales, op. cit., p. 16.

9 Browne and Cohn, op. cit., p. 5.

10 O. F. Peterson, *Leadership in Action*, National Training Laboratory, Washington, 1961, p. 27.

11 D. M. Hall, *Dynamics of Group Discussion*, Interstate, Danville, Ill., 1961, p. 3.

12 Robert R. Blake, Herbert A. Shepard, and Jane S. Mouton, *Managing Intergroup Conflict in Industry*, Gulf, Houston, 1964, p. 6.

13 Hall, op. cit., p. 5.

14 Herbert Thelen and Dorothy Stock, *Understanding How Groups Work*, Adult Education Association, Chicago, 1956, p. 8.

15 Browne and Cohn, op. cit., p. 9.

16 Peterson, op. cit., p. 20.

17 Henry Lindgrin, *Effective Leadership in Human Relations*, Hermitage House, New York, 1954, p. 40.

18 Ibid., p. 141.

19 Ibid., p. 151.

20 Adapted from material originally presented by the author in "Training to Lead: A Rationale," *Journal of Business Education*, January 1967.

CHAPTER 2

THE ELEMENTARY SCHOOL PRINCIPAL: KEY TO EDUCATIONAL CHANGE[1]

Kenneth A. Tye

Kenneth Tye has had a long involvement with the problems of the public school administrator. A former elementary school principal with a degree in administration from UCLA, Dr. Tye worked with principals throughout the five years of the League project.

This chapter highlights the central leadership role of the principal as he aids his faculty in preparing for and engaging in the change process. It is Tye's view that meaningful innovation in the school has the greatest chance of success if the principal is capable of creating an appropriate climate for change by facilitating communication, sharing decision-making power, managing conflict situations, and expediting problem-solving activities.

It almost goes without saying that the role of the elementary school principal is changing. There are new pressures being applied every day. State legislatures are calling for more accountability on the part of the principal and his staff, whatever that means. The community is asking for parity in decision making, whatever that means. Teachers are demanding more power, whatever that means. Above all, everyone seems to be suggesting that we decentralize, whatever that means.

There is one common denominator among all these demands for accountability, parity, power, and decentralization—that of educational decision making for change.

In studying the question of change in the school, we at |I|D|E|A| arrived at a variety of findings, many of which are discussed elsewhere in this volume. Perhaps the most important of these is that which has to do with the principal himself. We feel safe in generalizing that the principal can be a key agent for change in his school when he assumes the mantle of *leader* rather than that of *administrator* and when he organizes himself and his school to deal with the human processes involved in change.

Unfortunately, most principals have been trained as administrators rather than as leaders. The distinction, while subtle, is significant if the principal is to meet the demands of contemporary society. The role of the administrator is to accomplish established goals through the utilization of established means. The principal who can be judged as the best administrator is the one who can follow established policy and procedure and make others do likewise.[2]

The role of the leader, on the other hand, is to find and initiate new means to reach established goals or to formulate with the staff new goals for the school. How does the principal organize himself and his school for planned change? The behaviorists, the technocrats, the systems advocates—and they hold sway today—maintain that the key lies in planning. The way to heaven, used synonymously with planned change, is in preparing large charts with lots of boxes. In each box is listed something to do, an event. Each event, of course, is put in a time perspective. By going from one box to the next, one can easily see how we reach our goal, whether it be the completion of the SST, the Rolls-Royce aircraft engine, the rocket that will take us to Mars, or an improved school. The only problem with this approach is that people somehow have a way of wiggling out of boxes.

ORGANIZING FOR PLANNED CHANGE

Let me suggest another way of organizing for planned change. For lack of a better term, let me call it the "people approach" or better yet, "Happiness is what you do *with* other human beings, not *to* them."

Self-understanding

Perhaps the most important place for a principal to begin organizing for planned change is with himself. Suppose, for example, that a principal were to give himself a short true-false test on the following statements:

_____1   People need to be inspired or pushed or driven.

_____2 People need to be told, shown, or trained in proper methods of work.

_____3 People naturally resist change; they prefer to stay as they are.

_____4 People need to be released and encouraged and assisted.

_____5 People who understand and care about what they are doing can devise and improve their own methods of doing work.

_____6 People naturally tire of monotonous routine and enjoy new experiences; everyone is creative.

Perhaps the answers to these questions are obvious. Perhaps they are not. A principal who answered "false" to the first three statements and "true" to the last three, probably would be a leader whom Douglas McGregor would refer to as a "Y."[3] That is, he would believe that if people (in our case, teachers, parents, and children) are treated as responsible, independent, understanding, goal-achieving, growing, and creative individuals, they will become so.

The point, of course, is not that our principal had the right or wrong answers. It is, rather, that he knows where he stands with regard to those with whom he works. Further, it is that he attempts to make his behavior or "style" consistent with what he believes. "Know thyself," while it may seem a trite statement, is probably a good place to begin in organizing for planned change.

Climate

Once the principal knows where he stands he can move to establish a climate within his school.[4] (1) He can be formal and impersonal toward those with whom he works. In this case, policies and regulations become important. (2) He can emphasize goal attainment. In this case, he sets direction and lets others know what is expected of them. (3) He can be an example. In this case, he himself works hard and assumes that others will follow his example. (4) He can develop an esprit within the staff. In this case, he is very "human" and attempts to meet as many of the staff's needs as possible.[5] (5) He can be any combination of these things, as appropriate, utilizing policies and regulations, setting direction, being an example, and working for esprit, all as conditions or needs dictate.

The point, of course, is not that the principal is an authoritarian individual, is democratic, or is laissez-faire. The point is, rather, that he knows his people and his circumstances and, subsequently, determines and sets the climate that best allows those with whom he works the opportunity to perform their tasks.

There are those behavioral scientists who suggest that the main purpose of any organization is to provide good work for those it employs. Although we at |I|D|E|A| might not go that far, we would suggest from our data that in those schools in which the climate is open and in which the principal balances his initiation and consideration behaviors, more school improvement does occur.[6]

Communication

A major contributing factor to an open climate within an organization is the pattern of communications established by its leader. We have found that good communications are open, face-to-face, and two-way whenever possible, particularly when important matters are involved. (Unimportant matters can be relegated to memoranda.)

Listening, of course, is an important part of good communication. We communicate to others through our words and our nonverbal behaviors. Because perceptions differ among people, often the message which we intend to send is very different from that which others receive. To keep communications open, it is valuable to check such perceptions. Instruments such as those discussed by Bette Overman in "Criteria for a Good School" can be of value in testing one's perceptions of what people say as well as communication patterns. At the same time, it is wise to realize that more communication takes place through informal channels than through formal ones. The alert principal can gather a great deal of feedback in the coffee room or in the school corridor.

Communication with parents is of special importance in changing schools. Positive sanctions from advisory councils or PTA Boards are helpful. Tours, coffee klatsches, explanatory meetings, opinion surveys, evaluation reports, and newsletters are all means which, when used during the initial stages of change, reap great benefits during later stages, particularly if problems in the school should arise later.

An example of meaningful communication is evident in the case of one League district which recently passed its tax election with an over 80 percent favorable vote. Beyond the school's excellent program, such a vote can in good part be attributed to the fact that each principal has anywhere from 50 to 150 parent volunteers working in his building.

Conflict Management

Often, schools which attempt to change find themselves involved in various kinds of intergroup conflict. Conflict may arise from a lack of clarity with regard to role and task accomplishment definitions, or it may arise because of differences in values, philosophies, or perceptions. The typical administrator tends to suppress or avoid such conflict, assuming that it will go away. Suppressing conflict, however, usually results in some type of confrontation at a later date. And, because the conflict has been suppressed, the confrontation may result in irreparable damage to the organization.

When the climate and the communication system of a school are open, conflict of ideas can lead to new and better ideas. In such a setting, the principal can move in early, assisting others to talk through their differences, and head off damaging confrontations, converting them instead into opportunities for airing and examining differences in point of view while still maintaining a common purpose.

Decision Making

Griffiths suggests that the effectiveness of a leader is inversely proportional to the number of decisions which he must personally make concerning the affairs of the organization.[7]

In League schools, principals have come to believe that teachers should make *all* instructional decisions, since they are the ones who have the appropriate data about pupils. Such decisions include those about one's own role, instructional objectives, learning opportunities, materials, time, space, and classroom organization.

As a leader, the principal has a threefold responsibility in decision making: he monitors instructional decisions made by teachers, he serves as a facilitator for their decision making, and he acts as a transactional agent between and among levels of decision making.[8]

As a monitor, the principal sets forth procedures which will assist teachers. For example, if teachers wish to organize into an instructional team, the principal might advise them to (1) read what scholars and informed practitioners have written on the subject, (2) become familiar with the experience of other schools, (3) develop a long-range plan, and (4) pilot-test aspects of the plan.

As a facilitator of decisions, the principal provides the time, space, and atmosphere wherein instructional decisions can be made. He also serves as a resource person by knowing what information is available, which consultants are appropriate, where visits can be made, and so forth.

As a transactional agent, the principal transacts among instructional personnel or teams in such matters as time, space, materials, and paraprofessional personnel. He involves community members and interprets the school program to them. He informs teachers of policy decisions and institutional decisions of boards and districts which influence their instructional decisions. Conversely, he informs the district of teachers' decisions.

It is perhaps within such decision-making structures and processes that reside what we in education are truly seeking—professionalism and appropriate modes of decentralization.

STAGES OF PLANNED CHANGE

We at |I|D|E|A| do not believe that people naturally resist change. Rather, we believe that they go through various stages of behavior which ultimately lead them to the adoption of an innovation.[9] By being aware of these stages, by knowing where individual staff members are in terms of these stages, and by knowing what activities he himself can engage in as a facilitator for staff members, the principal can continue to move innovations forward and avoid individual resistance.

Initially, people become aware of a new idea. The principal can create such awareness or promote it with an article, book, film, speaker, and so forth. When an individual or group moves from awareness to active interest and information seeking, then the principal can provide more information. At this stage, a teacher from another school in which the idea has been utilized can be a valuable resource.

Once people have gathered sufficient information, they begin in their minds to evaluate the utility of the new idea for themselves. It is at this point that visits to successful programs in nearby schools can be of most value. If the idea is found to be worthwhile, people will want to test it. At this time the principal must provide in-service training through the utilization of appropriate resource personnel.

After the innovation has been adopted and integrated into the ongoing program, the principal will continue to assist by providing necessary services such as time, space, materials, and personnel. He will also give encouragement and serve as a transactional agent, translating the new program to parents, the district, and other staff members.

Such stages, although not rigidly prescribed, are important. Most of our change efforts which fail, and these are countless, result from our efforts to try something new without consideration of the human necessity to become aware, to become interested, and to evaluate.

PROBLEM SOLVING

Earlier in this discussion, some fun was poked at the systems people with the reference to boxes. Actually, the case was overstated. We *do* need rational problem-solving processes, and systems planning is a valuable tool. The danger occurs in those situations where change is planned at the top levels and then imposed downward. We at |I|D|E|A| are convinced that people change more easily when such change helps them to solve problems which are real to them. The principal should encourage his staff to use rational problem-solving procedures. The universal problem-solving model generally utilizes the following kinds of procedures:

1 Identifying a problem which has real relevance for the group
2 Defining the problem, its scope, and its implications
3 Considering a number of alternatives for solving the problem
4 Selecting one alternative for testing
5 Testing the alternative; keeping records of its results
6 Evaluating the results of the test in terms of its success in solving the problem
7 Recycling

Usually such a procedure is not employed by those of us in education. Instead, we tend to change by selecting one new alternative and installing it, whether it be a new instructional practice, new curriculum, or new organizational pattern. In many instances it fails. Although there are many possible reasons for such failure, one significant reason is our failure to use a scientific approach in solving our problems.

Problem solving is a difficult, often intense, time-consuming activity. Most educators have not truly been involved in it. The change-agent principal who wishes to create an atmosphere of scientific problem solving in his school should start by helping to identify problems which are real to the group, which are as nonthreatening as possible, and which are as well-defined as possible. He should keep his "antennae" up for real problems. At times, what appear to be problems are really only symptoms of more significant problems. Complaints about pupil behavior, for example, are symptomatic of a problem. Often, the problems reside within the school program itself.[10]

The staff which can utilize rational problem-solving procedures need have no fear of such things as accountability, PPBS, decentralization, or planned change.

CONCLUSION

This well may be the *decade of the principal*. Bureaucratic district structures and state and federal intervention have not markedly changed American education. Those of us at |I|D|E|A| strongly feel that we have demonstrated that the single school with its principal as leader *is* the setting for effecting significant educational change.

Well over 80 percent of the resources of education are vested in human beings. It is our feeling that the principal who invests his efforts in human activities such as self-understanding, setting a climate, building communication structures, managing conflict, clarifying decision-making roles, paying attention to each individual's capacity for change, and implementing problem-solving procedures will be the principal who will be a successful leader.

We at |I|D|E|A| believe that people are good, capable of commitment, capable of caring about their work, and open to change. The principal who develops a committed, caring, and open staff will find that these conditions carry over to pupil learning.

As John Gardner says about our capacity for growth and change: "Unlike the jailbird, we don't know that we've been imprisoned until we've broken out."[11] It is this challenge that is left with today's principals. Let's break out!

NOTES

1 Adapted from an address delivered to the Washington Elementary School Principals' Association, Spokane, Oct. 18, 1971.

2 James M. Lipham, "Leadership and Administration," in *Behavioral Sciences and Educational Administration*, Sixty-third Yearbook of the

National Society for the Study of Education, Part 2, University of Chicago Press, Chicago, 1964.

3 Douglas McGregor, *The Human Side of Enterprise*, McGraw-Hill, New York, 1961.

4 Andrew W. Halpin and Don B. Croft, *The Organizational Climate of Schools*, Midwest Administration Center, University of Chicago Press, Chicago, 1963.

5 Ibid.

6 For a more detailed discussion, see Ann Lieberman, "The Power of the Principal: Research Findings," Chapter 3 in this volume.

7 Daniel E. Griffiths, *Administrative Theory*, Appleton-Century-Crofts, New York, 1959.

8 For a good discussion of the role of the principal in decision making, see Donald A. Myers, *Decision Making in Curriculum and Instruction*, Institute for Development of Educational Activities, Dayton, 1970.

9 Adapted from Everett M. Rogers, *Diffusion of Innovations*, Free Press of Glencoe, New York, 1970.

10 A program for developing rational problem-solving procedures has been developed by Samuel G. Christie, Adrianne Bank, Carmen M. Culver, Gretchen McCann, and Roger Rasmussen in *The Problem Solving School*, Institute for Development of Educational Activities, Dayton, 1972.

11 John Gardner, *Self-Renewal*, Harper & Row, New York, 1964.

CHAPTER 3

THE POWER OF THE PRINCIPAL: RESEARCH FINDINGS

Ann Lieberman

During the five years of the League of Cooperating
Schools project, Ann Lieberman played an active role as
a liaison between the |I|D|E|A| research staff and the
eighteen League schools. Out of her involvement with
principals and teachers grew the study reported here. The
study viewed the single school as a social system and addressed the question of how much power the principal
has to influence this system. Teachers were asked to rate
their principals in terms of a variety of leadership qualities. These findings were then correlated with measures
of teachers' attitudes toward each other and toward
teaching as a profession, as well as with pupil perceptions
of teachers' own leadership styles, in order to determine
the influence of the principal's behavior on teacher attitudes and behaviors.

From these findings, a series of composite pictures
of principal leadership styles emerged, and the conclusion
was reached that through their handling of leadership,
principals do indeed influence the social system of the
school.

Leadership in large-scale organizations has fascinated researchers for
a long period of time. Conceptions of leadership have changed from a
concern with personality characteristics[1] to the effects of leadership
on morale and productivity.[2] The study of leadership in the school as
an organization presents different problems than the study of leadership in factories, hospitals, or the military. The goals of schools, as
opposed to those of such other organizations, are diffuse and hard to
define; therefore, the role of leadership is made quite complicated. In
the school, satisfactions come not from creating and seeing a specific
finished product, but rather from detecting sometimes subtle clues

that the pupil is growing and learning.[3] The complexity of leadership in the school is heightened by the fact that learning does not take place in an isolated state but instead appears to be influenced by many factors—teachers' attitudes, the curriculum, the principal, and the community. Within the school, the pupils, teachers, and principal relate to each other as part of a social system.

Although much has been written about the role of the principal as leader, little of the literature deals with his relationship to the whole school culture—to the teachers and, ultimately, to the pupils. If it is accepted that the principal holds the most significant leadership role in this social system, the school, then a central question emerges: How does his behavior affect teachers and pupils? That is, how much power does the principal really have?

Extensive personal observation of principals at work provided many opportunities to note the relationships which principals may establish with teachers. Some use staff meetings merely to inform teachers of decisions which have already been made; others engage the teachers in discussion and decision making about highly significant issues. Some principals stuff teachers' boxes with memos about everything from hot dogs on Thursday to how long children should stand at the "freeze bell"; others use the memo to distribute current articles on the magnitude of educational problems facing schools.

In investigating the power of the principal, then, it became clear that principals vary widely in their work relationships with their teachers. However, in order to answer the question of what these differences in the behavior of principals may mean to the whole school culture, it was first necessary to establish some categories of leadership by which such behaviors might be defined.

TEACHER PERCEPTIONS OF THE PRINCIPAL'S ROLE

The work of C. Wayne Gordon on the role of the *teacher* proved to be very useful in establishing leadership categories.[4] Gordon conceptualized the teacher's role in terms of three areas, or "orientations," defined as

1 Task: the extent to which the teacher emphasizes student fulfillment of classroom academic tasks.
2 Authority: the amount of authority kept by the teacher or delegated and shared with the students.

3   Expressiveness: the extent to which the teacher fosters a warm atmosphere in the classroom by taking into consideration the needs and
interests of the students.

Thus, Gordon saw the teacher's role as one in which the teacher
organizes the class for learning, deals with who should make what
decisions, and creates an environment in which learning can take place.

Because his concern lay with the effects of these three dimensions
of teacher leadership on pupil achievement, morale, compliance, and
voluntary activity, he asked pupils for their perceptions of their
teachers' behavior. He found that the teacher perceived as high to
middle on the task dimension, low on authority, and middle on the
expressive dimension tended to maximize all the effects of learning
gain as well as inducing high morale, compliance, and volunteer work.
On the other hand, the teacher rated high on task and authority but
low on expressiveness produced very poor results in learning gain as
well as pupil satisfaction.

The orientations which Gordon defined seem to be much like the
significant dimensions of the principal's leadership role. The principal
must organize the staff so that the school functions; he may choose to
make decisions unilaterally or to share decision making with his staff;
and he has the option of working behind closed doors or involving
himself with the staff as a group.

Thus, the leadership dimensions defined by Gordon were adapted
to fit the principal's situation (Table 3.1), and a questionnaire designed
to reveal teacher perceptions of the principal in each category was
devised. (See Part 1 of Appendix A for the complete questionnaire.)

Task

"Task" was defined as the extent to which the principal organizes activities and resources to promote ideas and to stimulate teachers'
thinking about changing school needs. Some questions to which
teachers were asked to respond were

1   At faculty meetings, does the principal talk about administrative procedures or about educational problems? For example, one may observe the principal who holds a weekly problem-solving meeting
(attendance voluntary), calling business meetings only when necessary; on the other hand, there is the principal who each week re-
ligiously holds a faculty meeting whose purpose is to rubber-stamp
inevitable decisions.

TABLE 3.1 DIMENSIONS OF LEADERSHIP

The Principal	The Teacher
Task	
The extent to which the principal organizes activities and resources to promote ideas and stimulation for teachers about changing school needs	The extent to which the teacher emphasizes student fulfillment of classroom academic tasks*
Authority	
The amount of decision-making power kept by the principal or delegated and shared with the teachers	The amount of authority kept by the teacher or delegated and shared with the students
Expressiveness	
The extent to which the principal fosters a warm atmosphere in the school by taking into consideration the needs and interests of the teachers	The extent to which the teacher fosters a warm atmosphere in the classroom by taking into consideration the needs and interests of the students

* Task orientation for the teachers is conceptualized by Gordon as the fulfillment of academic tasks. For the principal, this orientation was changed to represent the extent to which the principal organizes and promotes activities in the staff related to changing school needs.

2 Does the principal show that he is knowledgeable about changes in educational practices by his participation in staff meetings, task groups, or individual conferences?

3 Does the principal show interest in new developments in education by his support for teachers' use of new ideas, methods, or procedures?

Authority

The authority dimension was concerned with the amount of decision making which the principal keeps for himself, as opposed to how much he delegates and shares with the teachers. Answers to questions such as the following were sought:

1 How much direction does the principal give at faculty meetings? For example, in some schools in which the questionnaire was administered, the principal had all the teachers gather at the appointed time and announced to them that they would fill out the questionnaire ("Be honest," one of the principals said), while at other schools the

principal merely announced by the weekly bulletin that the questionnaires would be administered and did not pressure teachers to attend.

2   After the faculty has identified a problem area they want to work on,
    who usually decides how to proceed?

3   What does the principal do when he and teachers disagree about an
    idea in the grouping of students?

Expressiveness

Still another dimension was apparent at many schools. Consider the
difference between the principal who stays behind closed doors and
filters *everything* through his secretary (including paper clips) and the
principal who is available to teachers when they need him. To tap this
"expressive" dimension—the concern for the needs and satisfactions
of teachers as a group—questions such as the following were asked:

1   Is the principal usually fair or usually unfair when he decides things
    about teachers?

2   Does the principal show that he dislikes teachers in the school or not?

3   Does the principal make contacts with teachers in a way which makes
    them nervous and uncomfortable, or does he make contacts in a
    helpful manner?

In summary, teachers were asked to answer questions about their
principals in three major areas:

1   Task orientation: the extent to which the principal organizes activ-
    ities and resources to promote ideas and stimulation for teachers
    about changing school needs.

2   Authority orientation: the amount of decision-making power kept by
    the principal or delegated and shared with the teachers.

3   Expressive orientation: the extent to which the principal fosters a
    warm atmosphere in the school by taking into consideration the
    needs and interests of the teachers.

TEACHER MORALE AND PROFESSIONALISM

Having obtained some measures of how these teachers perceived their
principals, it was necessary to discover how their perceptions of the
principal's behavior seemed to influence them. It was assumed that the
ways in which teachers viewed their principals' behaviors on the afore-
mentioned orientations would affect their attitudes toward each other
as a group, as well as their attitudes toward teaching as a profession.

Classical leadership studies have documented the link between the behavior of the leader and staff working relationships and have isolated morale as an important effect of leadership regardless of the type of group being studied.[5] Morale has been defined as the degree of commitment, interest, and satisfaction of a group.[6] To gather data on this issue, the Gross scale was adapted. Gross, in measuring the *Executive Professional Leadership* (EPL) of principals, also measured teacher morale as an effect of leadership. Items 2, 3, 4, and 6 of Gross's index were included in the morale scale of this study. Teachers were asked questions such as

1   Do teachers spend time before and after school planning with other teachers?

2   Do teachers in this school feel a sense of pride in the school?

3   Do teachers respect the judgment of the administrator? (See Part 2 of Appendix A for complete questionnaire.)

If the work environment created by the principal produces variations in the degree of commitment teachers feel toward the school, it is reasonable to assume that the environment will also influence the extent to which teachers seek to better their skills as professionals. *Professionalism* was defined as involvement in teacher activities that have to do with bettering one's skills as a teacher, and an index of professionalism was devised. Some questions asked were

1   Do teachers in this school read educational journals and share their ideas with each other?

2   Are research findings used to help make decisions about the educational program?

3   Do teachers show their awareness of curricular changes by discussion and experimentation with new ideas? (See Appendix A, Part 2, for complete questionnaire.)

PUPIL PERCEPTION OF THE TEACHER

The final effort of this study was based upon the assumption that teachers' perceptions of their principal's behavior might influence their own behavior in the classroom. Pupils were asked to report their perceptions of their teacher's behavior in the three areas of task, authority, and expressiveness. Gordon's instrument, which was described earlier, was used for this purpose. (See Part 3, Appendix A for complete questionnaire.)

In summary, then, the study attempted to discover:

1 How principals differ in terms of teachers' perceptions of their task, authority, and expressive orientations.

2 Whether teacher perceptions of their principal's behavior in these three areas affect their morale and professionalism.

3 Whether the teachers' behavior on the dimensions of task, authority, and expressiveness—as perceived by their pupils—is related to the teachers' perceptions of their principal's behavior on the same dimensions.

These three major areas of concern reflect the internal school culture in much of its complexity. By collecting information from both teachers and pupils, it was possible to gain insights into both the formal and informal workings of the school as well as proceedings in the classroom.

PROCEDURES

A sample of thirty-one elementary schools in seventeen districts was used in this study. Fifteen schools were members of the League of Cooperating Schools and sixteen were from five additional Southern California districts.

Data were collected by means of two questionnaires. The first questionnaire, which combined questions of teacher perception of principal's leadership with an index of teacher morale and professionalism (Appendix A, Parts 1 and 2), was administered to 704 teachers. The second questionnaire, concerning pupil perceptions of teacher leadership (Appendix A, Part 3), was administered and read orally to 4,821 fifth and sixth grade pupils in their own classrooms.

FINDINGS

Principal Leadership Style

First, the principal leadership questionnaire was analyzed to discover how the three dimensions (task, authority, and expressiveness) were related to each other. Questions relating to each of the three dimensions had been constructed in such a way that they would yield a score of high, middle, or low. For example:

Does the principal help provide the necessary resources you need to achieve your educational goals, or are you left to your own devices?

1 I hardly ever get help. (low task)

2 I get some help, but not as much as I need. (middle task)

3 I get all the help I need. (high task)

Cutoff points for high, middle, and low were established, and Guttman scales were constructed. Guttman scales measure movement toward or away from the same underlying object. In this case, item responses were arranged from high to low task, high to low authority, etc.; that is, the choices under each question ranged from low to high. Mean values of the total frequency distribution were substantiated as cutting points. Each principal had a mean score. If his score was less than the mean, he received a point. Since each scale ranges from high to low, the higher the score, the higher the value on the scale. In this way each principal received a score on each dimension. It was then possible to see if any patterns in these orientations emerged.

It was found that the higher the task orientation of the principal, the higher was his expressive orientation; that is, the more the principal tried to mobilize the staff to look at their problems and practices, the more concern he seemed to exhibit for teacher satisfaction.

Secondly, the lower the authority of the principal, the higher his expressive orientation; that is, the more the principal shared decision making with his teachers, the more he seemed to be concerned with teacher satisfaction.

No significant relationship was found between the task and authority orientations. The results of the questionnaire appeared to indicate that a principal could organize his staff to look at its problems in school (high task) and tell teachers exactly how he wanted them to deal with these problems (high authority). Yet other high-task principals could encourage problem-solving behavior and have teachers deeply involved in bringing about necessary changes (low authority). This finding could suggest that different staffs need different types of leaders, or it could suggest the converse—different leaders mold the staff according to their own style of operating.

Once some connections among these orientations were found, an attempt was made to relate these findings to teacher morale and professionalism.

Teacher Morale and Professionalism

As with the principal dimensions, morale and professionalism scales were constructed by using the median response as a cutting point. These scores were then compared to principal scores on the three orientations. Findings were as follows:

Professionalism of teachers seemed to be related both to a high-task and to a low-authority orientation of the principal. Thus, a stronger feeling of professionalism was produced in teachers both when the principal mobilized his staff to look at its problems and when he shared decision making with them.

Teacher morale seemed to be related to the expressiveness of the principal. The more the principal cared and showed by his behavior that he understood the needs and satisfactions of teachers, the more teachers were able to work cooperatively.

No correlations were found between the authority of the principal and the morale of the teachers. The lack of any relationship here may provide a clue to the inactivity of so many schools which seem relatively unaffected by the changing world outside their gates. Teachers seem to need autonomy to function as professionals. Yet, this finding suggests that many teachers are happy when decisions are made for them. The process whereby a principal leads a staff from taking orders to participating in decision making includes a complex array of factors that have much to do with his establishing task-oriented activities and stimulating the staff with new ideas.

The Influence of Principal Leadership on Teacher Leadership

There was no evidence that teacher perception of the manner in which principals organized their staffs to look at their problems and school changes (principal *task*) had any relation to how teachers organized pupils for learning (teacher *task*). Nor was the fact that the principal may be perceived as caring for the needs and satisfactions of his teacher (principal *expressiveness*) related to the teachers' own preoccupations with the needs and satisfactions of pupils.

With respect to the authority dimension, however, there were correlations. Thus, when teachers gave their principal a high score on authority, they in turn received high authority scores from their students. Apparently, then, when teachers are given little decision-making power, they themselves are reluctant to give decision-making power to their students.

Composite Pictures

In order to understand more fully how the principal's orientations fit together and how these orientations relate to teacher behaviors, composite pictures were constructed, cutting across school lines and using all the data collected. This process resulted in eight "pictures" of schools, each characterizing the relationships which exist among principal and teachers.

At one extreme is the group of principals found to be high task, high authority, and high expressive (HHH). These principals organize the school around professionally oriented activities (working on new curricula, goals for the school, new grouping patterns, problem-oriented activities, etc.), tell the teachers how to proceed, and support them in the process. Interestingly, these principals apparently influence the greatest number of prototypes among their teachers. As reported by pupils, teachers working for these principals are also high on task and authority and highly expressive. One certainly must speculate on why this is so. Do principals of this kind seek out teachers like them, or vice versa? Or do these principals create such a whirlwind of excitement that teachers become influenced? More study needs to be done to discover the conditions under which this style might be most productive.

At the opposite extreme is the principal who was rated low on task, low on authority, and low on expressiveness (LLL). Where the principal was rated low on all three dimensions, two-thirds of the teachers reported that the staff generally does not work as a group. In short, everybody "does his own thing." At least one-third of the staff is highly professional. The attitude is, "Leave them alone and they produce." The atmosphere of the school is generally depressing and teachers feel less task-oriented toward their pupils than any others in the sample.

Between these two extremes lie several principal types, each of which has different effects on his staff. For example, the principal who is rated low on task but receives a high rating on the other two measures (LHH) is the leader who keeps the status quo with grace. The school is clean and well-ordered, and teachers enjoy many satisfactions. Coffee cups have names individually lettered on them, and procedures for everything from how to clean the blackboards to how to line up in the cafeteria can be found on the school bulletin board. Teachers appear to enjoy this type of principal. He takes care of the mundane aspects of school life. Morale is at midpoint, but teachers are reluctant to spend time with each other working to better the school program.

This principal (LHH) may be compared with his opposite—the man who is rated high on task but low on both authority and expressiveness (HLL). Such a principal has internalized the need to involve teachers and to provide stimuli for them. However, his low contribution to the teachers' welfare earns him some disapproval. Working with this kind of principal, teachers reported, means working hard but lacking satisfaction, in some part due to the principal's lack of support. Teachers recognize the need to improve their professional expertise but are resentful because the principal is unable to provide the social support necessary to balance an atmosphere of hard work with consideration for teacher satisfactions. Although 60 percent of the teachers reported high professional behavior on the part of the staff, 60 percent also reported low morale. The work gets done but at the cost of poor work relations among teachers.

What of the principal who is low on both task and authority, but high on expressiveness (LLH)? He is preoccupied with seeking the approval of his followers, and apparently, this preoccupation interferes with his ability to command teachers' respect. He is overly concerned with being liked; therefore, many of his decisions are not based on what is most effective for the school as a total entity. Morale of the teachers drops from middle to low, and professionalism varies, with 25 percent highly professional, 50 percent middle, and 25 percent low. One could speculate that the upper 25 percent of teachers work most productively with this principal. They take advanced degrees, are active union members, etc. Such teachers need a supportive principal. They do not need one who encourages professional growth, because they do it on their own. Nevertheless, there are other teachers on the staff who do need to be led to greater involvement, which would suggest that the principal individualize his leadership according to different teacher needs.

The reverse of such a principal may be seen in the principal who is rated high on both task and authority but low on expressiveness (HHL). This principal pays the price for his lack of understanding of the crucial importance of social support. Making demands on teachers without the accompanying attention to satisfaction leads teachers under this mode to react by low task orientation in the classroom. Teachers are at the middle of the morale scale; thus, they are characterized by a lack of pride in the school and often a lack of respect for the administrator.

Finally, the LHL principal can be compared with the HLH principal. The principal rated as low on task, high on authority, and low on expressiveness (LHL) spends much of his time on administrative procedures and little, if any, on organizing the school group to look at what it is doing. This principal is the one the administration periodicals decry as ineffective. He carries out orders unquestioningly and lacks an adequate understanding of teachers, of group life, and of what is happening out there. The greatest effect of this principal's leadership is that half of the staff feel they are functionaries just putting in time.

In contrast, the HLH principal is seen as one who views his role as primarily moving the staff by doing such things as having teachers visit innovative schools, organizing teacher groups who want to try new things, etc. That is, he feels that the major portion of his role is devoted to providing a stimulating environment for teachers. He has internalized the need to share decision making with his teachers (however difficult this might be) and goes out of his way to provide social support for them. The atmosphere of this school is generally permissive in that wide variations of teacher style are encouraged, and teachers are urged to develop as professionals. Teacher morale is high.

The HLH principal questions with his teachers various kinds of practices found in the school (for example, what kind of materials to use, how to group children, how to organize the school). Rather than telling the teachers what to do, he provides the type of environment and nourishment within which they can develop. This is a demanding role but offers the principal and teachers the challenges of working, studying, and struggling with the complexity of problems facing the school today.

Implications

Needless to say, these orientations, although referring to specific behaviors, do not take into account the myriad other demands and strains on an elementary school principal. On the other hand, perhaps they do get at some rather important elements of the principal's role.

The evidence was overwhelmingly in favor of principals developing a nourishing climate in which teachers will be able to come to terms with the many stresses of a rapidly changing society. It also seems clear that when the principal shares decision making with his staff, the teachers respond with greater professionalism.

It is still uncertain why or under what conditions teachers are influenced by the principal's task orientation, but evidence is overwhelming that when the principal involves himself in organizing the school to deal with its problems, gets teachers together, and encourages them to look outside the school, the teachers manifest greater professional behavior.

The instruments used in this study are available to principals for gathering information on principal and teacher leadership. (See Appendix A.) Perhaps a starting point for unraveling the school culture and recreating it could be to find out just where one stands in terms of the behaviors that do relate to teachers' excitement and participation in teaching. The principal leadership questionnaire can be such a start. Eventually, teachers too must become self-conscious enough to be concerned with not only *what* they do but also *how* it affects the students. The teacher leadership questionnaire can be used here.

This research has shown once again that the principal can provide a powerful leadership role in changing the school culture by attending to the various means of organizing the school to look outside its walls, to work toward shared decision making, and to provide consistently for the support and needs of the school faculty.

NOTES

1   Cecil A. Gibb, "Principles and Traits of Leadership," *Journal of Abnormal and Social Psychology*, vol. 42, 1947, pp. 267–284.

2   Robin Farquahar, Jack Culbertson, et al., *Educational Leadership and School Organization in the 1970's*, American Educational Research Association symposium papers, Minneapolis, Mar. 4, 1970; W. P. Lewin, Ronald Lippitt, and Ralph White, "Leader Behavior and Member Reaction in Three Social Climates," in Dorwin Cartwright and Alvin Zander (eds.), *Group Dynamics*, Harper & Row, New York, 1968; Hanan C. Selvin, *The Effects of Leadership*, Free Press, Glencoe, Ill., 1960.

3   Philip W. Jackson, *Life in Classrooms*, Holt, Rinehart and Winston, New York, 1968.

4   C. Wayne Gordon and Leta McKinney Adler, *Dimensions of Teacher Leadership in Classroom Social Systems*, University of California Press, Los Angeles, 1963.

5   Neal Gross and Robert Herriott, *Staff Leadership in Public Schools: A Sociological Inquiry*, Wiley, New York, 1965; Ralph M. Stogdill and Alvin E. Coons, *Leader Behavior: Its Description and Measurement*, research monograph, Ohio State University Press, Columbus, 1957; Lewin, Lippitt, and White, op. cit.; Daniel Katz and Robert L. Kahn, "Leadership Practices in Relation to Productivity and Morale," in Cartwright and Zander (eds.), op. cit.

6   Gross and Herriott, op. cit.

CHAPTER **4**

THE STAGES OF CHANGE IN ELEMENTARY SCHOOL SETTINGS

Ann Lieberman and David A. Shiman

Intensive involvement with the schools during the League of Cooperating Schools project provided the authors with the opportunity to observe the change process in a variety of school settings. They present a number of case studies to illustrate the pattern of change whose emergence they had witnessed over time. It is a pattern which contradicts the rational model of goal setting, implementation, and evaluation which currently receives attention in the field. The authors conclude that change in schools is encouraged by a number of conditions, such as the acceptance and support of the principal, the community, the district, and the teachers themselves.

Dr. Shiman teaches comparative education at the University of Vermont, and Dr. Lieberman is on the faculty of Teachers College, Columbia University.

During the 1960s and early 1970s, extreme pressure was placed on the school to change and to be accountable for its effectiveness.[1] We will not argue the legitimacy of this position,[2] but rather that it does exist and that schools are being pushed to answer and take responsibility for many of the inequities which exist in American society.

THE FORCES OF CHANGE

Evidence of this pressure could be seen in a large group of educators now named "radical reformers" performing the role of muckrakers—Kohl, Kozol, Herndon, Postman and Weingartner, Leonard, Silberman. The common theme of their arguments is that the school has become an institution totally insensitive to its pupil population, irrelevant,

49

"mindless," and in many cases injurious to the young who pass end-lessly through its doors.

To counter this situation, the federal government allocated mil-lions of dollars to educational improvement. The National Defense Education Act (Titles I, II, and III) has for some time provided some financial aid to improve education. In addition, under the Elementary and Secondary Education Act of 1965, regional laboratories were insti-tuted to create new instructional materials and new methodologies.

Professionals in the university also entered the battle to save the schools and to make them more relevant to our changing society.[3] At first in the fields of math and science and then in social studies and in English, university professors joined to update curriculum and create new methodologies and new ways of viewing subject matter. Added to these were such efforts as the rediscovery of Piaget, the implications of his theories for educational practice, and the importation of prac-tices from the British Infant Schools, known in this country as "open education."[4]

Other proposed reforms included reorganization of the school to meet individual differences by removing grade levels and expecta-tions,[5] the use of programmed instruction, "humanizing" the school, and even doing away with the school altogether, utilizing instead the entire community as a classroom.

Given these powerful and often conflicting forces impinging on the schools, a central question emerges: How does a school faculty attempt to cope with change? It was in recognition of the problems created by such forces that the League of Cooperating Schools was created in 1966. The major goal of the League was to provide an op-portunity for a staff of researchers and developers and eighteen school faculties to study the process of change in schools while attempting to improve them.

What the Literature Says

Our study began with a review of the literature on change. Such litera-ture ranges from generalized concepts about change,[6] including the stages through which an individual or a group passes, to more recent descriptions of strategies one might use to implement change.[7] Some, such as Katz and Kahn,[8] list types of change brought about through the use of information, feedback, or peer group reinforcement. Other writers view change from the position of the leader and define the leader as one who has either personal power or power by virtue of his position.[9] This description has been augmented by others defining the change process as one in which the activity or change is participative or coercive.[10] In such descriptions four elements are listed as representative of the change cycle: knowledge, attitudes, individual behavior, and group behavior.

Thus, we began our study of change armed with an ample supply of literature on the subject. As we were to discover in the ensuing five years, however, much of this literature deals with what the change process *should* look like or with what changes *should* be made. The reality, we found, can be grossly different.

Even those who describe change in educational organizations fail to take into consideration either the school as a culture[11] or the individual teacher and the values and demands of his job,[12] elements which we found to be overwhelmingly important. For example, Miles describes a sixteen-point process of change in schools which ranges from goal setting to forecasting long-range plans to diagnosing, supporting, and maintaining.[13] We found that such a description fails to take into consideration the realities of changes which occur sometimes fitfully, often irrationally, and most assuredly not in the order Miles states from one to sixteen. Neither does his description capture the nuances of day-to-day school life when a school faculty seeks to make changes.

Gross, in his case study of an innercity school, also describes a process of change.[14] His description of how a change in teacher roles is implemented in a school exposes the enormous gap between what a school staff actually does and what the change literature says about the process.

Our study was to involve us in those day-to-day nuances of schools coping with solving their own problems of change. Given the unique situation of getting to know eighteen different faculties over a period of five years, we were in a position to make various kinds of observations. As we observed, we looked for unifying themes that might emerge, a pattern which would allow us to describe the process of change as it really is.

We would like first to describe the pattern of change we observed and then exemplify the pattern by discussing three very different situations in which it appeared. Several cases of deviation from the pattern will also be presented. We will conclude with a discussion of the conditions and characteristics of the stages of change which we observed.

The Observed Pattern of Change

The process we observed was composed of five stages:

1   First, people talk about the possibility of bringing about some kind
    of change within the school. Some of the talk comes from teachers
    who are hoping to have changes legitimated from above. Some
    emerges from the stimulation of teachers and principals being to-
    gether. Some ideas come from outside consultants. During this stage
    there is a great deal of uneasiness. Expectations begin to rise.
    Teachers feel pressured to do something. The "Tell us what to do"[15]
    syndrome is rampant. Big ideas are talked about (self-concept, student
    decision making, individual differences). This stage is clearly Lewin's
    "unfreezing."[16]

2   Activity ensues. Some teachers begin to do something. One or two
    teachers may team. Some individualize their reading program. It is
    rare that the whole school participates (although we observed several
    examples of this). Usually a few people get excited about adopting
    a change, and with enough support, they do it.

3   Out of such activity, teachers begin to ask questions. The broader
    implications of the activity come to the fore. "Why am I doing this?"
    "Am I really providing for individual differences?" "Is this better than
    what I did before?" Discomfort is great at this time. The activity often
    calls upon both teacher and student to experiment with some new
    behaviors.

4   The whole program begins to look shabby. Teachers who have indi-
    vidualized reading find it difficult to justify giving thirty-six children
    the same spelling test. The stimulation of a successful team effort in
    one subject makes teaching alone much more difficult.

5   The large philosophical questions are asked. Teachers begin to deal
    with goals for the first time. Such questions are "Is our curriculum
    relevant to our student population?" "How can we organize the
    school to meet individual differences?" "How can we make our staff
    a cohesive unit?" "What will we do with teachers who won't
    change?" "How can I teach children to make decisions when I have
    been making all the decisions for them?"

These questions open up others, and the process begins again.
Dialogue takes place, activities are planned, and more questions
emerge.

This pattern looks substantially different from descriptions of
school innovations. Most such descriptions go like this: First you state

the objectives; then you provide the means for carrying them out; finally, you evaluate the extent to which the objectives have been accomplished. It is rational, neat, and flawless. It does not, however, square with reality.

Several social scientists have observed a pattern such as the one we saw. For example, in talking about groups, Weick[17] discusses the pattern of an organization as one in which the organizing of the group comes first and the reason for organizing becomes apparent later. Actions *precede* goals. Lindblom's[18] discussion centers upon the day-to-day activities of public administrators. He describes two methods in regard to decision making, policy formulation, planning, etc. These are the "root" method and the "branch" method. The root method is generally similar to the rational planning approach referred to above, whereas the branch method is similar to that described by Weick. Lindblom notes that the root approach is most often written about but fails to describe adequately the complexity of what most public administrators actually do.

Our observation leads us to agree most strongly with Weick and Lindblom. Proposals for change often assume a simplistic model of the school. In fact, any curricular, organizational, or instructional change involves a complex array of factors[19] and must take into consideration an accurate and actual picture of "life in classrooms."[20] Added to this, any change that looks different seems to involve teachers in community reaction. This involvement makes support by the principal important, since they take positions against the norms of the district or even their fellow teachers.[21] Such a complexity of events only becomes understandable *after* the change activity, when realizable objectives can be stated.

THREE CASES

Our definition of the stages of change came from both our participation in schools and from the voluminous case notes which we kept during the project.[22] We saw the stages take place in a variety of school situations, three of which we shall describe.

Being schooled in the rational model, we were quite unprepared when we saw teachers begin to team teach, change their reporting procedures, create a totally new classroom atmosphere, and years later begin to talk about the goals of the school.[23]

Independence School

Independence School was located in an urban-residential neighborhood within the Los Angeles area. Because the school building was condemned during the first year of the League enterprise because of earthquake hazards, teachers and their classes were spread out in three different schools until portable units were built in the schoolyard at Independence.

A court order to integrate the school gave Independence a population of 60 percent Caucasians and 40 percent from minority groups. The school was situated in an area that had already contained a considerable mix of students from many South and Central American countries as well as Chicanos and blacks. Socioeconomic levels ranged from blue collar to professional, and annual turnover of students exceeded 50 percent.

Independence's principal designed a reading program to be implemented, but before it could get off the ground, this principal was appointed to an assistant superintendency in the northern part of the state. The new principal, Arnold Z., took the position at the end of the first year of the League.

Teachers, in general, had been uncommitted to the reading program. When the principal left, so did the program. However, the flurry of activity over the reading program had made teachers anxious and ready to change even though they did not know exactly what to do.

Independence teachers wanted to try something new; they were encouraged to do so. Arnold Z., the new principal, had been known in the district as hard-working, innovative, and eager to have his school in the League. As such, he provided teachers with a great deal of support for trying a variety of educational alternatives, including individualization, team teaching, nongrading, and open classrooms. No school decision was taken to institute any specific type of change. Instead, those that did occur happened in piecemeal fashion. A few teachers experimented, talked with others about what they were doing, and more and more teachers mustered up the courage to try something new. There were no blueprints, no guarantees of success, and no clearly defined educational goals. The decision to act had been an outgrowth of dissatisfaction rather than careful planning. As one teacher said, "You have to have a certain amount of dissatisfaction with what you have right now. There's something wrong. . . . You get in and you try it. You try something different out of desperation. . . ."

In the beginning, many teachers did not fully understand the implications of the new instructional techniques they were trying in their classes. However, as they grew more comfortable with their new activities and began to realize what it meant to individualize or to move toward a nongraded, continuous-progress type of educational program, a whole series of new problems arose. Many of these were related to the problem of record keeping and reporting to parents. One teacher stated, "Serious discussion started last year because we knew that if we were going to have an augmented nongraded elementary program we would have to go to an ungraded method of reporting, with no grading either by letter grades or by grade level." Another said that when you begin to individualize the focus is less on grade level, and "that is what report cards generally turn out to be all about."

Again, there was dissatisfaction and frustration with an aspect of the school's program. This time, however, the teachers did not act out of desperation or without careful planning. They held numerous staff meetings and developed their own criteria for the new report card.

The process through which the new report card began to emerge was by no means smooth. The discussions were frank and open. The primary teachers chastised their upper grade counterparts for refusing to move away from a graded system and for failing to understand what a nongraded, individualized program entailed. The upper grade teachers reevaluated their initial proposals and finally came up with a set of criteria devoid of specific letter grades. The principal described the experience in the following manner:

> [It was] probably one of the greatest things that happened. . . . All our philosophies and pent-up feelings and emotions came out on the table. . . . There was some give and take, there were some tears, and there were some real moments when people were very frustrated. . . . The ultimate end was that we came up with a vehicle that they seemed to like.

It was an exercise which several teachers stated could not have taken place a few years earlier. Only in a nonthreatening atmosphere of mutual respect could such an activity be carried out.

What finally emerged was a reporting form with which no one was completely happy, but which was more in accordance with the instructional program as it was then proceeding. As reported by one of the teachers, it was based on the following criteria:

(1) We would give no letter or number grade as part of the report;

(2) We would be specific about what a child can or cannot do in a certain area of curriculum; (3) We would compare the child only with himself; (4) We would consider the use of a kind of accompanying guide wherein developmental levels and description are written for the teacher to "plug" into the report card; and (5) We would use the same reporting form or report card for the parent conference.

This was not a final document, but one which would be reexamined and reevaluated at some later date.

As the introduction of changes in the instructional program had brought about an examination of reporting procedures, so also the teachers found that the activity of rewriting their report card could not be isolated from other considerations:

[It] made us realize the close relationship between the report card and the course of studies and how you run your classroom.

A whole new series of problems emerged:

There had been a growing consciousness of the educational objectives on the part of both teachers and learners, brought about through the development of a reporting system that enlisted learner as well as teacher concerns.

It became apparent to many teachers that there was a need to define more clearly what sorts of pupils the school hoped to produce. Overall school goals and not merely classroom instructional objectives needed to be enumerated.

One's true philosophy of education comes out when you have to crystallize your thinking about reporting a child's progress.

However, the staff never took on the task of clarifying its educational philosophy and defining its school goals. As the report card–writing activity neared completion, so did the academic year. Although it was decided to postpone writing their school's goals until the following year, the task was again postponed in the fall. As one teacher said:

This kind of thing faded into the background and wasn't brought back. . . . That's something we should have worked on this year, I would say. But, there was a whole new set of problems, and there didn't seem to be the time.

The teachers immersed themselves in the pressing problems that confronted them during the first few months of another school year.

They had their new report card which seemed to serve their purposes better and they had a somewhat clearer idea of what they were trying to accomplish.

Independence and the Stages of Change

The experience of Independence typifies the stages as we have described. The teachers were agitated, heard many new programs described, visited other schools, and talked some more. A few teachers began to open up their classrooms and allow some student choices. Several different kinds of activities took place in several different classrooms.

Out of these activities teachers became very concerned that the report card did not reflect what they were trying to do. The report card thus served as a central theme for discussion. Little by little, with the report card as a backdrop, some teachers began to talk about more and more subject areas and different ways to use space, group children, and think about the school week. The big issues began to be raised.

The program was never spelled out. There never *was* a program as such, but rather an arduous dialectical process leading teachers from activity to questioning to still more activity.

Seastar School

Seastar represents still another kind of school. It was located in a small, long-established community within the metropolitan Los Angeles complex. About 20 percent of its 500 pupils came from minority racial and ethnic groups, and the school community represented almost equal proportions of blue collar, clerical, business, and professional occupations.

The teacher turnover was very low. The twenty to twenty-five teachers (with an average age of over forty) had a great deal of teaching experience. Many of the teachers had master's degrees or were currently attending graduate school. Several served on district committees writing curricula. This was a very sophisticated group. The principal, too, was about to complete his doctorate in curriculum studies.

This school, unlike Independence, was very self-satisfied. They liked what they were doing. The principal described himself:

I was a benevolent big daddy, but I was still the big daddy who used to make many, many decisions because the teachers expected me to make decisions and to tell them how to do things.

In the beginning of this school's League involvement the staff was very resistant. An announcement that the school was to participate in the League of Cooperating Schools appeared in the local newspaper *before* the staff had been notified. When Dave W., the principal, appeared at the first faculty meeting, the teachers voted *not* to be in the League. They felt they were already working very hard and could not see any advantages for them in participating.

The first year became a herculean effort to connect Seastar to this thing called the League. Meetings centered upon the faculty's attempt to explore the idea of individualization and what that might mean to the staff. There were several heated discussions about the changing population and the problem of discipline, and there was an attempt to find a goal for the proposed innovation. There was tremendous hostility in the group. Teachers had worked as individuals for a long time. Group commitment was nil. Several teachers suggested that the school begin to team teach. This seemed like a way of institutionalizing something which could lead to greater individualization.

In actual fact, the attempt at teaming provided a means for the school to gain district and parent support. As it turned out, however, after a year of experimentation most of the teams found themselves racked with arguments over philosophical and methodological differences, spiced with some enormous personality clashes.

Nor did matters go smoothly during the second and third years. Reflecting upon this period, the principal said:

The staff ran into lots of problems. Some of them became a little frustrated with the mechanical problems and others with personality problems. Some were just too insecure.

Major philosophical and practical questions were asked. Increasingly teachers became better able to transcend their own classrooms and look at the school program from a broader perspective. They had specific problems to react to and no longer felt merely compelled to do something out of a sense of frustration. They looked for answers to pressing questions such as, "How can you individualize and promote continuous progress in an essentially lockstep, graded system?" "Is it possible to describe a child as an A or B second grade student without denying the irrefutable fact that every child's rate of maturation and development is different?" Again, action on specific problems led to raising the larger issues.

Seastar and the Stages of Change

Seastar went through a long period of resistance to any new ideas. Then they went through a period in which they identified the locus of problems as the children (discipline, behavior problems) before they could begin to look at what was going on at Seastar and at themselves. Individualization and self-direction were the overall thrusts, but these concepts were too global to lead to action.

Instead, team teaching became the "ensuing activity" which we have identified as stage two, engaging teachers in intense dialogue as well as intense difficulties. However, the experience of working with other teachers provided many benefits. Several teachers for the first time experienced teaching with another adult, receiving stimulation and feedback. Some noticed how much richer the curricular offerings were when two or more adults worked together. Some teams worked out time for planning within the school day. Talking about the day or the week with someone else produced many new ideas, many sleepless nights, and in some cases a recognition that "sharing" children was difficult. Many found teaching impossible in a team situation.

Out of this activity, teachers and principals began to question everything about Seastar. The viability of the self-contained classroom began to be questioned in terms of student needs. Teachers began to talk about teacher style, learner style, use of time, student decision making. In short, Pandora's box opened. The process had proceeded fitfully from overall disequilibrium to an activity (team teaching) which dislodged people and failed for many, but which—more importantly—involved teachers in *real* questions, *self-imposed* as a result of changed circumstances.[24] Plans during the fifth year of the project included moving the entire school toward a nongraded program.

Dewey Avenue School

Dewey Avenue School belonged to a very large city school district and was situated in a stable, largely upper-middle class suburban residential area. Most of the 1,100 students were Caucasian. The main building was thirty-five years old, and additional classroom space was provided by bungalows in the school yard.

Stan M. had been principal for a year before the start of the League. He had a reputation in the district as being an excellent leader. He was interested in innovation and welcomed the idea of being a League principal; he enthusiastically announced to both parents and staff the exciting possibilities for the school as a result of League involvement.

Stan was very aware of the dynamics of running an elementary school. He was principal of a group of sophisticated teachers. He knew teachers were comfortable when he made decisions for them. What he learned was that teachers had to be intimately involved in developing their own programs if *real* changes were to take place. This learning came about through a series of steps initiated by the principal.

This school had an interesting pattern which again exemplifies the stages of change we have defined, but with some fascinating side roads. Stan began to talk about treating each child as an individual. Newsletters sent home began to praise the nongraded approach, "accepting each child where he is," "fitting the program to the child, rather than the opposite." The parents, who were essentially a professional group, felt that their school was on the cutting edge of educational innovation. Teachers liked what was being said but didn't really know what it all meant for them.

Faculty meetings became the scene of intense dialogue about individual children, the concept of individualized instruction, who should make what decisions, and so forth.

Three bold innovations were institutionalized during the first year. They sound trivial in the writing, but for those who know elementary schools, they were revolutionary moves. The playground was nongraded; that is, students were allowed to play anywhere they wanted. This caused children to break down age barriers; older children helped younger ones, and in some cases older children joined younger groups in which they were more comfortable. Teachers now had to deal with "other teachers' children."

Secondly, the textbook room became nongraded. That is, the labels were removed from the shelves and teachers were free to take books based on the needs of the children in their class, rather than thirty-five copies of the same series, according to grade level. This caused teachers to look at other materials outside their grade level and stretch the bounds of what was to be taught and learned.

The third innovation was to get parents to work in the library and have it open all day like a real library. With permission, students could then go at any time during the day *by themselves*.

These three innovations caused many consequences. A new resource, parents, began to come to the school. Students, freely going to and from the library, began to get a new sense of self and began working in new ways. Teachers began to see a wider range of students on the playground, and everyone began to get new insights into changing conditions in the school that would encourage individualization.

During the second year, a schoolwide project was launched. The entire school focused on math. All students were tested and placed in groups for mathematics based on achievement, rather than age or grade. Students were periodically tested and moved to new groups if test scores warranted it.

This program eventually eroded and became the prototype of the adage, "The more things change, the more they remain the same." However, out of this experience several teachers began to deal with such questions as

Do all children need to spend the same amount of time on a given concept?

Can some children work alone or in small groups without the teacher in front of the room?

Can several activities take place at the same time, in the same room?

Who needs a tight schedule? Teacher, or student, *or* some teachers and some students?

Few teachers and students were untouched by the "math" regrouping.

Dewey Avenue and the Stages of Change

In this case the principal took a leading role in bringing in new ideas and providing the support and enthusiasm for creating the dialogue among teachers and community. Stan was eager, excited, and knowledgeable about how to use resources in his school. Raised expectations created a powerful tension for change. Unlike the principals of Seastar and Independence, Stan brought about some visible changes which led to some immediate results, creating some new conditions for teachers, students, and parents. (Even custodians were involved in the changed playground conditions.)

The central activity at Dewey was the math program. Like the team teaching at Seastar, the program eventually died, but the activity was compelling enough to raise serious questions about the lockstep method of moving children mechanically from grade to grade, teacher roles, and so forth.

For some teachers, the classroom became too small to contain their growing ideas of what should be happening in school. The large halls became beehives of activity, often housing more children than the classrooms themselves.

During the fourth year of the League, we attended a June planning meeting. Sessions included such themes as

1   Creation of small units to handle phases of schooling.
2   What must be taught in school? What are the societal imperatives?
3   What kind of experiences should be a part of elementary school?

The big questions were being asked. Teachers were struggling with every conceivable philosophical, curricular, organizational, and instructional question current today. They had had four years of experimentation, supported by an outside group (the League). Innovative norms had been internalized by many. As we had seen before, the stages of change did *not* follow the rational model of stating what is to be done, engaging in activities for doing it, and assessing the extent to which objectives were accomplished; rather, change proceeded from dialogue to activity to questions arising out of the activity to a recognition that real changes shake fundamental assumptions about teaching, learning, staff relations, decision making, and more. These questions are raised not by imposed programs but by genuine voluntary engagement in activity.

Many activities we observed were failures. These failures, however, were the basis for crucial questions. This is not to say that one plans to fail, but that activities planned to change the conditions of teacher and pupil often have unanticipated consequences more powerful than those planned.

SOME NECESSARY CONDITIONS

We have suggested that in observing the process of implementing educational change, we have discerned a pattern which differs significantly from the descriptions of change in the literature. In observing those schools which exhibited these stages, we also observed some common conditions which existed, some basic elements which appeared as a part of the support system which seems to be necessary to encourage school change.

The community and its acceptance of change seemed to be one important variable. In those schools where change did take place, the community was open, willing, and eager to accept the changes.

District support also seemed to be an important element. In some schools that changed, district support came in the form of an encouraging phone call or an enthusiastic visit; in others it was money, programs, extra people, minimum days. At Seastar, for example, although the superintendent and principal were at odds, the district came through with a minimum day and some money to knock down some walls between classrooms. Independence had the support of district people as well as project funds coming into the school. At Dewey, there was no money, no substitutes, no minimum days, but the district superintendent in charge showed his approval of the school's efforts, and this seemed enough to keep both principal and staff moving and excited.

Principal leadership appeared to be a third crucial element. It would be naïve to state that there is a list of dos and don'ts, yet in schools that changed, the principal seemed to be intimately involved in facilitating the changes, in providing the support teachers needed, and in changing relationships among the staff members.

The teacher group represented a significant element as well. Somehow, teachers appear to need "early adopters," a group of teachers who will experiment and who, with support, can fail, pick up again, and learn through the process. Without this spark within some teachers, innovative activity never gets a chance.

THE DEVIANT CASES

Having repeatedly observed the stages of change, we kept asking ourselves why some schools never seemed to enter these stages, or why, having gone through the stages, they then appeared to take other directions. Examining two deviant cases gave us greater insight into this question.

In our deviant cases one or more of the support elements discussed above seemed to be missing. We do not mean to suggest that these elements are isolated and that therefore if a school has them change is inevitable, but rather that they interact in both obvious and subtle ways to form a configuration associated with school change.

Shadyside School

Shadyside, we feel, is a good example of a school in which, although the stages of change as we have described them occurred, the whole configuration changed when a few elements were disturbed.

This school was located in a low-income area of a unified school district in an urban area. Shadyside had 500 pupils, mostly Caucasian, in kindergarten through sixth grade. Shortly before the opening of the last school year of the League, the district adopted new plans for racial integration, and Shadyside was converted to a K–3 school. The number of pupils remained the same, but under the new plan the proportion of black and Mexican-American children increased, and many of the pupils came from outside the immediate neighborhood.

During the first year of the League, Russ D. was principal. He had very cautiously undertaken an individualized reading program. At the end of the year, Russ was transferred to another school. He was succeeded by Lucy K., a woman with more than twenty years of professional experience. She was genuinely respected by the faculty. They saw her as promoting and facilitating changes, engaging in a dialogue involving shared decision making, and also as highly supportive of their efforts.

> Our staff at Shadyside has a certain magic about them that makes an experimental program exciting.
>
> She [Lucy] continually redirected us to search for our own answers, and gave us great amounts of confidence in this search.

During the second year of the League, the school became an increasingly exciting place for children and teachers. The new reading program had been abandoned. Several rooms were experimenting with increased student decision making. Several groups of teachers were teaming, sharing resources. Teachers were open, questioning, wildly enthusiastic about their new learnings. The school talked about individualizing instruction, but it was clear that there was no one definition of what that was. To some teachers it meant differentiating by rate. To others it meant different students doing different things to reach the same ends. And to still others it came to mean different students doing different things to reach different ends.

Visitors came by the score to look at this school that was individualizing instruction and to talk with this highly motivated staff.

Lucy was very aware of growing problems in the district. She was concerned that other principals might be threatened by the innovative activity and the obvious contagion of enthusiasm and spirit at Shady-side. Her stance was to invite people to the school and have them view a changing school going through a developmental process, with all its problems and difficulties. In this way, the school would not boast of its successes but rather welcome people to come and join the struggle.

Lucy K. had the ability and sensitivity to excite the staff, question without threat, and work on any problem, however great or small. Her talents did not go unnoticed, for by the end of the third year of the League she was given a district position and was replaced by Brad C.

Brad was new to the principalship and came in very gently to look and learn. He was interested in innovation and liked the direction the school was going. The bubble burst, however, and little by little the tremendous enthusiasm and excitement waned. One teacher said:

> It's as if there is a huge fog enveloping the school. We can't seem to make a decision and get on with it.

About the new principal:

> Not persuasive. No direction under his nondirective technique. The program seems to be falling apart.

Our observation leads us to speculate that two disruptions turned this school from a beehive of excitement and activity into an endless maze of indecision and apathy. The first disruption was the arrival of Brad. Although sympathetic and supportive, he was just learning to be a principal. The teachers already had some clearly established needs, and Brad was administering instead of leading. He was learning with them, but they had grown used to a relationship with a leader who was both learner and teacher. Before Brad's arrival, meetings had been spirited and exciting. They became a drag.

One is tempted to ponder whether the change in sex of the principal made a difference. At Dewey Avenue, however, a popular male principal had been replaced by a female, and similar difficulties arose, so we discarded that explanation. This leads us to further speculate that the problem of a new principal in an innovative school where norms are changing is an extremely delicate one. The new principal steps into a situation in which teachers and principal have been experiencing some emotional and behavioral changes. Although we had seen it accomplished successfully at other schools, it happened only when the new principal filled a gap or recreated the position and legitimated a process consistent with his/her own style. Brad, because he was a novice, was just developing a style and therefore was concerned more with survival than with leadership.

The second disruption was a structural change. Shadyside was going to become a K–3 school, which meant that half the teachers would be leaving. The central problem of the school shifted from the innovative activity to, "Who will be here next year?" and, "How can the new teachers catch up?" This structural change, along with the principal's lack of clarity about his role, seemed to us to be most significant in Shadyside's failure to institutionalize change-oriented norms.

Fairfield School

Fairfield represents still another deviant pattern. In this case our speculations led us to isolate teacher characteristics as a possible source of the problem.

Fairfield belonged to a district that covered a small rural town. It serviced the low-income section. Its 1,300 pupils from K–8 were almost all Mexican-American. Most of the parents were farm laborers, but as more acquired permanent jobs the population became increasingly stable.

Ben U., the principal, had been at the school for more than fifteen years, several of these as a teacher. There was little staff turnover. The average age of the teachers was about forty-five. Several teachers had been at Fairfield for over twenty years, and most were Anglo-Americans. The principal once told our staff that all the people who don't make it anywhere else end up at Fairfield.

Initial visits by our staff associate indicated that attitudes toward change were hostile; yet even more than the classical resistance, there were statements indicating racial problems:

> Many [of the children] have little education. Some are too lazy. Some do not want to learn English even though they have opportunities to do so. Thank heavens my own children aren't like these. These Mexican kids aren't verbal, especially the lower class kids from Mexico. The children here can't be treated as individuals until they reach a certain age.

One teacher, eager for change, noted after a faculty meeting:

> Talked too much about sunflower seeds. Meetings are disgusting and

ridiculous. People don't seem to be interested in kids. They don't look upon them as humans.

(This attitude was still present at the end of the study.)

With the large amounts of money going to poverty areas, Fairfield got its share of new programs and consultants of all persuasions. Eight different consultants came to the school in the first year of the League, exclusive of our staff. This proved to be an irritant to teachers. They complained of differing sets of expectations from different consultants. Our hunch is that barraging a group of teachers with consultants is at best frustrating; at the very least, it gives teachers still another thing to complain about. They repeatedly stated that what they needed was equipment like tables and tetherballs, not "theory."

The principal, on the other hand, was very excited about the League. He felt that great things could happen at Fairfield with some impetus from the outside and a connection with other innovative schools. The district, too, fully supported Fairfield's membership in the League. We suspect, however, that this district, like others, saw change as a series of consultants and inputs, rather than as a process that engages people in voluntary activity so that the need for change emerges from the activity rather than from ideas being pushed from the outside.

Life at Fairfield seemed to be hampered by great physical difficulties. Teachers complained, for example, that there was no place where they could physically get together. The staff of forty did not fit comfortably into any of the rooms available. Communication was poor, at least partly because no opportunities existed to get together.

Engagement in activity was fitful. There were occasional twosomes who would team teach, teachers who periodically would "open" their classrooms, but for the most part traditionalism, the attitude of paternalism, and the inability to entertain new ways of thinking about teaching and learning held sway at Fairfield. It appeared that the norms of this school were so powerfully conservative that new ideas could not penetrate. This appeared to be so in spite of the fact that the principal changed radically during the course of the project from an authoritarian leader to one of extreme openness. Teachers noted:

Principal is not authoritarian; faculty is. Faculty likes the status quo. Teachers view parents paternalistically. Not overt prejudice; more— "What can you expect from these families?"

Split between the progressives (25 percent) and the traditionalists (75 percent).

The community of this school seemed willing to accept anything the school would do for their children and thus presented no problems.

The stubborn resistance to engage in activity which could change school life at Fairfield had its roots, we suspect, in a large staff of teachers, many of whom were of questionable competence. As we have stated, in a large school a nucleus of people is needed in the early stages to serve as "early adopters," teachers in the forefront who will try new things. This staff never had such a group to provide initial stimulus. Added to this lack of stimulation was a negative attitude about the children and their competence. On several occasions teachers voiced the opinion that any fault with what was going on in classrooms had to do with the nature of the children's homes.

In this case the principal grew to be a facilitator, district support was great and varied, and community support was quiet but not problematic. Our observations lead us to conclude, therefore, that it was the teachers who inhibited the school from entering the stages of change; they did so by their lack of leadership, low expectations, negative attitudes toward the children, lack of assuming responsibility for the school program, and lack of competence.

SUMMARY

The body of data which was gathered in this study answers some questions but raises others.

Having participated for five years with eighteen elementary schools going through a change process, we observed a pattern which engaged teachers in moving from dialogue to activity, to questioning their activities, to examining the whole school program, to engaging in large philosophical questions, commitments, and objectives.

Certain necessary conditions seem to accompany these stages. District commitment to change appears to be a prerequisite, although the commitment may take a variety of forms. A principal needs to be open enough to become aware of teacher, community, and district needs during the change process, and in particular he needs to be able to support teachers. Community support is necessary, even though its growth may be a process much like that undergone by the teachers, being facilitated by a principal who keeps the community informed. The teacher group, having a culture of its own, seems to need at least a few "early adopters" who can serve as an example for the staff. How many we cannot say. But our data strongly suggest that the norms of a teacher group can be so powerful that they can impede any kind of change process or facilitate it. We maintain that the problem is not the paucity of ideas for schools but the lack of knowledge regarding how to engage teachers in meaningful problem-solving activities.

We have tried to suggest that the stages of change interact in an extremely complex way with the necessary conditions for change listed above.

In Seastar, Independence, and Dewey Avenue, we observed that the stages and the conditions all interacted in ways consistent enough to make change possible, although the nuances of principal leadership, type of district support, quality of community support, and character-istics of teaching staff differed.

Shadyside represented a deviant case in that the stages of change and the conditions for obtaining them existed until the delicate bal-ance was upset by a new principal and a structural change within the teacher group.

Fairfield deviated in that all conditions except one seemed to be operative. Strongly conservative and paternalistic norms of the staff appeared to overpower the other supportive conditions (district, com-munity, and principal) for change.

We have tried not to be simplistic nor to overstep the bounds of our interpretation of both the data and our observations. Responding to the fact that there exists a paucity of conceptualizations about the process of change, we offer these data and interpretations as a basis for further exploration and as an aid to asking questions that relate the theory of change to the practice of change in elementary schools.

NOTES

1   For an excellent discussion of the social, political, and economic forces affecting schools, see J. Steele Gow, B. Holzner, and W. Pen-delton, "Economic, Social and Political Forces," in *The Changing American School*, Sixty-fifth Yearbook of the National Society for the Study of Education, Part 2, University of Chicago Press, Chicago, 1966.

2   In a tough-minded way, Michael Katz argues that historically the schools have always served to process children into their social class "slots." Michael Katz, *Class, Bureaucracy and Schools, the Illusion of Change in America*, Praeger, New York, 1971.

3   For a comprehensive review of the role of professionals in curriculum development see John I. Goodlad (with Renata Von Stoephasius and M. Frances Klein), *The Changing School Curriculum*, Fund for the Advancement of Education, New York, 1966.

4   For a comprehensive review of current philosophy and theories of learning as they relate to childhood, see John I. Goodlad, M. Frances Klein, Jerrold M. Novotney, and Associates, *Early Schooling in the United States*, McGraw-Hill, 1973. Model programs are also discussed and analyzed.

5   John I. Goodlad and R. H. Anderson, *The Nongraded Elementary School*, Harcourt, Brace & World, New York, 1963.

6   See, for example, Kurt Lewin's early description of the change process as including three sets of phenomena: unfreezing, changing, refreezing. Kurt Lewin, "Frontiers in Group Dynamics: Concept, Method and Reality in Social Science: Social Equilibria and Social Change," *Human Relations*, vol. 1, no. 1, June 1947, pp. 5–41.

7   Egon Guba discusses two general strategies: "experimental," in which the intent is to inquire into the possibilities of change, and "aexperimental," in which one inquires into the actualities. Egon Guba, "Methodological Strategies for Educational Change," unpublished paper presented at the Conference on Strategies for Educational Change, Washington, November 1965.

8   Daniel Katz and Robert L. Kahn, *The Social Psychology of Organizations*, Wiley, New York, 1966.

9   Amitai Etzioni, *A Comparative Analysis of Complex Organizations*, Free Press of Glencoe, New York, 1961.

10   Kenneth Blanchard and Paul Hersey, "Change and the Use of Power," *Training and Development Journal*, vol. 26, no. 1, January 1972.

11   An example of the results of failing to take into account the culture of the school can be seen in the demise of the "new math." For a description of the attempt to implement modern math, see Seymour B. Sarason, *The Culture of the School and the Problem of Change*, Allyn and Bacon, Boston, 1971.

12   Howard S. Becker, "The Teacher in the Authority System," *Journal of Educational Sociology*, vol. 27, 1953, pp. 128–141.

13   Matthew Miles, *The Development of Innovative Climates in Educational Organizations*, research note, Stanford Research Institute, Menlo Park, Calif., April 1969.

14   Neal Gross, J. B. Giacquinta, and M. Bernstein, *Implementing Organizational Innovations: A Sociological Analysis of Planned Educa-*

tional Change, Basic Books, New York, 1971. This book provides an excellent discussion of the literature on change, as well as a description of an actual attempted change in an elementary school.

15 Ann Lieberman (ed.), *Tell Us What To Do! But Don't Tell Me What To Do!* an |I|D|E|A| monograph, Institute for Development of Educational Activities, Dayton, 1971. Written by League teachers, this volume expresses the stages of change from their own perspective. In particular, it examines the feelings of dependence upon "authority" figures such as educational consultants of teachers who are in the beginning stages of adoption of an innovation.

16 Lewin, op. cit.

17 Karl E. Weick, *The Social Psychology of Organizing*, Addison-Wesley, Reading, Mass., 1969.

18 Charles Lindblom, "The Science of Muddling Through," *Public Administration Review*, vol. 19, 1959, pp. 79–88.

19 Such factors are discussed by Charles Bidwell in "The School as a Formal Organization," in James March (ed.), *Handbook of Organizations*, Rand McNally, Chicago, 1965.

20 The following references help to provide an accurate picture: Philip W. Jackson, *Life in Classrooms*, Holt, Rinehart & Winston, New York, 1968; Willard Waller, *The Sociology of Teaching*, Wiley, New York, 1965; Dan Lortie, "Teacher Socialization—The Robinson Crusoe Model," in *The Real World of the Beginning Teacher*, Report of the Nineteenth National Commission on Teacher Education and Professional Standards (NCTEPS), National Education Association, Washington, 1966.

21 Matthew Miles, "Some Properties of Schools as Social Systems," in Goodwin Watson (ed.), *Change in School Systems*, Cooperative Project for Educational Development (COPED), National Education Association, 1967.

22 For an extensive explanation of the history and research findings of the entire project, see Mary M. Bentzen and Associates, *Changing Schools: The Magic Feather Principle*, McGraw-Hill, New York, in press.

23 What teachers talk about and do during the change process has been documented in a series of films by Conrad Bentzen, entitled *The League*. For further information, contact the Institute for Development of Educational Activities, P. O. Box 446, Melbourne, Fla., 32901.

24 Amitai Etzioni, "Human Beings Are Not Very Easy To Change After All," *Saturday Review*, June 3, 1972.

CHAPTER 5

WORKING TOGETHER: THE PEER GROUP STRATEGY

Carmen M. Culver, David A. Shiman, and Ann Lieberman

This chapter traces the emergence of the major strategy used by |I|D|E|A|'s Study of Educational Change and School Improvement to develop the League of Cooperating Schools as a social system. The authors describe the evolution of three tactics to encourage League members to view one another as peers, capable of providing information and support to one another in their efforts to change and improve their schools, and able to function as a decision-making body for planning and carrying out its own activities.

The chapter recounts a growing awareness that in order to help the principals and teachers of the League to adopt new behaviors, the SECSI staff had to adopt new behaviors of its own, abandoning the traditionally paternalistic role of the interventionist and practicing instead the part of the facilitator who worked together with the schools.

While Carmen Culver edited *Changing Schools*, the League newsletter, David A. Shiman and Ann Lieberman served as field workers in the League. Dr. Culver is presently a consultant on the evaluation of an Experimental Schools Project for Ultrasystems, Inc., Newport Beach, California.

A teacher who visits another classroom to observe some innovative or imaginative program or teaching technique and then returns to his own room to try out what he has just seen may become discouraged and disillusioned. It just doesn't seem to work! One reason for this apparent failure lies in the fact that he has seen only the end product and has not been part of the process of growth that preceded it. He has not internalized the understandings and frustrations which the observed teacher had experienced during the development of the innovation.

An analogous situation may be seen in reports of research and discussions of new and effective educational strategies. The reader is presented with conclusions. Often for legitimate reasons, only those findings that were statistically significant or those change-promoting techniques that proved successful are presented to the reader. He is screened from methodological blunders and intervention failures. Even in reports of successes the reader may not be given an account of the process of research or development which took place. This is unfortunate, for we can gain a better understanding of both the successes and the failures when we have shared in the processes that were so much a part of the product. Only through such sharing can we insure that each new group of educational researchers or interventionists does not have to rediscover the wheel.

The aims of |I|D|E|A|'s Study of Educational Change and School Improvement—to effect and study the processes of change in schools —have been outlined in the Introduction. As project staff members, our role was to interact with the staffs of the eighteen schools of the League of Cooperating Schools as they attempted to bring about various changes which they saw as desirable. We believe that what we learned in the process can be of value to others. We did not enter into our relationship with these schools with a clearly defined model to implement and test. The intervention strategies which we ultimately adopted resulted from a frustrating, although illuminating, period of experimentation. We were able to test out and evaluate many of the traditional modes of intervention and to devise new and effective means of instituting and fostering educational innovation in both the classroom and the school at large. We learned that strategies which we and many like us had previously relied upon in our efforts to effect change in schools are not necessarily the best ways to reach teachers and to promote in them their potential for self-development and self-renewal.

The purposes of this chapter, then, are to share with the reader the development of those intervention strategies which we found to be most effective in helping to bring about change in schools,[1] to examine some implications of these strategies both for interventionists and for schools, and to present some suggestions for those engaged in the attempt to effect change in schools.

LOOKING BACKWARD

The overarching change strategy which ultimately emerged from our efforts was rooted in the creation of a social system whose members—the principals and teachers of the eighteen League schools—were encouraged to view each other as peers. This new peer group, in turn, was encouraged to adopt a commitment to educational innovation as a norm, with the members of the group mutually reinforcing this norm. Thus, whereas innovative behavior might be discouraged or at the least go unrewarded in a single school's own district, such behavior would be endorsed and supported by the new League peer group, whose membership cut across district lines.

Central to the success of this strategy was that membership in the new peer group be viewed by group members themselves as important and desirable. Without feelings of identification with the new group, its individual members would be apt to continue to hew to the change-inhibiting norms of their own districts. To accept the risks of disapproval and criticism from schools within their own districts, then, League members needed to perceive the League itself as highly valuable.

Three major tactics which emerged to increase the importance of belonging to the League were (1) the generation of opportunities for League members to serve as sources of information, inspiration, and aid to their fellow group members as well as to interested outside groups who were experimenting with educational innovations; (2) the development of the League as a decision-making body capable of planning and carrying out its own activities; and (3) development of effective interschool communication, especially the publication of a newsletter, to disseminate information about the new group to its members and to a wider audience.

Clearly, the peer group strategy called upon principals and teachers to adopt a variety of new behaviors—to lead instead of follow, to give information rather than merely receive it from the "experts," to make decisions instead of depending on the decisions of others. And just as clearly, the strategy called upon the |I|D|E|A| staff to adopt new behaviors as well, for the strategy was at odds with the traditional interventionist-client relationship. If the schools were to be able to behave in new ways, then we had to encourage them to do so by abandoning our own traditional role. Rather than acting as the sole source of inspiration and information concerning educational innovations, the decision makers who planned and executed League activities, or the experts who produced the newsletter for the benefit of the schools, we had to be willing to pull back, encouraging the schools in their efforts to fill these roles themselves.

To do this required a delicate balance, difficult to achieve, and neither our need to play a new role nor the means for doing so were clear to us at the start. As previously observed, the peer group strategy did not exist from the first as a fully developed model to guide our efforts. Rather, it became a fully cogent rationale only in the fourth year of the League, emerging from the failures, frustrations, and understandings of the early years. Even though we were an organization committed to the task of examining and supporting educational innovation, during those early years we showed through our selection of intervention strategies that we were ourselves tradition-bound. We were, after all, merely retread practitioners. Quite unimaginatively, we did at first what we knew and did not wander very far from the tried and true—or untrue—paths of the past.

The process of gestation, growth, and conceptualization of those first three years can perhaps best be understood in terms of the evolution of the three tactics mentioned above—the emergence of League members as sources of information and inspiration to their fellow group members, the development of the League as a decision-making body, and the increased communication among the schools, especially in their production of the League newsletter.

The Changing Sources of Information and Support

As the League began in the fall of 1966, we brought to it an implicit assumption: We were the "haves" and the schools were the "have-nots," and our task was to share with them what we knew so that they could benefit from it. We wanted to effect change in the schools, and so we set about devising methods for conveying information to the schools which would help them to change.

Although we did not want to impose or prescribe specific types of change, such as changes in instructional programs or techniques, we were nevertheless confronted with the need for a catalyst, a theme which would provide an element of common purpose for the League without threatening or alienating the schools. The theme of individualization of instruction seemed to lend itself well to our needs. Its rationale was based on solid research evidence on individual differences as well as the psychology of learning. But, perhaps more important for our purposes, individualization of instruction was an "unshackling topic." It defied precise definition and therefore meant different things to different people. It provided teachers and principals with considerable freedom in interpretation. We could suggest what individualization might entail without dictating the specific form that it should take.

With this theme in mind, we called upon outside experts to act as consultants. Their initial efforts were directed mainly at the principals, for we saw the principal as the key agent of change and sought to rely on him as the communication link between |I|D|E|A| and his staff. The task of the expert consultants was to share their knowledge with the principals and encourage them to promote changes in their schools. They reported research findings, discussed alternatives, and exhorted principals to think about the broader, more general issues involved in effecting change.

A second source of information was provided through field workers. These were principally graduate students from UCLA. In comparison with the experts, who generally met with the principals in the quiet of |I|D|E|A|'s office, the field workers made contact in the schools themselves. They were assigned to specific schools which they visited regularly twice a month. Their role was to help the schools in their efforts to identify some innovative project on which they wanted to work and to interpret relevant research findings to the schools. Perhaps most important, though, was the fact that the field workers raised questions and encouraged the teachers to do so as well. They sought to promote an atmosphere of creative disequilibrium in the school so that self-examination and open discussion could become legitimate and unthreatening activities.

Our unstated view of ourselves as the sole source of information began to fade as early as the end of the first year of the League. The schools, and particularly the principals, were urging more interschool communication as well as more direct contact of |I|D|E|A| staff with the teachers, for, despite the visits of the field workers, some teachers still had very little idea of what the League of Cooperating Schools was all about. One reason for their ignorance was that not all principals were serving as effective communication links between |I|D|E|A| and their own staffs. Some principals relied solely on the field workers to communicate with the teachers about the League, feeling themselves inadequate to do so. Other principals dittoed the materials and information they received at |I|D|E|A| meetings and passed them on to the teachers, while still others merely attended the meetings and communicated little if anything to their staffs. As a result, while some of the teachers were developing a tenuous attachment to this thing called "the League," others showed some resentment that their principal was involved in something of which they were not a part. This finding spurred us to consider new avenues of intervention which would more effectively bring the teachers into the project.

At the same time, we began more fully to appreciate the fact that although the eighteen schools were members of the same association, they had markedly different needs and interests. As champions of individualization in the classroom, we began to see that we needed to individualize our own strategies to take these differences among schools into account. For some schools, we believed that continued on-site intervention by the field workers and other |I|D|E|A| staff members was undesirable since it would promote a type of dependency upon |I|D|E|A| that we did not wish to encourage. However, we felt that other schools still needed this sort of attachment.

During the second year (1967–1968), we acted upon our first-year evaluations and began to modify some of our intervention strategies. We still did not have a clear idea of what our role should be and still had not meaningfully conceptualized an operational definition of the League. However, our experiences with the schools were making the League a much more cooperative venture. |I|D|E|A| would still provide the leadership, but it became evident that regardless of the form the League finally took, it would be a product of our interaction with the schools rather than of our exclusive direction.

The two most important changes made in our intervention strategies during the second year were our conscious attempt to include teachers in League activities and our new way of utilizing consultants. We invited teachers to an all-day conference at a large and prestigious hotel, where our staff was introduced and our director made a keynote address. At this conference, teachers took part in small group discussions in which they met teachers from other League schools. Many became aware for the first time that they were part of something big and that there were people who would support their attempts at innovation. In addition, teacher representatives were now asked to join the principals at the monthly meetings held at |I|D|E|A| offices. This provided them with the opportunity to participate with the principals as well as to meet as a separate group in special gatherings which we arranged for them. A third activity to involve teachers consisted of area conferences which were presented at different schools and which teachers helped to plan and organize to some degree.

The change in the utilization of consultants was related to the increased participation of teachers in League activities. The experts were still on the scene, and we continued to arrange for their visits and to suggest the topics on which they should speak. However, the content of their contributions was altered slightly, to focus on more specific instructional and organizational questions rather than on sweeping, all-inclusive themes such as "What is individualization?"

The role of the field workers also changed slightly. They no longer attempted to cover all the schools systematically, but worked instead with the staffs on the basis of need and interest. In small group discussions and workshops, they examined with teachers and principals specific aspects of instruction, such as team teaching, pupil grouping, and diagnosing pupil differences. Thus, their efforts were bent more on facilitating and organizing activities, and less on interpretation of research and provision of information to the schools.

While the use of these two types of consultants was undergoing modification, a third began to emerge. Teacher consultants made their appearance. We had begun to identify League teachers who not only had expertise in a variety of areas but who also possessed that enthusiasm characteristic of teachers who have found a good thing and wish to share it. They were given the responsibility of serving as discussion coleaders, along with |I|D|E|A| personnel, at one of the all-day conferences. This turned out to be an important event, for we discovered in them an untapped resource which could be utilized in our efforts to promote innovative changes in the schools. The discussion sessions were an outstanding success, and we immediately started planning to incorporate these teacher consultants into our intervention strategy.

The direct involvement of teachers in League activities added a new and exciting dimension to our experience. Teachers were beginning to know each other, develop relationships, and make plans for future contacts. Their appetites had been whetted; now they were beginning to want to learn what was going on in other League schools and to share their own experiences. And they wanted support. League principals, too, were developing a greater sense of identity as a group. Their attachments to the League became stronger, for they were beginning to experience isolation from the other schools in their districts, who were labeling League schools "funny farms."

Thus, by the third year (1968–1969), the League social system clearly was emerging, and we devoted much of our effort to developing and strengthening it. The use of experts as consultants was carried on and remained much the same as it had been in the second year. That is, they rarely interacted with principals to the exclusion of teachers, and they avoided global speeches on individualization and change, focusing instead on specific instructional topics, such as fostering inquiry in the classroom, open structure, or reading instruction.

It was through the expanded use of teacher consultants, however, that school staffs most effectively became involved in League activities. We saw that the increasingly active involvement of teachers in League activities was an important element in the task of weaning the schools from their dependency on |I|D|E|A|. We sought, therefore, to utilize the expertise of teachers, while at the same time diminishing our role, in an effort to strengthen the links among schools rather than the link between |I|D|E|A| and the individual school. For this reason, the use of field workers was discontinued. We developed a needs-resources inventory to aid us in identifying persons or schools to which teachers could turn for assistance or to observe particular instructional programs. This helped us to play the role of clearinghouse rather than consultant; we referred teachers' questions to their League peers rather than attempting to answer them ourselves.

Teachers also assumed increased responsibilities as program organizers and discussion leaders. Once during that year, for example, teachers serving as learning center coordinators in their schools met at a League school to discuss common problems and share ideas. At one of the area conferences, teachers ran a "show and tell" session, in which they described the educational program in their own schools. And on several other occasions, teacher consultants assumed the chairman's role in discussions organized at all-day conferences.

The teachers responded with enthusiasm to the opportunity to meet with fellow teachers; yet as we gave them increased responsibility for conducting discussion sessions, they expressed insecurity, saying that they did not know how to perform the function of group leader. Resisting the temptation to regain control, we instead provided them with some general guidelines for leadership. But we found that another form of help was needed as well. We had to convince them that they were in fact the right people to serve as group leaders, and we assured them that a group leader, no matter who he may be, must learn to lead.

We had identified and developed a theme, individualization of instruction, which served us well as an "unshackling topic." It had brought the schools into a dialogue with us and with each other. It had served as a point of departure, and the schools had interpreted it and used it in a variety of ways. That it no longer served as the principal focal point for discussion in the third year was not a matter of concern. In fact, we saw this as evidence that the schools were taking the initiative and identifying their own concerns, rather than depending upon us to do so.

Secondly, we had developed the concept of the League as a social system. The boundaries between and within schools were breaking down, and open, fruitful dialogue was taking place. New avenues of information and support had been opened which could enable schools to pursue educational innovations in a positive and unthreatening atmosphere. This is not to say that in fact all the League schools had become markedly innovative, nor that those who had done so had experienced no feelings of threat or discomfort at trying something new. As one teacher expressed it:

> When |I|D|E|A|'s new concepts were first introduced to our school, I had misgivings. We started putting these new concepts into action with great trepidation.[2]

However, it was a start.

Finally, our role as interventionists had been clearly defined. We were no longer the experts who descended upon the schools or who provided the impetus for their group meetings. We were instead part of a cooperative effort with the schools. Our task was to ensure that communication links among the members of the social system were strengthened and that the exchanges and visitations among schools became more frequent and more meaningful. The teachers, not the |I|D|E|A| staff or the outside experts, were becoming the active interventionists. We were becoming the coordinators. Through their increasing involvement, teachers were becoming aware that they had something of value to contribute. They could become the major source of information and support.

That the role of expert was a new one to the teachers was evidenced by their initial frustration. Annoyance and disillusionment with the |I|D|E|A| staff were frequent reactions to our refusal to provide directives. As one teacher expressed it, "Finally we became angry because |I|D|E|A| wasn't helping us by telling us what to do. Weren't they experts?"[3] In many cases, it was some time before teachers could view themselves as experts and begin to enjoy the fact that they did possess something of value to share with their peers. One teacher said:

> Our staff spent a year listening to experts who gave us no answers. How wise they were! They made us find our own way. . . .[4]

Another reported:

> It finally occurred to me that . . . it was really up to us. The change could only come from our creativity . . . and the motivation to change had to come from an individual or a group of individuals who want to plan together.[5]

In other cases, the metamorphosis was never achieved:

> I wasn't at all sure anyone knew what the discussions were about or where they were leading. It sounded terribly philosophical and that was boring. All I know for sure was that there were discussions. . . .[6]

We had hoped to increase the importance of the League by providing the opportunity for League members to act as sources of information and aid to outside groups as well as to other League members. As it happened, this opportunity arose from the teachers themselves. At the end of the third year, at one of the conferences, we had arranged for a group of teachers to meet to discuss changes in which they had been involved since the League had begun. It was our purpose to get a story for the League newsletter. But the teachers who met made it clear that they had a need of their own. They had come a long way in the previous three years. Many of them had painfully examined their teaching practices and found them wanting; they had made many new discoveries about themselves and about teaching. They wanted to share these experiences with other teachers.

We called the group together and encouraged them to write about their experiences. The group met six times during the next year, with an |I|D|E|A| staff member serving as liaison. In these meetings they hammered out a way of sharing very personally with other teachers the pain, frustration, and exhilaration that comes with examining and trying out fresh ways of working with children and with each other.

The initial meetings were a little strained. The teachers found themselves in a position of sharing their fears and failures as well as their excitements and successes. They realized that for most of them it was the first time they had fully exposed their innermost thoughts to other teachers, as well as to the |I|D|E|A| staff. At one meeting, struggling to express the tension which they had all felt between the desire to become self-directed and the opposing wish to lean on the |I|D|E|A| "experts," one teacher suddenly jumped out of her chair and announced, "You know what we should call our monograph? 'Tell us what to do, but don't tell *me* what to do!'" We laughed; but that became the title.

The same desire to share what they had learned with other teachers led a second group to produce a book on the theme of individualization of instruction. Preliminary discussions concerning this book made it clear that there was no one definition of individualization and no two teachers practiced it in the same way. Rather, in the foregoing years, each had evolved her own way of working, based upon a number of variables. Some individualized in a teaming situation, while others worked alone; some applied individualization to multigraded classrooms, others to self-enclosed situations, and still others practiced it in learning centers. Feeling that this variety could provide teachers in almost any situation with some ideas and some support for innovating, the group set about to write. The tone of this book is different from that of the monograph of the previous year. Whereas the monograph had dealt with the struggle to change, this volume is written from the point of view of teachers who *have* changed. It contains explanations, encouragement, suggestions, recommendations. In this book, then, the teacher as the source of information and inspiration comes of age.[7]

The Changing Locus of League Decision Making

Although many teachers did emerge as leaders, their initial reluctance to take leadership positions and to see themselves as valuable resources seemed to us to be related to the passive role which the teacher traditionally plays. Teachers are so used to being "done to" that they are not accustomed to seeing themselves as decision makers. And yet, it was considered of great importance in strengthening membership ties in the League that the League group be developed as a decision-making body which would plan and carry out its own activities.

One way to increase the capacity for decision making in the League was to develop it in each of the schools. Thus, during the last two years of the League (1969–1971) we began to emphasize the importance of full-staff involvement in the affairs of each school by espousing a process which we called *DDAE*. DDAE referred to the steps of dialogue, decision making, taking action, and evaluation which we saw as necessary to the development of each staff as an actively functioning body.[8]

Meanwhile, in the League itself, teachers had gradually been assuming a greater share in determining the activities they wanted and in planning to bring those activities about. It was in the fourth year, however, that their role as decision makers was more sharply accelerated by the formation of the Teacher Activities Group (TAG). This group, consisting of volunteers from the schools, took on the responsibility of providing the direction which conferences and workshops would take. Interestingly enough, the "TAG group," as it was called, began by declaring that we could no longer treat the teachers as a monolithic whole. It was felt that League teachers fell into at least three groups, and that this had to be considered in the planning of conferences. There was one group of new teachers, who had joined school staffs after the League had begun and knew little about the League. The TAG group felt that these teachers needed the inspirational messages about innovation and about the League as a powerful mechanism for change which older League members had received earlier. A second group was characterized as those who were willing to experiment with innovations such as individualization of instruction, but needed more help on how to go about it. And a third group was defined as being in an "advanced rut," having changed considerably through the adoption of innovative practices but now seeking more new ideas. This group was now asking questions such as, "Under what conditions does this seem to be a worthwhile change?" They were concerned with the evaluation of innovations they had adopted and the effects of these innovations on children.

The conferences, said the TAG group, had been good for support and for the exchange of ideas, but why not provide for the differences that existed in these three groups of teachers?

It has been previously observed that from the first year of the League the |I|D|E|A| staff had recognized the need to approach the schools on an individualized basis. And yet, here were the teachers themselves pointing out the need to individualize along different lines. One may speculate that in some cases they perceived of the League as an entity more clearly than we did, for it will be noted that the groups defined by the TAG members cut across school lines.

It was to provide for these various groups that the TAG members drew up a plan for activities, to take place once a month for five months. One such activity was an orientation meeting for teachers who were new to League schools or who simply wished to learn more about the League. The meeting was an informal one, with "old" League teachers relating to the newcomers their experiences with the League. Another activity was a series of Saturday morning meetings with |I|D|E|A| staff members. Each meeting was devoted to a specific topic, such as team teaching or humanizing the curriculum, and was attended by teachers especially interested in that subject.

One All-League Conference was planned that year, and a nationally known consultant was invited to speak. Although we ourselves contacted the consultant, it was the teachers who decided upon the kind of interaction they would have with him, taking into consideration the three previously identified teacher groups and their varying levels of commitment and understanding. Area meetings followed which featured small-group discussions of materials and methods of approaching various subject areas.

During the fourth year the TAG group also exercised an important decision-making function in regard to interschool visitations. In earlier years, we at |I|D|E|A| had made the decisions concerning which schools were "worthy" of being visited. We encouraged visitation to schools which we expected would provide teachers with stimulation and support to try new ways of doing things in their own schools. But in the fourth year it became clear that the teachers had rather specific expectations of their own for these visits. These the TAG group drew up as standards: Visitors should be able to interact fruitfully with fellow League members and come away with ideas and materials; visitors ought to question what they see at the host school as well as seek answers to their own problems; and the host school ought to set aside time to welcome and interact with its visitors.

Thus, teachers were now asking much more of their League peers. Whereas once they had looked to us to provide answers, now they were asking for a dialogue of a very sophisticated nature with other teachers. They wanted to feel free to ask questions, to challenge each other as to the validity of innovations which they saw demonstrated, to find out about the problems they could anticipate if they tried the same innovations. More than that, they were asking their fellow League members to welcome them; they felt they were special and wanted to be treated as if they were. The importance of League membership and the teachers' awareness of themselves as members of a group seemed clear at this point.

The fifth year (1970–1971) opened with a meeting of the Teacher Activities Group to evaluate the activities of the previous year and to plan for the coming one. It was agreed that, like individualizing instruction in the classroom, providing for individual teachers in the League was difficult. As the minutes of that meeting noted:

> Our greatest difficulty is in individualizing for teachers. We do okay with three groups, but when we try to break out we have problems. . . . It was felt that we must do a better job of getting to individuals at our area conferences and larger meetings, and provide group meetings that are real discussions, not lectures by discussion leaders.

The concern that "lectures by discussion leaders" still hung on is evidence of both the persistence of tradition and the desire of teachers to assume an increasingly active role. It was to satisfy this desire that a variety of workshops and conferences led by teachers themselves was planned. One teacher, for example, discussed her experiences with innovative practices in a British Infant School, while another demonstrated techniques for establishing various classroom environments. Our role in such activities was to serve as a liaison and attempt to match needs with resources. In this we were not always successful. At times, we found that we had an imperfect understanding of the teachers' needs, with the result that they were disappointed by what fellow teachers had to offer. And one or two such workshops, while planned, were cancelled owing to lack of interest.

An All-League Conference this fifth year derived from the requests of teachers through their representatives in the Teacher Activities Group. In the morning, there was a wide variety of discussion groups designed around differing teacher interests. These sessions, led by teachers, were in general very successful. An afternoon session on accountability, however, failed to provide the teachers with opportunities for active involvement. Speakers talked in generalities and did not invite teacher participation. Unintentionally, the style of presentation of this afternoon session repeated that of our very first League conference. The experts spoke, the teachers listened. It is notable that, impressed as the teachers had been with a like presentation during that first year of the League, in this last year the lack of opportunity for active involvement proved disappointing to them.

During the spring of the League's final year we worked with the Teacher Activities Group to plan a two-week period of visitation, called the League Fortnight. Each school played host on a different day, and visitors were invited to spend the entire day. After school, many of the schools held workshops with teachers presenting their specialties.

The Changing Nature of the Newsletter

The development of teachers as sources of information and support and the emphasis upon increased decision making by League members in planning and carrying out their own activities were two tactics which emerged to increase the importance of the League. A third tactic was the publication of *Changing Schools,* the League newsletter. The newsletter was seen as a means of disseminating information about the League to its members and to a wider audience. And in fact *Changing Schools* was distributed, both nationally and internationally, to some 2,000 libraries and individual educators.

The evolution of *Changing Schools* reflects the evolution of the peer group strategy itself. The first few issues carry many of the earmarks of the traditional, institutional newsletter and betray the "have–have not" assumption remarked upon earlier as well. Volume one, number one provides an example. The masthead is formal, schematic, and of a green often seen on the walls of classrooms. The photographs feature |I|D|E|A| staff members and expert consultants, and |I|D|E|A| personnel are listed, by title, on the front page. The lead article, which makes reference to "|I|D|E|A| Headquarters," is devoted to an explanation of the formation of the League. Three additional articles discuss individualization of instruction: two of these deal with approaches to individualization, and the third reports on a speech delivered on the subject by an outside expert-consultant. A bibliography of readings on individualization is presented. Finally, a map showing the location of the League schools is given, together with a listing of the schools and their principals.

This first issue set the tone of the newsletter for the first two years or so. Each issue attempted to assert the importance of the League by tying it to |I|D|E|A| as a prestigious, nationwide organization, by expounding the unique quality of the League, and by offering the thinking of experts on innovative issues. Toward the end of the second year, the newsletter began to mirror our view of the principal as the key agent of change in the school by devoting articles to that subject and by featuring interviews and photographs of the League principals themselves.

During the third year, our attempts to draw teachers into more active participation with the League are very evident in *Changing Schools*. Thus, one issue was devoted to "the changes that teachers in League schools have been experiencing as well as their attitudes and perceptions of those changes."[9] For the first time, League teachers were quoted at length, with accompanying photographs, and reports of innovations in the schools focused upon the efforts of the teachers. Although still presenting material on principals and on the League concept, subsequent issues that year featured articles written by teachers themselves, in which they reported innovative classroom strategies which they had been trying.

Our effort to focus more heavily on teachers that third year was aided by the fact that we had developed a more systematic means of communication with the schools. Whereas previously information had been gleaned from informal discussions with principals and teachers, or by visits of |I|D|E|A| staff to the schools, we now had instituted *League Reports*. These were written reports, submitted twice monthly to |I|D|E|A| by teachers. Each school made its own decision about how reporters were to be selected. Some rotated this function, while others selected one or two teachers to serve for the entire year. Reporters were paid $25 for each report. They were to provide specific information concerning staff discussions of school matters and contacts made with other League schools. This information was treated as confidential. However, it did provide leads which we could follow up for newsletter articles.

The last two years of the League brought even more dramatic changes to the newsletter. Feedback indicating that many teachers simply were not reading the newsletter spurred us to develop ways to make it more relevant to their concerns and to give it a much more active role in emphasizing the peer-consultant relationship of League teachers. For this reason, a number of changes were made.

First, we changed the method of distribution. We found that one reason some teachers were not reading the newsletter was that they were not receiving it. We had been sending *Changing Schools* directly to teachers' homes, but with new teachers frequently joining school staffs and others moving, our mailing lists were never current. A more efficient method—and one which was less time-consuming and less costly to us as well—was to send the newsletter in bundles to League reporters in each school, who were charged with distributing them. It was hoped that this method would have an additional psychological benefit of providing a catalyst for discussion among teachers, when they saw their fellow teachers receiving and reading the newsletter.

Secondly, we asked for the help of League reporters in getting more information to us. We explained that we were interested in learning more about the needs and resources of each school and in receiving articles written by teachers. We asked them to encourage their staffs to submit material through them and assured them that we were eager to publish their ideas, their contributions, and their needs. Each League report, then, was to be divided into material which the school wanted to release to other schools and material which it wished to keep confidential.

Finally, we made a number of changes in the format and the content of the newsletter itself. We felt that one way to make the teachers feel that it was indeed their newsletter was to make it less formal. To this end, we scrapped the green "institutional" masthead in favor of a magenta one which featured a child's drawing of a schoolhouse. We used casual photographs of teachers talking together, as well as occasional pictures of children. And we strove for less formal diction in an attempt to personalize the newsletter and to avoid the stance of the experts preaching to the "have nots."

We also attempted to make the newsletter more timely. That is, we felt that perhaps one reason *Changing Schools* had not been widely read was that it tended to concern itself with events which had already happened—League conferences which had taken place the previous month, interschool visitations or workshops which had passed, and so forth. For this reason, while still reporting on past events, we also focused on activities to come. For example, one column entitled "TAGlines" reported on plans being made by the Teacher Activities Group for upcoming events. Another regular feature, borrowed from daily newspapers, was a section of want ads, called "LCS Classified." This column drew upon the League reports to present short entries concerning the needs and resources of the schools and urged teachers to contact each other directly to give or receive help. Some samples:

ART PROGRAM—multi-media approach, highly individualized. Contact Pat Thompson, Cucamonga Jr. High.

E.M.R. teacher experienced in group leadership and helping group define objectives. Palm School.

Teachers working on narrative reporting form. Would welcome suggestions. Banyan School.

Names, addresses, and telephone numbers of each school were included in each issue to encourage interaction.

The desire for timeliness as well as greater informality led to another change in the newsletter halfway through the fourth year. Up to that point, *Changing Schools* had been printed by a local shop. The tasks of conferring on layout, supplying photographs, and the printing itself created a lag of at least six weeks in the production of the newsletter—this in addition to the time required to collect the information and actually write copy. This made it very difficult to keep readers informed of coming events and to supply relevant information concerning needs of the schools. We made the decision, therefore, to produce *Changing Schools* in the |I|D|E|A| office. Although the process of layout and reproduction took more of our time, and while we regretted the loss of means for using photographs, this method did allow us to produce more issues in a shorter time span.

Throughout the last two years, in issues with titles like "Teacher-to-Teacher" and "With a Little Help from Your Friends," the message of the newsletter was reiterated. It is perhaps best summed up in an editorial: "Because they are involved in educational change, League teachers have special problems and questions. But for the same reason, they also have special ideas and answers. In their attempts to innovate, teachers may turn to the results of research or to consultant help. But there is another vast resource upon which League teachers can draw—each other."[10]

The contribution of *Changing Schools* to the peer group strategy is, of course, somewhat difficult to gauge. Certainly it is clear that when invited to contribute to the newsletter, many teachers were willing to do so. Succeeding months brought increasing requests for needs-resources items to be printed, as well as manuscripts by a variety of teachers. As in their reaction to leadership of discussion groups and to acceptance of themselves as "experts," we found among contributing teachers a hesitancy concerning whether or not they had anything of value to write about, coexistent with a desire to write it anyway and a feeling of pleasure that they should become published authors.

Data gathered during the spring of the League's final year also indicate that *Changing Schools* may have helped to support the peer group strategy. They show that by far the majority of teachers was reading the newsletter and that a high correlation existed between readership and the perception of the League as an organization devoted to the exchange of ideas among peers. They also show that readership of the newsletter was highest in those schools which had most fully developed the processes of dialogue, decision making, action, and evaluation (DDAE) among the staff.

Some Findings

Throughout the League project, data collected from the schools helped us to determine their feelings about the League and provided guidance in our development of strategies. We found that as early as the second year of the League, teachers were expressing an awareness of the potential of their peers as resources. When asked to rank four different types of League activities, 50 percent of the randomly selected sample of teachers listed visiting other League schools as most important, while only 10 percent said that it was better for |I|D|E|A| to spend its efforts giving solutions to specific classroom problems rather than helping the school staff to use a problem-solving approach to find its own answers.

During the final year of the project, League teachers were asked to indicate what they felt to be the major advantages of the project and to offer some general evaluation of their five-year experience. The opportunity to have contacts with other teachers in the throes of change, to exchange ideas and help each other—both in one's own school and in other League schools—stood out as the single most important advantage, receiving the highest percentage of responses in over 72 percent of the schools.

An average of about 40 percent of the teachers took advantage of the opportunity to meet with other League teachers at workshops and conferences during the last two years of the League. This figure ranged much higher in some schools and was as low as 9 percent in the least active school. During the final year of the project, about one-third of the teachers visited other League schools. When we consider the fact that some of the League schools were separated by as much as 250 miles and were 60 miles from the nearest League school, this figure appears quite substantial.

Finally, teachers who had transferred out of League schools were asked to compare their past and present experiences and to comment specifically on their League experiences. Although this survey sample was very small, the responses are worth reporting because of their near unanimity. All stated that their peers in League schools had been receptive to new ideas and willing to try out new programs, while only

18 percent found this to be the case in their present school. Also, 91 percent felt the League teachers had been supportive and helpful in their efforts to try something new, whereas only 37 percent found this to be the case in their present school.

Responses by these transferred teachers to a question regarding what being in a League school had meant to them show a definite pattern:

> There was a constant flow of ideas which came from teachers on the staff of our school and other League schools. This does not exist now and I feel frustrated. There does not seem to be the excitement in my work this year.

> Opportunity for lots of verbal exchange, many visits; chance to be "where it's at" in education. I miss it!.

> It gave me infinite freedom to do many of the things I wanted to do. . . . I also enjoyed the contacts made with League people and other schools and felt the joy of sharing ideas on a high plane. I would like to be included in League activities, should it be possible.

And finally,

> Last year we functioned as a group. . . . There was more enthusiasm about what kids were doing. This year most people complain.

The availability of teacher resources, the chance to talk, and the opportunity to grow were the major benefits these teachers accrued from their League association.[11]

SOME IMPLICATIONS OF WORKING TOGETHER

In the preceding pages we have discussed only some of the events, tactics, and experiences involved in the evolution of our major strategy for change. Although we have taken care not to gloss over the problems and failures, we nevertheless feel quite certain that the brevity of the foregoing history may make the development of the peer group strategy appear deceptively simple. In fact, however, the utilization of such a strategy must take into consideration four key elements, each of which is extremely complex. These are (1) the culture of the school; (2) the role of the principal; (3) the role of the teachers; and (4) the philosophy of the change agent or organization.

Waller's classic work[12] as well as Sarason's contemporary work[13] insightfully describe the culture of the elementary school. Teachers face a group of students who have purposes of their own and somehow must excite these young people about a variety of subjects, while at the same time having to legitimate their authority. The situation has become increasingly stressful today because the goals of the school are often unclear and in many ways contradictory. Teachers are being asked to teach children to "learn how to learn" and also to teach them the cultural imperatives, the "three R's." Ideas for achieving these goals are proliferating in the field, but the means to implement the ideas are almost nonexistent.[14] This situation leaves teachers in a position of raised expectations concerning what they are supposed to do, but with little opportunity to develop ways of doing it, and with no one in the school responsible for helping them.

Nor is experimentation on one's own encouraged. The school culture, like that of other small-scale organizations, inhibits innovators. Teachers are rewarded for keeping their shop in order—not for experimenting with new ideas or new curricula.

Another alternative, that of working together with fellow teachers, is inhibited as well. Teachers are separated from each other by the physical structure of most schools—the ubiquitous "eggcrate" classroom—and thus are not accustomed to working together. As a matter of fact, too much openness, too forthright an appeal for help, might create contempt among one's peers, who are used to working alone and in a sense protecting their own domain, their classroom.

It is only natural, then, that teachers should look outside the school to the "experts" for ideas and direction. From them, it is felt, one can get help with no strings attached, even though most of the ideas received do not take into consideration the uniqueness of one's school, student population, or community.

The principal, too, is in an extremely difficult position. He or she is being called upon to have his teachers individualize instruction, team teach, and so forth. Yet, typically the principal is just learning about these innovations himself. His traditional role is that of decision maker for his school; yet, if he is to help his teachers to adopt innovative behaviors, he must share some of this decision-making power with them. Since he is unable to tell them what to do, he must instead try to create a climate in which they can be free to experiment.

Given these complexities, a peer group strategy can fill a very large gap. Nevertheless, the interventionist is apt to find that the strategy is in conflict with the culture of the school and with the traditional expectations and roles of teachers and principals. More than that, he is apt to find that the strategy is in conflict with his own traditional "expert" role. Thus, it is necessary that he not only accept the notion of the teachers as expert, but that he consciously work at the peer group strategy, symbolically, physically, socially, and philosophically. This means finding teachers with expertise and convincing them that they possess it. It means creating situations in which their expertise, in as many areas and on as many levels of sophistication as possible, can be demonstrated to other teachers. It means encouraging teachers to think and to write about their shared experiences to convey them to others. And finally, it means learning how to facilitate instead of direct.

|I|D|E|A| attempted to combat many of the forces of tradition by creating a countervailing force consisting of many schools in a variety of districts, drawn together into a new social system. This is not necessarily to say, however, that it is impossible to create such a social system within the single school or within the single district. The League provided impetus and support for change within the schools, but it nevertheless was up to each school to adopt the new behaviors which would allow change to occur.[15] While they draw upon our experience with the League, then, the following suggestions for action are intended for implementation within the single school and/or district. None of the suggestions is simple, and all are demanding in terms of the amount of time, effort, and ingenuity they require of the interventionist, as well as of the school.

SOME SUGGESTIONS FOR ACTION

1   There is much that teachers can learn by visiting fellow teachers in their own school, watching them teach, and discussing with them what they are attempting to achieve.[16] Such visitation can only succeed in an atmosphere of openness and free exchange, however, in which teachers feel safe enough to open their classrooms. If such an atmosphere is to be promoted, the principal must be encouraged to facilitate discussion with his staff concerning classroom problems, to support teachers who are experimenting with innovations, and to provide substantive help.[17] As a simple example of the kind of help which is needed, the principal and assistant principal can take over classes for an hour or two to free teachers for visitations. In schools with team teaching, one team member can be released for a part of the day to go to other classrooms.

2   Teacher involvement in the school's decision-making process is crucial if the staff is going to be able to work effectively together. The

staff can be encouraged to elect a representative teacher steering committee, which meets regularly with the principal to discuss questions of teacher concern. This group might give the principal feedback and input regarding changes in the direction of the school's program (for example, toward open structure or team teaching) that he might be contemplating. It might also take as one of its tasks the responsibility for creating ad hoc committees to deal in depth with specific problems confronting the school. Furthermore, it might provide information for the principal regarding the types of consultant expertise needed to help the school's instructional program. Finally, this committee might organize faculty meetings which would be run without the presence of the school's administrator. This could result an an openness of discussion that sometimes is lacking when the principal is present and would insure that the topics examined are of particular concern to the teachers.[18]

3   A similar sort of teachers' committee might be organized at the district level. As in the case of the single school, this committee might play a major role in suggesting and organizing districtwide workshops and conferences which would genuinely serve teacher needs.

4   A series of school "open houses" could be organized, not for the pupils' parents but for teachers from nearby schools. Teachers from one or two schools at a time might be invited to come to a school, meet with their fellow teachers, visit classrooms, and exchange ideas. Such a plan, carried out systematically throughout the district or even across district lines, could create communication bridges to facilitate the types of dialogue and idea exchange described in this chapter.

5   A new type of intradistrict workshop could be organized in which teachers would work together to develop new skills. Summer sessions might be devoted to microteaching workshops.[19] Each session might have a particular theme, such as the inquiry method, the use of behavioral objectives, the humanistic curriculum, and so forth. Teachers would first study the technique or subject matter and then plan short lessons together which embody the principles of the new approach. Next, some teachers would teach the lesson while others observed. Afterward, the teachers would meet to evaluate what had happened and begin planning again. The benefits of this type of learning experience are considerable.[20]

6   The district could be encouraged to publish and circulate a newsletter similar to Changing Schools. Such a publication, written principally by teachers, could be used both to identify outstanding teachers and to disseminate new ideas. Reporters with functions similar to those of the League reporters could provide material from each school.

7   A conscious effort could be made to identify skilled teachers in the various schools to serve as teacher-experts. These might include a creative reading teacher, an imaginative art instructor, a teacher who has successfully individualized her math program, or one who has integrated music and social studies or has created spelling games, and so forth. Frequently, the necessary resources exist in that district or in a nearby one, and there is little need to hire an outside consultant. It might be necessary only to hire a substitute teacher to replace the district's own talented person, who would then do consultant work. As we have found, such teacher-experts can serve as discussion leaders or demonstration teachers at workshops and conferences, sometimes much more effectively than an outside consultant. The identification and utilization of a core of teacher-experts would give teachers something rarely present in the school—recognition for outstanding work.

8   There are times, of course, when outside consultants will be wanted. When this is the case, they could be utilized in a variety of ways which would promote the sorts of teacher interaction and cooperation advocated in this chapter. As suggested above, teachers might be involved in both the identification of needs and the selection of the consultant. Access to consultants might not necessarily be confined to teachers in a particular school. While the problems of a single school are sometimes unique, teachers in other schools often are grappling with the same sorts of issues. Bringing teachers together from different schools enhances the possibility of wider dissemination of new learning and strengthens interschool communication patterns as well.

NOTES

1   The history of the League project is treated in detail in Mary M. Bentzen and Associates, *Changing Schools: The Magic Feather Principle,* McGraw-Hill, New York, in press.

2   Ann Lieberman (ed.), *Tell Us What to Do! But Don't Tell Me What to Do!* an |I|D|E|A| monograph, Institute for Development of Educational Activities, Inc., Dayton, 1971, p. 1.

3   Ibid., p. 5.

4   Jane O'Loughlin, "Five Years of Individualization," in David A. Shiman, Carmen M. Culver, and Ann Lieberman (eds.), *Teachers on Individualization: The Way We Do It,* McGraw-Hill, New York, 1973.

5   Lieberman (ed.), op. cit., p. 5.

6 Ibid.

7 David A. Shiman, Carmen M. Culver, and Ann Lieberman (eds.), *Teachers on Individualization: The Way We Do It,* McGraw-Hill, New York, 1973.

8 The concept of DDAE is discussed more fully by Bette Overman in "Criteria for a Good School," Chapter 12 in this volume, and by Bentzen and Associates, op. cit.

9 *Changing Schools,* published by Research and Development Division, |I|D|E|A|, vol. 3, no. 3, February 1969.

10 *Changing Schools,* vol. 4, no. 1, December 1969.

11 A complete presentation and discussion of data relating to the League may be found in Bentzen and Associates, op. cit.

12 Willard Waller, *The Sociology of Teaching,* Wiley, New York, 1965.

13 Seymour B. Sarason, *The Culture of the School and the Problem of Change,* Allyn and Bacon, Boston, 1971.

14 Neal Gross, *The Implementation of Educational Innovations,* Basic Books, New York, 1971.

15 In "The Stages of Change in Elementary School Settings," Ann Lieberman and David A. Shiman discuss necessary conditions of change in the single school. (See Chapter 4 in this volume.) In "Criteria for a Good School," Bette Overman presents an instrument for assessing the extent to which the school is engaging in processes necessary to self-renewal, Chapter 12 in this volume.

16 The ability of teachers to adopt certain teaching behaviors from the experience of observing their utilization by other teachers is discussed in Carmen M. Johnson, "The Effects of Analyzing Instruction on the Classroom Performance of Teachers," unpublished doctoral dissertation, University of California, Los Angeles, 1971.

17 The importance of support from the principal is discussed by Kenneth A. Tye in "The Elementary School Principal: Key to Educational Change," Chapter 2 in this volume. Schools wishing to develop skills of systematic and collaborative problem solving may also be referred to Samuel G. Christie, Adrianne Bank, Carmen M. Culver, Gretchen McCann, and Roger Rasmussen, *The Problem Solving School,* Institute for Development of Educational Activities, Dayton, 1972.

18 The use of teacher groups for decision making and problem solving is discussed more fully by Roger Rasmussen and Adrianne Bank in "Mobilizing Group Resources for School Problem Solving," Chapter 6 in this volume.

19 A discussion of microteaching can be found in Walter R. Borg et al.,

The Minicourse: A Microteaching Approach to Teacher Education, Macmillan Educational Service, Beverly Hills, 1970.

20   This suggestion derives from the Planning-Teaching-Observing model developed by Robert H. Anderson and others at Harvard University. The following works contain more information about this model and variations of it: Johnson, op. cit.; John D. McNeil, *Toward Accountable Teachers: Their Appraisal and Improvement,* Holt, Rinehart & Winston, New York, 1971; and Robert Goldhammer, *Clinical Supervision: Special Methods for the Supervision of Teachers,* Holt, Rinehart & Winston, New York, 1969.

CHAPTER 6

MOBILIZING GROUP RESOURCES FOR SCHOOL PROBLEM SOLVING

Roger Rasmussen and Adrianne Bank

The authors of this chapter advocate the use of teacher groups as a powerful force for change within the single school. They demonstrate how such groups can be of use in problem solving at various levels and discuss reasons that group resources are infrequently mobilized for problem solving in the school. Their exploration of a variety of approaches to development of group resources leads them to conclude that although each has advantages, each is incomplete without the others. The chapter ends with a call to the single school to accept the responsibility for finding the means necessary "to transform potential group power into actual group power."

Both authors were involved in the development of |I|D|E|A|'s Problem Solving School Program, an organizational training program designed to develop group skills in problem solving and promote a school climate of trust and self-confidence. Adrianne Bank currently is serving as a specialist in educational program planning at the Center for the Study of Evaluation, UCLA. Roger Rasmussen is completing doctoral studies in management, with a special interest in the social system of the school.

Where does the power to change lie within the single school? Does it lie with the principal? Or with others? Does it depend on individual talents, on principles of organization, on physical facilities? Taken together, the various chapters in this volume which are addressed to this question indicate that each plays a part in the change process. The purpose of this chapter is to provide an additional perspective. We believe that a major underdeveloped source of power to change education for the better exists in group problem solving. When the group resources of teachers within each school are mobilized for efficient and effective problem solving, they can make meaningful contributions to long-term goals of change and school improvement.

After clarifying what we mean by "group resources," we will define three types of problems for which teacher groups are useful and explore the potential of group resources for solving each type of problem. Then we will suggest some reasons why group resources tend to remain underdeveloped in so many schools. Finally, we will review several approaches to mobilizing the group resources of teachers, pointing out some of the features associated with success in each, as well as some of the difficulties.

WHAT ARE GROUP RESOURCES?

As used in this chapter, the term *group resources* refers primarily to the resources of the adult professional and paraprofessional staff of the school. Obviously, there may be student groups interested in solving school problems, and the possibility of joint student-teacher problem-solving groups also exists. Outside of the school there may also be interested persons who can become involved in problem-solving activities related to the school. Some of the ideas in this article may apply to such groups, but we are concerned here mainly with problem-solving groups composed of adult school employees—teachers, student teachers, administrators, counselors, aides, etc.

Our discussion is further limited to groups which meet together *specifically for the purpose of solving problems*. When teachers listen to reports or hear about decisions at faculty meetings, they are not a problem-solving group even though they are meeting together. When teachers in the lunchroom complain that the school is poorly maintained, they are not a problem-solving group, although again, they are meeting together.

A problem-solving group may be large or small. It may consist of the entire faculty or of a few individuals. The meetings of problem-solving groups may be structured or quite informal. Groups may be ad hoc—temporarily called into existence for the purpose of dealing with a particular situation—or they may exist on a formal, continuing basis to discuss and resolve particular kinds of school problems.

THREE TYPES OF SCHOOL PROBLEMS

Group resources can contribute significantly to the solution of three major types of problems which occur in schools. First, there are many problems on which individual teachers must act independently to solve. For these problems, groups can serve as consultants to the individual problem solver by providing ideas and insights into the causes of the problems and suggesting a variety of possible solutions for the individual teacher's consideration. Secondly, there are problems for which small groups of teachers can find excellent collective solutions. The range of possible solutions to teachers' problems often becomes much greater when the responsibility for action can be shared by a group of teachers working together. Finally, there are problems whose solution requires group commitment to a particular strategy by the entire staff of the school. Here, effective group problem solving is likely to increase both the quality of the solution and the staff's commitment to it. We will try to show in some detail why groups have so much to offer in solving each of these three types of problems.

In this discussion, the problem-solving process is regarded as consisting of four phases: identification of the problem; search for and selection of strategies; action; and evaluation.[1] During the first phase, the problem is defined and its causes analyzed. In the second phase, possible solutions are considered, a particular course of action is selected, and the details are worked out. In the third phase, action is taken. Finally, the course of action itself and the outcomes of that action are evaluated.

Within this problem-solving framework, let us look first at some of the reasons why group resources are a great potential source of power in helping the individual teacher solve problems which he has identified and on which he alone must act.

The Group as Consultant to the Individual Problem Solver

Let us say that a teacher has a problem with one of his students: the child reads poorly, seems anxious when called on to read aloud, and avoids reading whenever possible. This kind of problem is often considered to be the teacher's individual problem. After all, each teacher is supposed to be a professional who knows how to handle this type of problem without help from others. It may be true that the professional responsibility for helping the child does belong to the individual teacher, but this responsibility should not be construed as preventing the teacher from using a group of his colleagues as consultants in the problem-solving process.

The advantages of using colleagues as consultants are many. First, when a teacher presents his problem to a group of fellow professionals, he is necessarily forced to clarify his own thinking about the problem. The continuing need to make oneself understood by others is, in itself, a valuable source of motivation for the individual to approach his problem in a systematic way.

A second advantage of using a group of colleagues as consultants is the group's capacity to provide the individual with alternative perspectives on the problem at each phase of the problem-solving process. In the example given above, for instance, there are many ways in which the problem can be defined. Is the desired goal to have the child reading up to grade level? Up to his own potential? Is the goal to have the child develop confidence in himself as a reader regardless of his current level of reading accomplishment? Or is the goal to have the child feel more at ease when he is the focus of attention in the group?

There may be alternative causes of the problem as well. Perhaps the child has an undetected physical incapacity, or perhaps he has not mastered certain skills prerequisite for reading. The range of environmental conditions which may be contributing to the problem is wide: How are the child's parents influencing his behavior? What about his school peers? Is there something which the teacher is doing which contributes to the problem? A single teacher, if he acted alone to diagnose and solve such a problem, might settle too quickly on a particular definition of the problem and its causes, with relatively little exploration of alternative definitions and their implications.

The group can usually see more sides to a problem than any one person can, especially in areas which require social judgments.[2] Different individuals are sensitive to different aspects of human reality. Through their own life experiences, or through training, people tend to become very perceptive in some areas and to develop recurrent "blind spots" in others. Thus, one teacher may be more sensitive than another in understanding a child's difficulties in making friends, simply because he has coped with similar problems in his own life; another teacher may "tune in" on the child's ambivalence about his own achievements; another may be sensitive to his needs for adult approval.

Many times, the individual teacher has trouble making an accurate diagnosis of his own contribution to the problem. Sometimes a teacher may be burdened with guilt feelings of personal responsibility for a problem which others can see is not within his sphere of influence. At other times, he may not see how his own attitudes and assumptions in the classroom are contributing to the problem, even when this contribution is quite obvious to others. In either of these situations, the perspective of others can be helpful to the individual teacher who wishes to find a good solution to the problem by making an accurate diagnosis of its causes.

Group resources can also be a source of power in helping the individual teacher search for workable alternative strategies for dealing with his problem. In the present example of a child's reading difficulties, a group of teachers would almost certainly be able to identify more ways of dealing with the problem than could any one person.

Finally, group resources can be a valuable aid to the individual after he has taken action, at the point where he tries to evaluate his efforts to solve the problem. As in other phases of the problem-solving process, a group can bring a diversity of viewpoints to evaluation which makes it both more complete and more accurate. The group can provide the teacher with perspective in determining how much progress has been made in solving the problem. The group can also point out to the individual teacher the discrepancy which may exist between the course of action he claimed to have followed and the one which he actually did follow.

We have suggested that the discipline of describing his problem to a group can help the individual to gain insight into the nature of his problem and that a group's capacity to generate alternative perspectives can help the individual teacher in problem identification, strategy selection, and evaluation. The action phase—that of actually doing something about the problem—still remains with the individual teacher. However, even in this phase groups can offer social support and encouragement to the individual in his attempts to take action. Innovative or creative action to solve a problem sometimes requires that the teacher behave in unaccustomed ways. Group support and encouragement can help him find the strength to try something new.[3]

The Group as Seeker of Collective Solutions

Let us now look at a second type of problem for which group resources can be helpful. There are many problems in schools which are identified by individual teachers but which can be solved most effectively if more than one teacher takes an active part in the solution. In the first type of problem we discussed, the individual teacher alone was responsible for acting to solve the problem, and group resources were used only to help him clarify the problem and to provide alternative perspectives. In the second type, the *group* takes responsibility for solving the problem, and the role of group members is broadened to include action-taking as well as consultation.

When a group of teachers rather than an individual teacher accepts the responsibility for solving a problem, the possibilities for action often are greatly enlarged. For example, consider the additional kinds of action which a group might take to solve the reading problem which was presented earlier. A member of the group with older students might volunteer to train one of them to tutor the child. A member with younger students might have the child come to his room or area for remedial work in reading. The group might schedule a regular time when this student and others like him could get special attention. One teacher in the group might undertake advanced training in solving reading problems, while another teacher concentrated on handwriting and composition skills.

Consider another example: a problem of chronic conflict between a teacher and one of his students. The teacher can, by himself, try to understand the causes of the problem and try to devise a strategy to deal with it, or he can use his colleagues as consultants to clarify his problem and to get alternative perspectives before he himself takes action. If, however, the problem is redefined so that a group of teachers becomes willing to share the responsibility for successful action in solving the problem, a wide range of possible courses of action emerges.

It might be that the conflict between this particular teacher and child is simply a personality clash which is unique to these two individuals and could be resolved by changing the student to a different classroom; or it might be that a "cooling off" period for the student in the library or under the supervision of another teacher might work. Perhaps a group of teachers with similar problems might work together to get an outside resource person into the school to help them all learn to deal more effectively with such situations.

A group of teachers can bring a broadened range of spatial, temporal, and financial resources to bear on many problems as soon as they are defined as collective or group problems rather than as individual problems. A single teacher may not have the space to set up a reading lounge or a game area for his students, but a group of teachers who have students with similar needs or problems may together be able to find the space for such a solution. A single teacher may not have the time to investigate new materials in particular subject areas suited to the needs of special children, but a group of teachers might be able to enlist outside help for that purpose or divide the work involved in some manner. Advantageous use can be made of special talents and of school resources in schools where individual problems are redefined as group problems and resources are mobilized for their solution.

The Group as Participant in Policy Making

Finally, let us consider the third type of school problem, for which the mobilization of group resources is highly desirable. These are problems in which it is recognized that the entire faculty must cooperate in order to implement the solution. Many problems in allocating common resources, in curriculum development and coordination, in community relations, and in the setting and enforcement of standards for student (and faculty) behavior are of this type. The formulation of solutions to such problems is often made by the principal, who then requests the faculty to carry out his policy decision. However, we are suggesting that group resources be mobilized for these problems not just at the stage where policy is implemented, but also earlier, when the policy is being formulated.

The power of a group in relation to this type of problem comes in part from the kinds of group resources which we have already discussed—the capability of the group to clarify the problem, to offer alternative perspectives, to achieve greater accuracy in analyzing problems requiring social judgment, and to exercise greater flexibility in applying resources to solve problems. An additional resource which groups have in relation to shared or common problems is the feeling of commitment of group members to an action agreed upon by the entire group. Effective problem-solving groups generate powerful forces in support of implementing schoolwide policies which might otherwise have only paper reality.[4]

There are at least three reasons for this power to implement: (1) Group members who have actively participated in the examination of the problem and the search for solutions are familiar with the reasons for the agreed-upon solution and can be more effective and more flexible in implementing that solution. (2) Group members who have been influential in arriving at a solution to a problem are likely to feel personally responsible for carrying out that solution in the best possible manner. (3) Group members are likely to apply informal pressure on one another to carry out the solution in addition to providing one another with support and encouragement.

BARRIERS TO THE EFFECTIVE MOBILIZATION OF GROUP RESOURCES

Since the potential power of groups for solving many types of school problems is so great, why are faculty problem-solving groups so rarely used for school improvement? Most teachers work alone with their students, rarely interacting on a professional basis with one another,[5] and school problems requiring solutions through group effort often simply go unsolved.[6] We believe that a number of interlocking forces are at work which impede group problem solving in today's public schools, including—on the part of teachers and administrators—feelings of vulnerability and powerlessness, problems of time, space, and money, and underdeveloped group skills.

Feelings of Vulnerability

In some schools, problems are considered to be natural occurrences, a regular and necessary part of organizational life and nothing especially to fear. Teachers openly discuss their own problems and what they believe to be the school's problems, with the expectation that this will enhance both their own effectiveness and that of the school. The principal often asks advice of his faculty members and tries to improve his own effectiveness as an educational leader by seeking staff opinions of his leadership practices.

In other schools, problems are more often treated as evidence of inadequate job performance. Teachers hesitate to discuss their classroom problems, though of course everybody has them. Attempts to identify school or group problems are frequently taken to be accusations or personal criticisms of individuals. The principal is not eager to confront his own weaknesses and makes it clear that he does not want to know what teachers think of his leadership or how it might be improved.

We believe the second school portrait is more typical of schools today than the first. The emotional climate in this second type of school is one in which many people feel vulnerable and try to avoid exposing themselves to real or imagined criticism or sanctions against them. Such a climate makes effective use of group resources unlikely because people do not feel safe enough to discuss candidly their individual and common problems in a group setting.

External criticism is certainly one factor which contributes to feelings of vulnerability in many schools. Stinging criticisms of school practices, and of individual teachers and administrators as well, have been made in recent years by conservative community groups, liberal intellectuals, and nearly everyone in between. In addition, today's parents and children are certainly more willing to express their complaints than were the parents and children of the previous generation. The teacher or administrator who has never been put on the defensive, has never monitored his speech and actions for fear of outside criticism, is rare indeed.

Lack of clear measures of student learning as criteria for teaching performance is another factor which contributes to teachers' feelings of vulnerability in schools. Where objective criteria are not used, one must substitute subjective judgments of teaching performance. Such judgments can make the teacher more vulnerable in two ways. First, the teacher himself may not know how good a job he is doing; his sense of self-confidence never has a firm base. Secondly, because subjective judgments are by definition based on the *appearance* of good teaching rather than on any firm measure of actual teaching performance, the art of impression management assumes major importance in helping the teacher without tenure to retain his job. Many a teacher is driven to pretend that the situation in his classroom is much better than he knows it to be, and this kind of pretense leads naturally to feelings of vulnerability: "What if they find out how little my kids are really learning?"

Emphasis on classroom control in lieu of student learning as a criterion for teacher performance is another source of vulnerability for teachers, especially in an age when the authority of the teacher is very much in question and the danger of student rebellion is imminent in some classrooms. Role expectations virtually force the teacher to assert his authority over students who are yearly growing less willing to accept such assertions.

Finally, a lack of serious institutional commitment to the improvement of teacher performance leads to marginal competence or to the outright incompetence of some members of the faculty. Incompetent or marginally competent teachers usually know it and are understandably afflicted by feelings of vulnerability. The system allows their teaching to stagnate or deteriorate and cannot protect them from the personal insecurity which must come from being at or below a minimum standard for the profession.

Feelings of Powerlessness

Many teachers and administrators are so depressed by feelings of their own powerlessness to deal personally with their day-to-day problems or to influence the students in their charge that they have little motivation to involve themselves in faculty problem solving to improve the school or even their own immediate working environment.

One external source of feelings of powerlessness is the lack of meaningful decision-making authority at the level of the individual school, a situation still found in too many districts. Some districts have regulations so thorough in their specifications of what will go on at the individual school that there are no decisions of any real consequence with which faculty groups might concern themselves. Happily, the trend seems to be away from such detailed district regulation of school activities and budgets and toward increased autonomy and decision-making power in the individual school.

Another external source of feelings of powerlessness among school personnel is students who are in school only because the law requires it and who have no interest at all in education, particularly as the school's teachers or administrators define it. After recurrent failures, in the face of student hesitation to accomplish "reasonable" educational objectives demanded by the larger society, many teachers and administrators have all but thrown in the towel. Their defeated and resigned attitude does not make it easy for them to be effective participants in or leaders of group problem solving.

Sometimes the source of feelings of powerlessness is to be found in the working relationships among adults on the school staff. Teachers and administrators can, at times, feel that others on the school staff are blocking, discouraging, undermining, or simply failing to support their attempts to create change in the school. When this happens, the resistance or apathy of other staff members makes the problem seem even larger, and feelings of hopelessness and powerlessness are a common outcome.

Problems of Time, Space, and Money

As teachers and principals know only too well, most schools have problems of time, space, and money which can seriously inhibit the employment of group resources to solve school problems. The sheer logistic problems of housing and supervising hundreds or thousands of warm bodies on a finite budget can severely limit the opportunities of school staffs to meet together during the school day. The recent upsurge in teachers' economic bargaining powers has led to growing resistance among teachers to spending after-school or vacation hours for school-related meetings without pay. In addition, the financial status of most school systems today does not allow them the luxury of paying teachers extra to engage in group planning and problem solving outside of the regular school hours.

In many schools, the present organization of the school day almost totally precludes opportunities for teachers to confer with one another about the problems which they confront. Teachers do tend to have more time today than in the past for planning instruction or preparing materials during the school day, but they still have little opportunity to schedule their free time so that it coincides with that of other teachers with whom they would like to work.

The unavailability or inflexibility of time for group problem solving often is paralleled by the unavailability or inappropriateness of physical facilities. Lunchrooms, cafeterias, auditoriums, and school libraries tend to be less than ideal as meeting places for professional activities. Teachers' lounges often are overcrowded and may be improperly equipped for effective meetings. Private offices for teachers are rare, as are other facilities for small group discussions.

Although group problem-solving activities do not in themselves require large amounts of money—except perhaps to purchase extra time for meeting—a small amount of discretionary money can be quite helpful to acquire the occasional services of a consultant, to build a professional library of books and journals, to buy sample materials, and so forth.

Underdeveloped Group Skills

Another barrier to the effective use of group resources for school improvement is that, quite simply, many teachers and school administrators lack the group skills which are necessary for effective task-oriented collaboration with other adults. There are several reasons for this. First, relatively few university courses, preservice training programs, or inservice programs give serious attention to developing such skills. Second, the relative infrequency of serious group problem-solving efforts in schools today gives teachers and administrators little chance to develop their group skills through practice. Finally, a social norm of avoiding or smoothing over interpersonal conflicts is often found in our schools (as in our culture generally). This norm limits the amount individuals are likely to learn about their effectiveness as group members from their experience with others.

What exactly are we talking about when we use the term "group skills?" For a group to act effectively as a consultant to the individual problem solver, the problem solver must be able to decide when, how, and how much to use the group to help him, based on the nature of his problem and on the time, interests, and special abilities of group members. As consultants, members of the group need to know how to offer ideas and feedback to the problem solver in a way which is helpful to him. Also, like the problem solver, they must be able to balance the individual's need for consultation with the group's time, willingness, and ability to provide it.

For a small group to be effective in solving a common problem, it must be able to approach its task in an inquiring, yet efficient manner and at the same time be able to satisfy at least partially the social needs of its members.[7] This implies two related kinds of skills which are needed for effective small group problem solving: skills in structuring the task and skills in dealing with interpersonal dynamics and individual feelings so that each person can feel satisfaction as a result of his participation in the group's work.

Finally, for a group as large as a total faculty to be effective in solving its common problems, members must have all the skills needed for small group problem solving, plus at least one more: either the skill of structuring problem-solving activities to permit effective participation by the total school staff or the skill of effectively representing the wishes of the total staff on a smaller body or council.

Skills in structuring a group task are important regardless of the type of problem and are especially important as group size increases. Structuring the sequence of discussion is one such skill. All too often, meetings get bogged down in endless discussions concerning proposed solutions before the problem has even been described in such a way that everyone understands it. Likewise, meetings often get sidetracked into arguments about a single proposed solution before the alternative solutions have been considered.

In addition to the skill of structuring activities in an appropriate sequence, there are many other structuring skills which can be of value in mobilizing group resources. Techniques for distinguishing between issues based on misunderstanding and issues based on value differences do exist. So do techniques, such as brainstorming, which help group members freely generate alternative approaches to an issue. Likewise, there are systematic procedures for reaching agreement among group members on priorities or preferences. Very important, too, is the skill of reaching closure on a decision and moving the group along to its next problem. Knowledge of these techniques is requisite for effective mobilization of group resources.

Yet another set of skills—skills in dealing with interpersonal dynamics and individual feelings—is important, regardless of the type of problem or the size of the group. Those who already have some experience with shared faculty problem solving know that group effectiveness can be hindered by an amazing variety of interpersonal factors. Sometimes those with strongly felt positions or those who are especially articulate dominate the group discussion, leaving others to silent frustration. Sometimes alliances among group members provide the meeting with a "hidden agenda" which diverts the group's attention from the main order of business. Sometimes group members do not feel free to express their feelings and opinions openly. Sometimes the group's anxiety about its own progress leads members to avoid coming to grips with the task. Some of these problems of interpersonal dynamics can be reduced by appropriate structuring of the task, but others must be confronted more directly.

Learning to deal directly and effectively with interpersonal problems in a group setting is, we believe, difficult but not impossible for the average group of teachers. Some of the practical ways by which individuals and groups can learn the necessary group skills we have outlined here will be discussed in the next section.

APPROACHES TO MOBILIZING GROUP RESOURCES

We have suggested that a substantial gap exists between what school faculties might gain from effective use of faculty group resources and the present practices of many schools. We have suggested some reasons why this gap exists: feelings of vulnerability and powerlessness; problems of time, space, and money; and underdeveloped group skills. Here we will describe some approaches which can be used to increase a school's power to change by mobilizing the faculty's use of its own group resources.

Practical measures which schools can use to mobilize group resources for problem solving can be classified into two main categories: (1) *training experiences* for individuals or faculty groups, and (2) *structural changes* which facilitate group problem-solving efforts. We will try to show that a combination of training experiences and structural changes in the school represents the best overall strategy for improvement.

Training Experiences

Let us look first at some of the training experiences which have been used within organizations to minimize unproductive competition and secretiveness and to train individuals in the skills necessary for making effective use of group resources.

Sensitivity Training   One type of experience which has been used by many business organizations, but which is less widely used by school staffs, goes by the generic label of "sensitivity training."[8] Since 1946, when this type of training experience first appeared, there have emerged a number of variations in the goals and methods of sensitivity training. Within this diversity, however, is a common thread of purpose: to increase the individual's awareness of the factors which influence his own behavior and the behavior of others in group settings. There is also a common methodology: the discussion of "here and now" problems by small groups, assisted by specialists trained in group processes. These groups are often composed of people not previously acquainted with one another and removed from their normal organizational environment.

A number of studies and articles suggest that sensitivity training has important limitations as a method for organizational change.[9] Although sensitivity training often has positive personal consequences for individuals, many have difficulty incorporating their learning into their everyday organizational behavior. For one thing, sensitivity training does not usually devote much attention to the structuring skills necessary for task accomplishment. In addition, the deep and open sharing of feelings which occurs in some successful sensitivity groups is not easily duplicated in organizational settings, nor is it always appropriate. In cases where the entire staff of an organization has been mandated to participate in sensitivity experiences, there sometimes develop serious rifts between those who find the experience deeply meaningful and those who feel antagonistic toward it.[10] Such reactions have caused the National Training Laboratories to recommend that training should be voluntary rather than based on the wishes of an employer.[11]

Sensitivity training has not been used extensively in schools either to improve the social climate or to train individuals in specific skills. Individuals within schools who have participated in such experiences have often benefited, but the extent to which sensitivity training has influenced the effective mobilization of group resources within schools so far probably has been slight.

Consultant-Led Organizational Training   A different kind of training experience, the purpose of which is to develop organizational teamwork for problem solving, is exemplified by the school organizational training program developed by Schmuck and Runkel.[12] Organizational training differs from sensitivity training in that the focus is on organizational tasks which need to be accomplished and organizational problems which need to be solved, rather than on personal growth and development or the quality of interpersonal relationships per se. In contrast to sensitivity training, organizational training can be thought of as "broad" rather than "deep."[13] Organizational training tends to be less stressful than sensitivity training for individuals as *persons*, although it may generate considerable stress for individuals as *role performers* within an organization.

The specific training program reported by Schmuck and Runkel was a seventy-hour inservice training program conducted at a junior high school in Oregon during the 1967–68 school year. The purposes of the program included establishment of a continuing series of school activities for improving communication among faculty, wider participation in group meetings, development of new forms of faculty-initiated organization within the school, development of more productive working relationships among formal role levels, and improvements in classroom instruction.[14]

The program began with a six-day training session in August, attended by all but two members of the school staff. Small group exercises to increase faculty awareness of interpersonal and organizational processes occupied the first two days. During the remainder of the session, three groups of faculty members worked through a systematic problem-solving sequence of description, diagnosis, search for alternative solutions, action planning, and simulated tryout for three problems which the faculty had identified as hampering school functioning. They were (1) unclear role definitions for principal, vice principal, counselor, and area coordinator; (2) failure to utilize fully staff resources, especially between academic areas; and (3) lack of interest and participation in faculty meetings.

In December, a second day-and-a-half training session was devoted to strengthening problem-solving skills by improving communications between teachers and administrators and between the professional staff and service personnel (cooks, custodians, secretaries). In February, a third day-and-a-half session was held, during which work continued on the organizational problems which had been identified in August.[15]

Data were collected to assess the outcomes of this training program. It was found that working relations between the principal and his faculty had improved significantly, faculty meetings were now characterized by more candor and inquiry,[16] the Principal's Advisory Committee had taken a stronger role in school problem solving, and a number of faculty members had become interested in group dynamics and leadership skills as well as in adapting what they had learned about group process to the classroom. Possible negative outcomes included some dissatisfaction with the increased length of faculty meetings and a lack of interest by some faculty in further organizational training.

This program apparently succeeded in developing a more open climate for communication among the faculty and in developing specific problem-solving skills. Unlike sensitivity training, it focused on organizational problems and involved all the people who worked regularly together. It provided an opportunity for integrating new behaviors and skills in the work setting and then supported those behaviors and skills by review sessions throughout the year.

The Problem Solving School Program A similar, although a shorter and less expensive organization training program has been developed by |I|D|E|A|.[17] |I|D|E|A|'s Problem Solving School Program (PSS) takes about thirty hours of faculty time over the course of a school year. Half of this time is oriented toward the mobilization of group resources for solving *classroom problems* where the individual teacher has the responsibility for action, and half of the time is spent with *school problems* whose solutions are a shared faculty responsibility.

The primary objectives of the program are long term: (1) to promote a school climate of trust and self-confidence, which constitutes a precondition for effective group problem solving; and (2) to teach a number of specific individual and group problem-solving skills. An additional, short-term objective is to enable participating schools to identify and solve some specific school and classroom problems during the training program itself.

The activities in which group resources are mobilized to help individual teachers solve their classroom problems include (1) a series of structured meetings at which three or four teachers discuss problems in a systematic fashion; (2) readings in a programmed instruction format concerning alternative procedures and strategies for problem solving; and (3) schedules for classroom practice in applying these strategies. The activities in which group resources are mobilized to solve schoolwide problems include (1) three 1-hour "team-building" activities for the entire faculty; (2) a sequence of six problem-solving meetings in which the faculty identifies a school problem, formulates some strategies for dealing with it, and evaluates its problem-solving processes and outcomes; and (3) a second cycle of meetings devoted to a new schoolwide problem.

A "Development Team" of three teachers selected by their peers is responsible for coordinating the various activities of the PSS program. The work of the Development Team is directed by a handbook which contains detailed guidelines for each activity.

The Problem Solving School Program has undergone two years of field testing and can presently be used by the faculty of an elementary school independent of consultant help. Of the six elementary schools which participated in field tests during the 1971–72 school year, we believe that four have experienced significant positive changes in school climate and in their problem-solving skills. Teachers at these schools report less defensiveness about classroom problems and more use of other teachers as resources in solving them. Conflicts between union and nonunion teachers, between specialist and regular teachers, between upper and lower grade levels, and between teachers and administrators have been reduced, freeing faculties for a more unified attack on their schoolwide problems. Both broader faculty participation and more skilled faculty leadership of school meetings have been observed.

Five of the six participating schools accomplished at least one significant schoolwide change as a consequence of participating in the PSS program. One school established a permanent representative advisory council to work with the principal on problems of general concern. One school brought about a lasting improvement in student behavior during the lunch hour by changing its cafeteria rules to emphasize positive reinforcement rather than punishment. One group planned how they would fund, supply, and staff a resource center for their school. One school created a successful "student court" system which dramatically reduced out-of-class fighting and damage to school property. One school upgraded its physical education–recreation program by giving greater attention to playground skills and providing more alternative activities for youngsters during the recess period.

Like the Schmuck and Runkel program, the PSS program takes place within the organizational setting where the skills are to be used. It attempts to change the social climate of the school toward willingness to use group resources for problem solving and at the same time to increase the skills of the school faculty for effective utilization of group resources. Because it is self-directed, it encourages the emergence of faculty leadership; however, the professional support, conceptual inputs, and timely feedback which a consultant could provide are missing.

Neither of these types of organizational training programs deals with the structural impediments to group problem solving in schools: the lack of time, space, and money for continuing group problem-solving activities. Schmuck and Runkel reported that the demands which their program made on the personal energy of teachers during the regular school year was one of its principal weaknesses. They recommended that "vacation times" should be set aside during the school year for organizational training. The complaint most often voiced about the shorter PSS program has also been the amount of afterschool time which the meetings consume. When group problem solving is added on to a work day already overloaded with tasks, many teachers feel too tired to do their best.

In the short term, strong administrative support in the form of released time for participation seems to be the only way to make organizational training a viable strategy for change. In the long term, teachers themselves may apply their new problem-solving skills to find ways of relieving the intolerable time constraints and workloads which many of them face.

Structural Changes

Training programs alone seem insufficient to help schools fully realize the benefits of group problem solving. Structural changes also are needed. One kind of structural change is to create special times on the school calendar for faculty groups to meet. Another structural change is to redefine teaching as a group-coordinated activity by adopting team teaching.

Creating Special Times for Group Planning and Problem Solving Changing the school calendar to make time for professional meetings during regular working hours is not always as difficult a task as it may seem. Some schools already have freedom to schedule the beginning of classes an hour or two later, to dismiss students early one day each week, or to schedule a pupil-free day once a month if they wish. As the apparent nation-wide trend toward school decentralization grows, the individual school is likely to have increased freedom to make many of its own scheduling decisions.[18]

Structural changes made at the district level can also foster faculty-directed problem-solving efforts within each school. For example, teacher employment can begin in the fall two or three weeks before students arrive to allow adequate time for faculty planning and decision making. A longer school year, with regularly scheduled pupil-free planning days (or planning weeks) during the year, is another alternative.

These structural changes presume, of course, that school faculties either have or can develop the attitudes and group skills necessary to make productive use of their planning and problem-solving time. Here, structural changes and training experiences can effectively complement each other, the one providing the real opportunity for group problem solving, and the other encouraging the attitudes and skills needed to make full use of the opportunity.

Team Teaching One type of structural change in schools which directly increases the role of group problem solving in the instructional process is the adoption of team teaching. Since the term is quite often misunderstood, a clear definition of team teaching is in order. We will follow Shaplin's definition:

Team teaching is a type of instructional organization, involving teaching personnel and the students assigned to them, in which two or more teachers are given responsibility, working together, for all or a significant part of the instruction of the same group of students. . . . The phrase *working together* specifies a close working relationship among the teachers of a team for planning, instruction, and evaluation. . . . Joint planning may occur at the committee or departmental level, but if the teacher teaches *his* students and conducts *his* own evaluation, the conditions of joint instruction are not met.[19]

Team teaching can be a powerful force for helping teachers to use group resources to solve classroom problems. The team can act as a consultant to its individual members, helping each person to sharpen his thinking and broaden his perspectives for dealing with instructional problems; or the team can bring more flexibility and resources to bear on group problems which would have been defined as individual problems in the traditional school organization.

Teaching teams are, of course, likely to encounter many of the same barriers to effective problem solving which affect other school groups. Time is required for coordination of activities, especially when the team is new. Group skills in structuring the task are needed to keep the planning process efficient, and skills in dealing with interpersonal relationships are helpful in negotiating the give and take of shared decision making.

Some form of training to accompany the transition to team teaching seems to be desirable. L. Jean York has published a programmed learning module that deals explicitly and exclusively with the problem of making team meetings productive.[20] The module contains articles, question-and-answer self-tests, and transcripts of team meetings with a study guide to help the reader understand what to look for. Finally, a transcript of an interview with a teaching team with some provocative study questions completes the unit.

There are, of course, variations in the ease or difficulty with which teachers accustomed to running their own classrooms adapt to the interdependence of a team-teaching situation. Nevertheless, as long as the teacher's decision to join a team is freely made and not dictated by administrative fiat, the transition process seems to be relatively easy. Keith recently studied teachers' perceptions of the role strain under which they worked, both in team and self-contained classroom settings.[21] He found, as might be expected, that strain tended to be higher in new teams than in established teams and that there was higher strain in teams where there was low agreement on the teacher's role in the educational process. In a similar vein, Johnson and Hunt suggest that the initial fear of exposure to peers which some teachers experience when they begin team teaching tends to subside as the team develops.[22] In fact, many teams have reported an exciting increase in problem-solving abilities once they passed beyond the initial transition stage.[23]

SUMMARY AND CONCLUSIONS

We have suggested that groups of teachers meeting either on an ad hoc or on a continuing basis to solve problems can be a powerful force for change within the school. We have outlined some of the ways in which such groups can be of use: as consultants to individual teachers who have problems for which they believe themselves responsible for solving; as seekers after shared solutions for those problems which can be redefined as involving collective responsibilities; and as participants in problem definition and analysis for those problems whose solution requires schoolwide implementation.

We have listed three general reasons why group resources are infrequently mobilized for problem solving. The social climate of the school, characterized by feelings of vulnerability and powerlessness, hinders the professional discussion of problems. The usual organization of the public school, in which there is neither adequate teacher time available for group discussion, nor places in which to meet, nor money to spend for materials or outside expertise, is a second obstacle. Finally, within the faculty of the elementary school, the skills needed to initiate and sustain effective group problem solving are rare indeed.

The usual remedies have been piecemeal. Sensitivity training attempts to teach interpersonal skills to individuals, but there are often problems of transferring learnings to the setting itself. Organizational training within the school setting appears to have promise for changing the social climate and helping teachers to become proficient in problem-solving skills, but it does not satisfactorily address questions of time, space, and money, all of which are needed if group problem solving is to become a continuing resource. On the other hand, those who are interested in restructuring the organization of the school rarely attend to the influence of social climate and level of group problem-solving skills. It is clear that training experiences and structural change are most effective when they occur together and that either approach alone has significant drawbacks.

The responsibility for building a program which will help teachers overcome their fears about revealing and discussing their problems, which will provide the time, facilities, and discretionary funds for group problem solving, and which will teach the necessary skills, remains with the single school. With some awareness of the ways in which mobilizing group resources can change and improve the school and with a knowledge of the obstacles which must be surmounted, school staffs can find the means necessary to transform potential group power into actual group power.

NOTES

1   The conceptualization of problem solving as a series of phases or steps goes at least as far back as Robert F. Bales and Fred L. Strodtbeck, "Phases in Group Problem-Solving," *Journal of Abnormal and Social Psychology,* vol. 46, 1951, pp. 485–495. Several current conceptualizations of the steps in problem solving are reviewed in Ronald G. Havelock, *Planning for Innovation through Dissemination and Utilization of Knowledge,* Center for Research on Utilization of Scientific Knowledge, University of Michigan, Ann Arbor, 1971, pp. 59–69.

2   Harold H. Kelley and John W. Thibaut, "Group Problem-Solving," in Gardner Lindzey and Elliot Aronson (eds.), *Handbook of Social Psychology,* vol. 4, Addison-Wesley, Reading, Massachusetts, 1969, pp. 1–101. Kelley and Thibaut review a number of studies which have shown group conclusions to be more accurate than individual conclusions in social judgment tasks. Their analysis is that "these beneficial effects occur only for problems of multiple parts and for group members having noncorrelated (complementary) deficiencies and talents." (p. 69)

3   For further articulation of this point see Ronald Lippitt et al., "The Teacher as Innovator, Seeker and Sharer of New Practices," in R. I. Miller (ed.), *Perspectives on Educational Change,* Appleton Century Crofts, New York, 1967.

4   A classic study which supports these assertions is D. Katz, M. Maccoby, and N. C. Morse, *Productivity, Supervision and Morale in an Office Situation,* Survey Research Center, University of Michigan, Ann Arbor, 1950.

5   Matthew Miles, "Some Properties of Schools as Social Systems,"

in Goodwin Watson (ed.), *Change in School Systems,* NTL Institute, Washington, 1967, p. 12.

6 John I. Goodlad, M. Frances Klein and Associates, *Behind the Classroom Door,* Charles A. Jones, Worthington, Ohio, 1970, p. 68.

7 Robert F. Bales, "The Equilibrium Problems in Small Groups," in Talcott Parsons, R. F. Bales, and A. Shils (eds.), *Working Papers in the Theory of Action,* Free Press, Glencoe, Ill., 1953, pp. 111–161.

8 The reader interested in recent developments in sensitivity training theory and practice should see R. J. Golembrewski and A. Blumberg (eds.), *Sensitivity Training and the Laboratory Approach,* F. E. Peacock, Itasca, Ill., 1970.

9 For a critical review of research on the effectiveness of sensitivity training, see J. P. Campbell and M. Dunnette, "Effectiveness of T-Group Experiences in Managerial Training and Development," *Psychological Bulletin,* vol. 70, 1968, pp. 73–104. Also, see the series of articles titled "Sensitivity Training and the School Administrator: A Special Section," *The National Elementary Principal,* vol. 50, no. 6, May 1971, pp. 46–77.

10 See Richard A. Schmuck and Matthew B. Miles, *Organization Development in Schools,* National Press Books, Palo Alto, Calif., 1971, pp. 21–22.

11 NTL Institute, *Standards for the Use of Laboratory Methods,* Washington, 1969, p. 9.

12 Richard A. Schmuck and Philip J. Runkel, *Organizational Training for a School Faculty,* Center for the Advanced Study of Educational Administration, University of Oregon, Eugene, 1970.

13 See Roger Harrison, "Choosing the Depth of Organizational Intervention," *Journal of Applied Behavioral Science,* vol. 6, 1970, pp. 181–202.

14 Schmuck and Runkel, op. cit., p. 35.

15 Ibid., pp. 4–7.

16 See Roger Rasmussen, "Alternative Means of Analyzing the COPED Meetings Questionnaire to Measure Participants' Perceptions of School Faculty Meetings," unpublished paper, 1972, p. 22.

17 Samuel G. Christie, Adrianne Bank, Carmen M. Culver, Gretchen McCann, and Roger Rasmussen, *The Problem Solving School,* Institute for Development of Educational Activities, Dayton, 1972.

18 See, for example, Anthony N. Barata, "Decentralization in Urban School Districts," in Frank Lutz (ed.), *Toward Improved Urban Education,* Charles A. Jones, Worthington, Ohio, 1970.

19 Judson Shaplin and Henry Olds, Jr., *Team Teaching,* Harper & Row, New York, 1964, pp. 15, 17.

20 L. Jean York, *Prerequisites for Good Planning Sessions in Team Teaching,* Leslie Press, Dallas, 1971.

21 P. Keith, "Sources and Correlates of Role Strain Among Teachers in Varied Settings." Paper presented at the 1970 annual convention of the American Educational Research Association, Minneapolis.

22 Robert Johnson, Jr. and John Hunt, *Rx for Team Teaching,* Burgess, Minneapolis, 1968. Cited in L. Jean York, *The Background, Philosophy and Purposes of Team Teaching,* Leslie Press, Dallas, 1971, p. 16.

23 Shaplin and Olds, op. cit., pp. 72–73.

CHAPTER 7

BEYOND TEACHER MILITANCY: IMPLICATIONS FOR CHANGE WITHIN THE SCHOOL

Samuel G. Christie

Samuel Christie served as coordinator of |I|D|E|A|'s Elementary School Appraisal Study, which produced *The Problem Solving School,* a program designed to develop the school as an effective problem-solving organization. In this chapter Dr. Christie traces the recent history of growing teacher militancy and poses the question of the implications of this militancy for the working relationship of the principal and teachers in the single school. He argues that teacher militancy has served a useful purpose in breaking down the paternalistic relationship which has existed between administrators and teachers and thus clearing the way for the establishment of co-operative relationships. Dr. Christie emphasizes the need for principals to become willing to share decision-making authority with their teachers and the need for teachers to accept this responsibility.

Samuel Christie is a member of the faculty of the School of Education at Indiana University, Bloomington, Indiana.

One of the salient issues in education during the decade of the sixties was the growing militancy of teachers and the resulting redistribution of power between teachers and governing boards and between teachers and administrators. During this period the number of teacher strikes increased every year. From a rate of 5 per year in the early sixties it had risen to 131 by 1969.[1] However, as we entered the seventies we saw a *decline* in strike activity. In 1970–1971 there were only thirty-nine teacher strikes,[2] while the number of agreements negotiated continued to climb 34 percent during 1969.[3]

These figures prompt one to raise several questions about teacher militancy and teacher-management relationships. Has the period of confrontation passed? Has the nature of the demands changed? Has the scene of the conflict between teachers and boards of education and teachers and administrators shifted from the central office to the school? These questions must be considered along with the more basic questions about the results of teacher militancy; in particular, how has this new militancy, which frequently has resulted in open and hostile confrontation between teachers and principals, affected the operation of the schools?

One result of the new militancy of teachers is that it has brought an end to the myth that teachers and principals are united in a common purpose. We must consider whether or not the hope for cooperative relationships between the two groups has all but vanished. As teachers have gained more power in direct negotiations with boards of education, principals have complained that their interests have not been attended to. Thus we must ask whether or not the principals will become an organized force at the local level, a development which could intensify the conflict between teachers and principals.

As we examine these questions we shall look first at the development of the conflict as it erupted during the sixties and as it moved from one scene of battle to another—from confrontations over the issue of the right of teachers to negotiate to NEA-AFT rivalries over the right to represent teachers.

We shall next look at issues that relate more directly to the operation of individual schools and examine the nature of the conflicts between teachers and principals. Here we shall discuss implications of the conflict model that was used through the early period of teacher militancy and the positive possibilities inherent in a consensus model of conflict resolution.

TEACHER MILITANCY

The Opening of the Conflict

Inasmuch as schools have seen little change in the first sixty years of this century, the new wave of teacher militancy descended on education with the swiftness of a revolution. As the mid-sixties approached, the idea of teachers striking was an alien thought, not only to the public but perhaps even more so to teachers themselves.

The long period of nonmilitancy, perhaps even antimilitancy, ended in 1965 when the teachers of New York City struck the nation's largest school system. This strike seemed to provide the catalyst needed to inflame the long-smoldering discontent of teachers throughout the nation. The militancy of teachers spread rapidly. Demands for negotiated contracts and for salary increases were frequently met with retorts from boards of education that they could not negotiate, that the law would not allow it, and that this would be surrendering authority delegated to them by the people.

The attitude of many boards of education was reflected in the following statement of the National School Boards Association's *Beliefs and Policies:*

> The Authority of the board of education is established by law and this authority may not be delegated to others. Strikes, sanctions, boycotts, mandated arbitration, or mediation are improper procedures to be used by public school employees who are dissatisfied with their conditions of employment.[4]

In 1965 the president of the NSBA clarified this statement in a speech to the Association by stating,

> It is time for teachers to decide whether they are calling for joint *responsibility* with boards of education—or whether they are saying we have joint *concerns* with boards of education, and we want our opinions to be heard and our counsel to be carefully considered before decisions are reached by the board. If it is the latter school boards can give their support.[5]

The demands by teachers, however, were clearly not the latter. Teachers were not willing to present their opinions and hope that the board would make decisions acceptable to them. As the militancy of teachers and the intransigency of boards met head on, the nation witnessed an ever accelerating rate of strikes. There were 33 the year following the 1965 New York strike, 80 the next year, 114 the next, and 131 in 1968–1969.[6]

The sovereignty arguments advanced by boards against teachers had simply given way to new realities. According to Robert Doherty, an expert in industrial labor relations who has studied the teacher movement,

> The teachers, to the extent they have become organized for something other than "more of the same," have in effect said, "To hell with all your legalistic arguments; we now have the muscle through organization to get something better than the shabby deal we have been getting for years past, and we hereby demand something better!"[7]

State legislatures quickly reacted to the situation, prodded to a great extent by the NEA, which had long been an effective influence in state politics, by passing legislation that either "permitted" boards to negotiate with teacher organizations or mandated that they do so.[8]

Although the move to enact state legislation was in part a strategy to relieve the intensity of the conflict in local school districts (by at least "allowing" school districts to negotiate), it was also the scene of another battle that was going on at the time, that between two national organizations fighting for the allegiance of teachers. Thus, teachers in many of the nation's schools were party to a three-cornered conflict, between local affiliates of the NEA and the AFT, and between the duly elected negotiating council and the board of education.

The Battle for Teacher Allegiance

In terms of numbers, the NEA had a head start in the battle. It had three-quarters of a million members while the AFT had less than one-tenth as many (60,000). However, the AFT had some advantages that helped it overcome the tremendous disadvantage in numbers. First, the strength of the AFT was concentrated in the large urban areas where teachers tended to have more militant attitudes toward management. Secondly, the NEA had traditionally built strength at the state level and did not have strong teacher-oriented local affiliates. The NEA included administrators and teachers in the same organization and was susceptible to the AFT charge that they were in effect a company union and thus did not represent the exclusive interests of classroom teachers.

Although the NEA hotly denied this charge, it must have carried some weight with teachers, at least in urban areas. This was demonstrated in New York City in late 1961 when an election was held to determine which organization would represent teachers in negotiating with the board of education. The NEA with 30,000 members received 9,770 votes, while the AFT with 5,000 members received 20,045 votes.[9] Thus the AFT became the sole bargaining agent for the teachers of New York City. As a result of this election many of the AFT locals throughout the country believed that they could win representation elections in spite of being outnumbered and began to press for these elections and for collective bargaining.

At this time the NEA opposed collective bargaining, but they too got the message from the New York election. In 1962 the NEA endorsed the idea of "professional negotiations," a procedure that supposedly differed from collective bargaining in that it was not tied to "labor precedents." Soon the NEA, with its greater strength at the state level, began to pressure legislatures to pass statutes consistent with the idea of professional negotiations. The key demands in their position were the inclusion of administrators in the negotiating councils, the regulation of teacher negotiations by a state educational agency, and the setting of no limits on the scope of negotiations. This latter item was also AFT policy. Myron Lieberman points out that "actually the resulting legislation sometimes served as much to block the AFT as to advance meaningful bilateral negotiations, but the overall effect was to promote collective negotiations between teacher organizations and school boards."[10]

The NEA was only moderately successful in getting administrators "legislated" into negotiating councils, partly because the issues to be negotiated were not always limited specifically to education, but pertained to labor-management relations in municipalities as well.

With both NEA and AFT claiming to be the real representatives for teachers, the conflict focused on representational elections to be conducted within the schools. Thus, the issue was not to be settled in the legislature but moved into the schools with full force as each organization hurled charge and countercharge. The AFT accused the NEA of being in cahoots with administration and the NEA responded with the charge that the AFT was a front for the AFL-CIO.

In a confidential memo to NEA affiliates Dick Dashiell, an NEA staff member, had this to say:

> When considering the elections in Detroit and Cleveland—or in any other city which involves the AFT—it is essential that you understand that the American Federation of Teachers is a front in the drive of organized labor to take over the teaching profession in the United States.[11]

At the same time David Seldon, an AFT official, sent this statement to union members:

> The education association will immediately recognize the drive of your union toward collective bargaining as a challenge to their preferred status. The usual intimate relationship between the board, the superintendent, and the leaders of the association means that you must be ready to take them all on, if need be.[12]

Although the NEA in philosophy was much closer to boards of education than organized labor, the board was certainly not viewed as an ally by Dashiell when he told affiliates:

> Don't depend upon a board of education to set up ground rules for an election that are fair to the professional association. It will often play one organization against another until a choice has to be made—under its rules.[13]

This statement sounds as militant and distrustful of the board as do union statements. Actually, the main point of the message from Dashiell to the NEA affiliates was that they were going to have to change their image and that they must lose some if not all of their identification with administrators. If they did not do this, they would continue to lose elections.

And that image did begin to change, most noticeably from the viewpoint of administrators. In two short years after the Dashiell memo, an open letter to the president of the American Association of School Administrators appeared in *The Nation's Schools*. This letter gave the administrator's view of the change in NEA:

> NEA is as militant and strike-happy and sanction oriented as are teacher unions. Like teacher unions, NEA does not want administrators among its members. Unlike teacher unions, NEA is stuck with them. But not for long. Each year, NEA grows ominously close to tossing them out. It has no choice. Supervisors, especially superintendents, not only represent management, they are management. To expect AASA and NEA to function sensibly as one organization under one roof is like expecting the National Association of Manufacturers to sign up as a division of the AFL-CIO. We should live so long.[14]

Although the NEA has changed drastically in the eyes of many administrators, this change did not come soon enough to keep the AFT from winning the majority of contested representation elections, both in and outside of larger cities. The AFT won exclusive representational rights for teachers in such major metropolitan centers as New York, Philadelphia, Detroit, Boston, Cleveland, Chicago, Washington, and Baltimore.[15] Then, at the annual NEA convention in July 1967, a significant step was made in creating an image of militancy for the organization. The association reversed its position of the past with respect to teacher strikes. It passed a resolution that called for the NEA to offer all the services at its command to affiliates that had gone out on strike provided that there had been bargaining in good faith.

At long last the NEA made the difficult decision it had been attempting to head off. It had become evident that the often repeated statement that "administrators and teachers were not in basic conflict, but were members of the same team," was an ideal, not a reality. The decision at the 1967 convention was the result of a final recognition of this reality. The organization would serve either the teachers or the administrators; it could not serve both.

The NEA lost no time in moving to emphasize its changed position. Before the year was out the NEA president went to Montgomery County, Maryland, walked the picket line with teachers, and in the words of the superintendent of that district, "helped fan the fire for a strike."[16] The following year in Florida, the NEA sanctioned the first statewide strike in the nation. Since that time the rivalry between NEA and AFT gradually has subsided. The demands which the two organizations make on behalf of teachers are more and more alike as they seemingly move closer to an eventual merger that has been predicted for some time.[17]

The Decreasing Strike Activity

As the conflict between AFT and NEA has become less intense, the strike activity of teachers has fallen off. (It was noted earlier that the rate dropped from 131 to 39 between 1969 and 1970.) Although the talk of merger and the lessening of conflict between the two organizations may have some bearing on the decrease in strike activity, it seems more likely that the decrease is a result of the natural development of the negotiation process. In the early sixties *all* the districts involved in negotiations were in the beginning stages of establishing new relationships between labor and management. As each side learns more about both the bargaining process and the limits of its demands on the other side, the likelihood of strikes diminishes.

Teachers are *seemingly* less militant, probably because they need not push so hard as they once did to get the same results. An indication of this is the change in the type of issues that are negotiated. Typically, when a teacher negotiating council and a board of education first open negotiations, the issues are procedural: recognition of a bargaining unit, procedures for negotiations, procedures for resolution of an impasse. As these issues are settled, the negotiations deal more and more with substantive issues. Between 1966 and 1969 the percentage of agreements over procedural issues declined from 74.6 to 57.6 percent.[18] This decline could provide part of the explanation for the decrease in strike activity. Procedural issues are more basic, and they tend to deal more with the legitimacy of the teachers' right to bargain.

It should also be noted that there have been differential rates of increase within the substantive areas of negotiation, which indicates a move away from basic economic issues. Certainly a decrease in strike activity does not mean that teachers have stopped expanding the areas in which they are demanding participation in decision making. On the contrary, during the period when strike activity decreased, teacher demands increased significantly in the area of instructional programs. Although the rate of increase was 34 percent for the total number of agreements negotiated from 1969 to 1971, agreements in the area of instruction were up 72 percent. Salary agreements were up 43 percent; personnel, 40 percent; and fringe benefits, only 10 percent.

These percentages are consistent with the observations of one superintendent of schools who said, ". . . the subject matter falls conveniently into three categories: money, time, and rights. Interestingly enough, in that order, boards are inclined to give ground."[19] The move to redress the balance of power within education seems to be entering a new phase in which the battle will give less emphasis to money and will focus more on what many say was the central issue all along, the rights or the power of teachers.

This brief history of the decade of militancy has been traced to demonstrate the nature of this power struggle with its attendant conflicts, the kinds of concerns teachers have, the demands they have voiced, and the gains they have made as a result of their demands. Also, this brief history documents the lack of trust that has existed between teachers and administrators.

During this period of militancy that we have been describing, there has been notable success for teachers. They have gained more equitable pay and a greater say in decision making. These gains have been made not because they were based on just claims (although in many cases the claims were just) or because board members saw them as a way of improving education. Rather, they were made because teachers mobilized their strength and demanded that they be granted.

Even though the conflict has brought gains for teachers, it has made life miserable for many of those involved. It has resulted in bitterness and even hate in some instances. It has not only pitted teachers against board members and administrators but has also resulted in open conflicts and recriminations among teachers.

A superintendent in Michigan who experienced this type of conflict recounts some of the bitterness that he witnessed:

Michigan today is no place for the faint-hearted nor for the superintendant who needs to feel loved and revered by his teachers. . . . The ugly, discrediting, unwarranted innuendo unleashed against boards and administrators has been a necessary device of negotiating teams to rally the troops when it appeared they might be losing interest. . . . We know that deep divisions have been created within the teacher ranks. Highly professional teachers who protested the recklessness of the militants have found that they were not exempt from innuendo and attack.[20]

What we are apparently witnessing in education today is the open acknowledgment that conflict is a part of the normal situation in schools. Ever since education became public in this country it has put forth a facade of cooperation, consensus, and commonality of interest and purpose of everyone within the educational enterprise. The reluctance to admit that there has been conflict among teachers, principals, and boards of education has had the effect of suppressing rather than resolving the conflict. This suppression has created frustration, and frustration can lead, as in this case, to aggression, hostility and destructive acts. Although the leaders of teacher organizations have exaggerated their claims that "you can't trust the administrators," this appeal would not have met with such a sympathetic ear if the feeling had not been genuine on the part of teachers.

The problem of trust between teachers and administrators is real. The typical response of administrators, particularly early in the movement, was to deny its existence. One NEA field representative reported that it was common practice when he visited a district to be invited to the superintendent's office and advised that, "Things are different here. Our teachers are happy."[21]

But, as former New York City superintendent Bernard Donovan warned, "In the first place we just have to decide that negotiation is here to stay—period. . . . Those of you who do not have it now, watch out tomorrow morning."[22]

And Charles Young, a superintendent in the Midwest, cautioned, "Don't delude yourself about the presence of conflict in your district. It's there."[23]

Prospects for Future Militancy

Myron Lieberman, who has studied the militancy movement quite closely, has analyzed the prospects for the decade of the seventies in light of the merger of AFT and NEA. In his view, this merger will reduce some tendencies toward militancy and increase other tendencies. In some areas, the AFT-NEA conflict will be replaced by intraorganizational conflicts within NEA that can promote just as much militancy as before. His view is that teachers will control both the state and national organizations that will result from an AFT-NEA merger. This will place great pressure on teachers to join the merged group and will probably lead to a dramatic increase in organizational membership. According to Lieberman:

> With greatly increased membership and resources—none of which are needed to fight a rival organization—and without the internal constraints inherent in administrator membership or control, the new organization will probably pursue more militant policies in behalf of teacher interests than anything we have experienced thus far in either NEA or AFT.[24]

On the other hand, the merger will tend to awaken the capacity of dissident members, particularly in local affiliates, to criticize their own leadership for not driving a hard enough bargain.

On balance, Lieberman believes militancy will continue to rise rather than subside. This is a view shared by Terry Herndon of the NEA who says, "One thing cannot be overlooked; there will be no reprieve in the aggressive behavior of teachers . . . and they will become *more* militant and *more* aggressive in asserting their rights to have some full measure of partnership in deciding the new directions and revision of educational planning."[25]

Thus on the basis of these observations, made by people who have both studied and been involved in the rise of teacher militancy, it would seem evident that teachers will continue to press aggressively for full participation in many areas of policy making in education.

MILITANCY AND THE IMPLICATIONS FOR CHANGE

We have noted thus far the effects of this movement on the educational institution generally. One may also ask, What does this new militancy mean for the operation of the school? How does it affect the working relationships of principals and teachers?

One of the most significant changes that affect teacher-principal relationships is the provision for a grievance process to settle disputes. Grievance is in effect a declaration that rights of teachers have been violated. In order to set up grievance procedures there must be some formal definition of these rights. Perry and Wildman note that in the school districts they studied, conflict between teachers and boards over grievance procedures usually concerned two matters: first, determining the types of claims which may be processed through the grievance procedure (that is, identifying the areas in which administrators, particularly principals, must be bound by these procedures); and second, determining whether arbitration to resolve the grievance, if any, should be binding or advisory.[26]

Although some teacher organizations have attempted to include in the grievance process all board policies and administrative procedures, the areas covered by grievance are usually limited to those specifically stated in the negotiated contract. One of the issues frequently included in these contracts is the amount of extracurricular time that is required of teachers. Since the principal has the responsibility to see that certain duties outside the classroom are carried out, this can make his task more difficult. The negotiated contract can and usually does change the conditions under which these arrangements are worked out. These changes do limit the discretion of the principal, particularly one who is used to making decisions without consulting teachers.

The establishment of grievance procedures will affect most directly those principals who have acted arbitrarily in the past, and this is the way it should be. However, there can be some negative effects. For example, teachers may willingly give extra time for the sake of a project or program in which they are interested, but they may as a result be accused of "rate-busting" by teachers interested in enforcing the terms of the negotiated contract. The establishment of work procedures by the process of negotiation and the existence of teachers functioning as "shop stewards" certainly can affect the cooperative relationship between teachers and principals.

In addition, negotiations that establish detailed procedures can limit the freedom of both teachers and principals. In order for principals and teachers to reach decisions together there needs to be a cooperative attitude in which concessions can be made by both parties. Detailed procedures laid out in advance, whether they are the product of the bureaucracy of the school or of the teacher organization, limit the freedom of principals and teachers to define the situation and to set their own limits for agreement.

The establishment of grievance procedures, although generally achieving a good end, has in some cases resulted in an intensification of the adversary relationship between teachers and principals. When this occurs, a sense of negativism pervades the climate of the school. Many observers have commented on the debilitating effect this adversary relationship has on the schools and have called for alternative methods of resolving conflict.

Proposals for Conflict Resolution Within Schools

Williams,[27] for example, has proposed that an academic model, with a decision-making process patterned after that in institutions of higher education, is most appropriate for schools to adopt. Griffiths[28] has suggested that bargaining should be confined to salary, fringe benefits, and personnel matters and that faculty committees should be formed to advise administrations on matters of curriculum and instruction. Boyan[29] and Madden[30] have made similar proposals. Madden suggests that distributive bargaining, which is basically a conflict model, is appropriate for economic issues and that integrative bargaining, which is essentially problem solving, is appropriate for matters of curriculum and instruction. The proposals of Williams, Boyan, Griffiths, and Madden all have a common element. They stress the need to set educational policy with more emphasis on cooperation, on consensus rather than on conflict.

A criticism often leveled at those who stress consensus is that this perpetuates the status quo, that consensus means more often than not a suppression of conflict. Yet, one must ask, are there no alternatives to the kind of conflict resolution that continually separates people into different camps, that stresses their differences over their similarities or common interests?

Mary Parker Follett, an outstanding pioneer in human relations, advanced theories about conflict resolution that offer such an alternative. She conceives of conflict not necessarily as "a wasteful outbreak of incompatibilities, but a normal process by which socially valuable differences register themselves for the enrichment of all concerned."[31] She proposes three ways to deal with conflict. One is domination, which means victory for one side or the other. The second is compromise, which means that both sides give up something to have peace. The third is integration, which means that a place is made for each desire as both parties seek to find and use elements in the conflict situation that are of benefit to both.

She believes that conflicts not only exist in all organizations but also serve a useful function if they are integrated. The first step toward integration is to bring conflict out in the open and to examine the symbols used and the realities to which they refer. It involves dropping the general dispute and centering on proposed activities.

Mary Parker Follett's ideas on integrating conflict have influenced many, among them administrative theorists, game theorists, and those interested in the theories of collective negotiation.

Distributive and Integrative Bargaining

Walton and McKersie[32] have applied concepts similar to those of Follett in developing their theory of labor negotiations, in which they place bargaining on a continuum from distributive to integrative.

Distributive bargaining occurs when the parties perceive that gains by one side will be made at the expense of the other. It is a win-lose proposition with antagonists participating in a struggle to decide who gets how much of a scarce resource, usually money.

Integrative bargaining, on the other hand, is entered into with different assumptions. In this case the belief is that mutual benefits can be developed through the exploration of alternatives. The net rewards for both parties can be increased. In other words, the total array of rewards or benefits can be increased so that both sides get more as a result of the bargaining process.

Walton and McKersie, however, do not see certain issues as purely appropriate for either distributive or integrative bargaining. Instead, they see many factors that will determine what kind of bargaining will occur. They tend to view the bargaining relationship as evolutionary with the distributive model stressed more frequently in the beginning stages of the bargaining relationship and the integrative model utilized more frequently as the relationship "mellows," as the parties to the bargaining become more experienced.

The move toward integrative bargaining will occur when both parties perceive this to be of mutual advantage. It is not likely to occur as long as one side questions the legitimacy of the other or when there is a lack of good faith in bargaining by either party. In integrative bargaining common interests are stressed, and alternative solutions are sought which will promote those interests. When bargaining of this nature is established, the need for grievance procedures will gradually diminish.

However, if in the process of working toward solutions, hidden agendas begin to surface, it is likely that one or both parties will feel that their private interests are threatened and the negotiation process will revert to distributive bargaining.

At the present time, few negotiations in education could be characterized as integrative. It does little good, however, to point out to teachers and administrators that different behavior on their part, behavior directed toward integrative bargaining, would be more rational, would be better for education. There seems to be a rather deep feeling among teachers that one cannot really trust administrators. There is little doubt that in the past most administrators have taken a paternalistic attitude toward teachers. It will take time for this attitude to be eradicated from teachers' minds; teachers must experience first hand, not just one time but over and over, evidence of good faith, of a willingness on the part of administrators to involve teachers in decisions without hidden agendas and to abandon all thought of manipulating them.

Although bitter conflicts among teachers, administrators, and boards of education have occurred, and although they have had many ill effects in the short run, these conflicts have served a useful and necessary purpose. They have set the stage for change. Now that teachers have "stood up" to boards of education and to administrators and have refused to submit to any form of paternalism, the possibility of bargaining among equals is available. This is not to say that conflicts will not continue to exist. Even though teachers and principals may stress common interests, they still have conflicts that must be resolved. If they basically trust one another, the conflicts can be settled by problem-solving activities and consensus decision making. Therefore, a central question for educators remains: How can a climate be promoted in which teachers and principals operate from a base of common interests and a feeling of trust in each other?

The Role of the Principal

To answer the above question, let us look to the school principal who, by his response to the present conflict situation, can alter significantly the effects of bargaining in his school.

The principal occupies a most difficult position in the educational organization, that of middle management. On one hand he is charged with the responsibility of administering the policy of superiors—the superintendent and the board. On the other hand, he is charged with the responsibility of transmitting views of teachers to the administrative hierarchy so the teachers can have an effect on future policy decisions.

That middle managers often neglect the latter responsibility, representing teachers, is documented by the fact that teacher labor unions exist. Even with the best intentions and a less hierarchical organizational structure, the conflicting interests existing between a district office and teachers force principals to walk a tightrope between administrative disfavor and teacher discontent.

Until recently the discontent of teachers was only a vague potential which permitted principals to follow the existing reward system, in which the criteria for promotion were more often than not conformity to bureaucratic rules and maintenance of the status quo. English and Zaharis have noted, "In all too many cases, particularly large city systems riddled with nepotism and seniority clauses, the chief criterion for selecting principals is organizational docility."[33] They note further that in times of stress, when the frequency of societal demands for change increases, the bureaucracy responds by "tightening up" job descriptions. "Those at the apex pass new rules, refine standards, issue more dicta, adopt various mandates and policies, and add more personnel. . . ."[34]

As real as these restrictions are, they are sometimes exaggerated and sometimes serve as an excuse for teacher inaction. In his study of the culture of the school, Sarason found, "Too frequently the individual's conception of the system serves as the basis for inaction and rigidity, or as a convenient target onto which one can direct blame for almost anything. The principal illustrates this point as well or better than anyone else in the school system."[35]

In spite of the strictures of bureaucracy, in spite of the loss of discretion by principals which is brought on by negotiations, the principal still occupies a position of authority and can influence the climate of the school. Assuming that he is willing to take some risks, he has a considerable degree of freedom to decide which rules to enforce and which rules to ignore.[36] He is free to extend more opportunities for teachers to participate in decisions; he is free to initiate a structure of openness within his school; he is free to work closely with other principals in his district to gain more autonomy for individual schools, to work to change the criteria for granting and receiving institutional rewards.

Toward an Open Structure

Perhaps the foremost way for a principal to influence the climate of a school in a favorable manner is to involve teachers in the decision-making process. A change from authoritarianism to cooperative decision making is not just a change in the style of leadership; it reflects a change in organizational structure. As the role definitions of both teachers and principals change, the expectations one has for the other change. Teachers are expected to take more initiative and assume more responsibility for the welfare of the school, and principals are expected to gather and to share with teachers openly the information which is needed to participate meaningfully in making educational decisions.

Cooperative decision making is a part of the "structural openness" defined by Likert.[37] The organization with an open structure has a high degree of communication both vertically and laterally. It is in evidence when teachers voice to each other their true concerns regarding their own work relationships with colleagues and identify the forces that block their success in teaching. The maintenance of a closed structure, on the other hand, is associated with a higher incidence of teacher militancy, as Gans has shown.[38] In addition, the hierarchical relationships attendant to that structure have been found by Bridges and others to inhibit group productivity in problem solving, efficiency, and risk taking.[39]

The changing of the hierarchical school structure can be significantly aided by the school superintendent. Elliott Jaques[40] in his studies of change in an industrial organization has found that the leadership of the top executive influences the leader-follower relationships all the way to the shop floor. Ann Lieberman, in Chapter 3 of this book, has reported similar findings in the school setting, noting that authoritarian teachers are more frequently found in schools with authoritarian principals. Thus, in schools, superintendents affect principals and principals affect teachers.

As important as the superintendent is for setting this tone at the top of the organizational hierarchy, the school should be the *major* focus for change. The individual school with its principal, its teachers, and its students has its own culture, its own social system, and its own goals. It has an organic structure that makes it a viable unit for change. If nothing changes in the school, it matters little that the district is "innovative."

A district administration can buy new materials; it can disseminate information on new ideas to the school; it can hold inservice workshops. All these things can happen and still make no difference in the way schools function, in the kind of experiences children have in the classroom. This is not meant to imply that the district makes no difference at all. It is perhaps too much to expect of principals and teachers to act without district support and encouragement. Still, principals can act on their own, they can take initiative, and they can give teachers more freedom, provided, of course, they know how.

Implementation of Participatory Decision Making

Often it is assumed by advocates of democratic decision making that all the principal has to do is to *decide* that he is going to institute this change and announce it to teachers. It is not that simple. Teachers may be suspicious of the principal's motives, particularly if he announces or mandates change to democratic decision making. Issuing mandates in the name of democracy will probably be viewed by teachers as inconsistent and may be seen as another example of the lip service that has been given to the concept too often in the past. On the other hand, it should be recognized that some teachers do not want to accept the responsibility that goes with decision making, at least not all at once, and would rather leave it to the principal.

Another difficulty that principals must guard against is the tendency to abdicate *their* leadership responsibilities. Jaques observed this phenomenon in a factory he studied:

> Higher management was striving to eliminate practices by which some people gave orders to others without taking their views and feelings into account. This was considered contrary to both social conscience and practical efficiency. Their troubles arose because they had confused sanctioned authority with unsanctioned autocracy and in so doing had undermined the processes necessary for executive work.[41]

When confusion such as this develops, a principal may be reluctant to give orders even to implement policies or practices already agreed on. In this case he may be viewed by teachers as being weak and incompetent.

These examples are meant to illustrate the point that principals will have to work at extending participation to teachers. They often must change lifelong behavior; they must be truly sensitive to the feelings of their subordinates; they must in each instance think through their decisions and consider the impact they may have on teachers.

Many principals will need help at this and not just in the form of patience on the part of teachers. Some principals can make this change with the help of written materials, which can vary from books on organizational development and change to programmed procedural materials that provide guidelines and exercises to facilitate organizational problem solving. Products of this nature only recently have been developed but offer great promise for reaching many schools.[42]

Principals who need more than written materials may find process consultants helpful. These consultants may be found in some graduate schools of education or schools of management. Schmuck and Miles[43] in their book on organizational development in schools have listed in the appendix the names and addresses of 151 of these consultants.

SUMMARY AND CONCLUSIONS

In this chapter we have discussed the use of militancy by teachers and have talked of the implications it has for the schools of this country. We have documented this struggle briefly, noting the development of the conflict with first one set of antagonists, then another. The conflict has at times been bitter, and the fight has not always been limited to teachers and administrators. It has sometimes been included in the NEA-AFT struggle and in teacher-teacher conflicts.

Many educators decry the new militancy on the part of teachers. They take the position that the adversary relationship is inimical to the purposes of the school, that with this development there is little hope for cooperative relationships between teachers and principals. We take no such view. We believe that a paternalistic relationship has existed between administrators and teachers throughout the history of organized education in this country. That relationship has become intolerable to a vast majority of teachers. As long as this paternalism either exists or is perceived to exist, the relationship will be one sided, a situation in which cooperative give and take is not possible. Thus the paternalism must be changed before truly cooperative relationships can be established. Teacher militancy where it has occurred has changed this; therefore, it has served a useful purpose.

Without this militancy the change would have been a long time coming, if ever, because it is a change in power relationships and power is usually taken, not given. Now that teachers have become more powerful, they will probably not have to resort to militant action as often as in the recent past. Because their power is real they can influence decisions without resorting to force.

The change in the distribution of power external to the school can be a motivating force for internal change, a change that may strengthen the school. This will not be accomplished without a great deal of patience, hard work, and understanding.

In the future teachers will continue to affiliate with district-wide teacher organizations and principals with district administrators' councils, or in more and more cases, principals' organizations. The teacher organizations will continue not only to promote but also to define the interests of its members. They will make subtle demands on teachers that they not cooperate too openly with principals, who are the enemy and would subvert their interests. Principals' organizations will function in the same way: they will support principals' claims to traditional prerogatives of decision making and wider discretion in administering the school.

Thus both principals and teachers face role conflicts and must recognize that in some cases their own individual interests are not served by strict adherence to the dogma of the external organization. Both principals and teachers have a stake in the schools where they work. They depend on one another. They have a common interest that the school do well, that children become effective learners, that a work environment be maintained such that both teachers and principals can function to the best of their individual abilities.

The reaction of the principal in the face of these changes which are occurring and which will continue to occur is a key element in determining the effect they will have on his school. The principal can significantly affect the viability of his school, can help to develop an internal strength, by voluntarily sharing decision-making authority over such matters as assigning duties, establishing budgetary priorities, and choosing new strategies and materials for the instructional program, and by accepting conflict over these matters as legitimate and resolving it, rather than smoothing it over or ignoring it. If principals encourage shared decision making, teachers who desire a greater voice in the affairs of the school can satisfy their needs without resorting to an external ally, the teacher organization. With shared problem solving and leadership distributed among teachers, it will be less likely that a "police" function will be necessary to guarantee that the terms of collective bargaining are observed. This policing *both of teachers and the principal* is a great source of conflict and a reminder to all that administration and staff are in different camps. Although this is a source of strength for the district-wide teacher organization, it weakens the schools because the school grows stronger as the resources of both teachers and principals are brought together.

Although we have discussed at some length the conflicts which face teachers and principals and have pointed out the history of paternalism that has existed in our schools, we believe that as schools move beyond teacher militancy there is reason for optimism. We believe that the changes resulting from the militancy of teachers can be beneficial to education, provided both principals and teachers view this as an opportunity for establishing a working relationship among professionals.

We think the effects will be positive where a principal seeks ways to involve teachers, to share with them the responsibility for building a better school, and where teachers accept this responsibility with an openness of their own and are willing to examine all alternatives before reaching decisions and willing to change their own behavior if necessary.

Even if we are beyond teacher militancy we are not beyond conflicts. However, we are moving beyond the paternalism of old, and this will provide us with the opportunity to recognize and use conflict as a force for change.

NOTES

1   National Education Association, *Negotiations Research Digest,* January 1970, vol. 3, no. 5, p. 1.

2   The data on 1970–1971 strikes were compiled by examining the NEA pamphlet *Facts On File* for this period.

3   National Education Association, *Negotiations Research Digest,* November 1971, vol. 5, no. 3, p. 3.

4   Harold Webb, "The National School Boards Association and Collective Negotiations," in Stanley M. Elam, Myron Lieberman, and Michael H. Moskow (eds.), *Readings on Collective Negotiations in Public Education,* Rand McNally, Chicago, 1967, p. 198.

5   Ibid., p. 200.

6   National Education Association, January 1970, p. 3.

7   Quoted in Robert Bendiner, *The Politics of Schools,* Harper & Row, New York, 1969, p. 110.

8   Myron Lieberman, *When School Districts Bargain,* Part I, Public Personnel Association, Chicago, 1969, p. 3.

9   Ibid., p. 2.

10 Ibid., p. 3.

11 Dick Dashiell, "Lessons from Detroit and Cleveland," in Elam, Lieberman, and Moskow (eds.), op. cit., p. 305.

12 David Selden, "Winning Collective Bargaining," in ibid., p. 333.

13 Dashiell, op. cit., p. 303.

14 Bendiner, op. cit., p. 110.

15 Charles R. Perry and Wesley A. Wildman, *The Impact of Negotiations in Public Education*, Charles A. Jones, Worthington, Ohio, 1970, p. 13.

16 Homer O. Elseroad, "Professional Negotiations in Montgomery County," in Patrick W. Carlton and Harold I. Goodwin (eds.), *The Collective Dilemma: Negotiations in Education*, Charles A. Jones, Worthington, Ohio, 1969, p. 132.

17 Stanley M. Elam, "Prospects for an NEA-AFT Merger," *The Nation*, October 1965, pp. 247–249. Also see Myron Lieberman, "Implications of the Coming NEA-AFT Merger," in Carlton and Goodwin (eds.), op. cit., pp. 44–57.

18 National Education Association, November 1971, p. 3.

19 Charles R. Young, "The Superintendent of Schools in a Collective Bargaining Milieu," in Carlton and Goodwin (eds.), op. cit., p. 105.

20 Ibid., p. 106.

21 Terry Herndon, "The Future of Negotiations for Teachers," in Carlton and Goodwin (eds.), op. cit., p. 65.

22 Bernard E. Donovan, "Speaking of Management," in Elam, Lieberman, and Moskow (eds.), op. cit., p. 65.

23 Young, op. cit., p. 104.

24 Lieberman, "Implications of the Coming NEA-AFT Merger," op. cit., p. 50.

25 Herndon, op. cit., p. 64.

26 Perry and Wildman, op. cit., p. 210.

27 Richard C. Williams, "Teacher Militancy: Implications for the School," in Philip K. Piele, Terry L. Eidell, and Stuart C. Smith (eds.), *Social and Technological Change: Implications for Education*, Center for Advanced Study of Educational Administration, Eugene, Oreg., 1970.

28 Daniel E. Griffiths, "Board-Superintendent-Teacher Relations: Viable Alternatives to the Status Quo," in Frank W. Lutz and Joseph Azzarelli (eds.), *Struggle for Power in Education*, The Center for Applied Research in Education, New York, 1966.

29 Norman J. Boyan, "The Emergent Role of the Teacher and the Authority Structure of the School," in Roy B. Allen and John Schmid

(eds.), *Collective Negotiations and Educational Administration,* Arkansas Press, Fayetteville, Ark., 1966.

30 George Madden, "A Theoretical Basis for Differentiating Forms of Collective Bargaining in Education," *Educational Administration Quarterly,* Spring 1969, vol. 5, no. 2, pp. 76–90.

31 Cited in Bertram M. Gross, "The Scientific Approach to Administration," in *Behavioral Science and Educational Administration,* Sixty-third Yearbook of the National Society for the Study of Education, University of Chicago Press, Chicago, 1964, p. 48.

32 Richard E. Walton and Robert B. McKersie, *A Behavioral Theory of Labor Negotiations,* McGraw-Hill, New York, 1965.

33 Fenwick English and James Zaharis, "Crisis in Middle Management," *NASSP Bulletin,* April 1972, vol. 56, p. 5.

34 Ibid., p. 2.

35 Seymour B. Sarason, *The Culture of the School and the Problem of Change,* Allyn and Bacon, Boston, 1971, p. 134.

36 English and Zaharis, op. cit., p. 2 .

37 Rensis Likert, *The Human Organization,* McGraw-Hill, New York, 1967, pp. 4–10.

38 Thomas G. Gans, "Teacher Militancy, the Potential for It, and Perceptions of School Organizational Structure." Paper prepared for the annual meeting of the American Educational Research Association, Chicago, April 1972.

39 Edwin M. Bridges, J. Wayne, and David J. Mahan, "Effects of Hierarchical Differentiation of Group Productivity, Efficiency, and Risk Taking," *Administrative Science Quarterly,* September 1968, vol. 13, no. 2, p. 305–319.

40 Elliott Jaques, *The Changing Culture of a Factory,* Redwood Press, London, 1970.

41 Ibid., p. 276.

42 One example of this kind of material is Samuel G. Christie, Adrianne Bank, Carmen M. Culver, Gretchen McCann, and Roger Rasmussen, *The Problem Solving School,* Institute for Development of Educational Activities, Dayton, 1972. Another is the SPECS package produced by the Center for the Advanced Study of Educational Administration of the University of Oregon, and a third is the rural school project at the Northwest Regional Educational Laboratory. These products are described in greater detail by Rasmussen and Bank in Chapter 6 of this book.

43 Richard A. Schmuck and Matthew B. Miles, *Organization Development in Schools,* National Press Books, Palo Alto, Calif., 1971.

CHAPTER 8
THE SCHOOL WITHOUT A PRINCIPAL

Gary J. Hoban

The author builds a case for an "unthinkable" idea—the school without a principal. Arguing that the view of the principal entertained by most teachers, the inhibitions the principal feels about participatory decision making when he alone is held accountable for decisions made, and the absence of a strong bond of identification between principal and teachers all militate against the principal's role as key agent of change in the school, Dr. Hoban outlines a plan for school reorganization which eliminates the principalship.

Dr. Hoban served as a staff specialist to |I|D|E|A| and is currently coordinator of publications for the San Diego County, California, public schools.

It is indisputable that the position of principal is firmly established in the administrative structure of most American schools. Whether the principalship is given as a reward for long and faithful service or whether it is viewed as an important leadership post in the school, it is a venerable institution, one not to be treated lightly. To suggest that the principalship has undergone change over the years and that, in many cases, the occupants of that office have not kept abreast of educational development as much as they might have is acceptable criticism. However, to suggest that the position of school principal is an entirely outmoded concept which should no longer be a part of a school's administrative structure is at least controversial and in the eyes of many school people unthinkable.

Nevertheless, the time has come to consider seriously the possibility of eliminating the principalship from the list of roles to be filled in the school. This suggestion is not made as part of the political rhetoric, some of it no doubt justified, of disgruntled militant teachers.

Rather, it is made in light of the new realities which must be acknowledged by those educators truly interested in effecting the innovations which will permit a school to perform its essential function: to provide for the education of children and young adults.

It is impossible for one familiar with education not to be sensitive to the plight of the principal today. Regardless of the personal strengths and weaknesses he brings to the job, the principal is, as he has been dubbed so often, "the man in the middle." Not only is he straddling the middle ground between the central administration and the teachers in his school, but he is also subject to the pressures and counterpressures of parents, students, and special interest groups. Perhaps in the not so distant past the principalship was a meaningful, if not terribly dynamic, educational occupation. The position invested its occupant with paternal authoritarian rights such that the main task of the principal was to rule *his* school and to assure his public that all was fine in *their* school. Today, however, is not the era of administration by public relations, although there are many schools which are still administered with this objective in mind. With the current popularity of the accountability movement, the principal increasingly must share, if not completely shoulder, responsibility for the success or failure of the educational program in his school. In a more stable situation, this new responsibility is trying enough. In a volatile situation, where political considerations are of prime concern or where social conditions are so bad that educational achievement is of minor consequence in the school, the principal's major task is nothing short of survival.[1]

Although the complexity of the principalship today—with all of its many pressures—cannot be denied, it is not sufficient merely to bemoan the uncomfortable middle ground the principal must occupy. There are many who suggest that the best way to handle this increasingly ambiguous role experienced by the principal is to strengthen his role, to recognize that he remains the most powerful and influential figure in the individual school. These defenders of the principal point out, justifiably, that in the traditional school context it is the principal who is the most effective innovator because, by virtue of his leadership position, he has the opportunity to guide his staff toward providing better education for the children in his school. Also, some studies have shown that it is the principal, contrary to what one might expect, who has more progressive educational values than do the teachers he supervises.[2]

This defense of the principal and other suggestions for improving the role of the principal, however, are based on the assumption that the traditional administrative structure of the school has been established for all time. It may be true that, in light of the existing situation today, the principal is a key agent in promoting the needed changes for the revitalization of education and that he does hold more progressive values than do the teachers in his school; but it is also true that a long-range view of education might produce an alternative to traditional defenses of the principalship or to the supportive palliatives which attempt to firm up the tenuous middle ground now gingerly occupied by the principal. Simply put, educational reform must not always be in the context of the existing system. It may be that the system, or at least a significantly visible part of it, needs changing.

THE TRADITIONAL ROLE OF THE PRINCIPAL

The difficult, tenuous position of the principal already has been mentioned. However, a closer examination of the problem of the principal suggests that his position does not ultimately enhance innovation and adaption to new educational realities; it may, in fact, impede them. There are several areas of the traditional role of the principal which warrant critical discussion: the type of person who becomes principal, the authority-responsibility of the principal, and the nonteaching resocialization of the principal.

The Type of Person Who Becomes Principal

When one attempts to describe the individual who becomes a principal, it is difficult to avoid resorting to a stereotype. However, as much as one might wish to deny it, stereotypes are often rooted in reality. That is, while a stereotype might be an exaggeration of fact, it does reflect a dominant pattern of characteristics found in whatever is being described—and such it is in the case of the principal.

Common teacher prejudice would have it that the typical school principal, whether at the elementary or secondary level, is a former teacher with a physical education background or at the very least with a physical education orientation (recent survey shows, however, that most principals have a social studies background[3]). This physical education orientation is often cynically thought to be consistent with the imperatives of a moral athleticism which closely approximates the standards of conduct expected of a Boy Scout. Put another way, the typical principal from the perspective of teacher stereotype combines the stern values of the American Gothic with the easy ambience of Rotarian good cheer.

Of course this picture of the principal may go beyond the limits of permissible stereotype and may in effect be, to the militant teacher, an appealingly grotesque caricature. However, it cannot be denied that despite the many studies and good words written about the principal's leadership role—ideally progressive—a good many principals are ardent defenders of the status quo. And to be an ardent defender of the status quo, when one's occupational role definition calls for it, one usually has the personality and value structure most adaptable to such a role. There is an administrative type, though it may not be universal.

The administrative type, whether he be the principal of an easily dominated staff (one which may in fact want to be dominated) or the visible, vulnerable, authoritarian symbol to be resisted by militant teachers, is a ready target for detractors. Since school districts are not unlike most organizations, the orientation of most people who remain within them for any length of time is one of acquiescence to bureaucratic control. Few principals emerge from the ranks of teaching as the result of creativity or impressive academic backgrounds. Indeed, these latter characteristics may be a detriment to an administrative career, since it is better to keep highly qualified teachers in the classroom, as they are hard to find. For the most part, as stereotype would have it, the principal is a personification of the Peter principle—that is, he has risen to his level of incompetence—who has parlayed his hierarchical orientation along with his reasonable social ability into a higher paying educational job.

Although there are many who would reject this stereotype of the principal as being plainly untrue and not reflecting actual facts, that is not the issue. The issue is that there are many individuals who *believe* that this stereotype represents the truth, and it appears that their numbers are growing, especially in the ranks of teachers who are being drawn to the more militant movements. Since this negative picture of the principal exists and may be proliferating, the status of the principalship is diminishing, and as the status of the principal diminishes, the traditional power invested in the office no longer provides the reservoir of leadership potential it once did. Thus it is now possible and in some places fashionable to deny that the principal is the instructional leader of the school. In these situations, then, the principal can no longer be counted on to be the innovative leader in the school. To the skeptical teacher, be he reactionary in his resistance to change or radical in his advocacy of it, the principal can as easily be seen as the critical impediment to, rather than the inspiration for, educational improvement.

The Authority-Responsibility of the Principal

Whatever one's image of the principal is—be it the more derogatory stereotype suggested above or a more flattering paternal picture from the past—there are few who would suggest that the principal does not exercise broad discretionary authority within the school. By the same token, the principal does have a great deal of responsibility for the effectiveness of the educational program within the school. And, of course, the authority and the responsibility of the principal are interrelated.

In the traditional system, the principal exercises virtually all decision-making power within the school—from deciding how to keep the building clean to determining how closely a district curriculum guide is to be followed. The extent of this authority is of course a result of the historical movement in education to consolidate schools into well-functioning units which are parts of a larger, well-functioning bureaucracy.

While the administrative style of a benevolent autocrat had its place at one time, it is questionable whether such an administrative style is acceptable today. The resistance of teachers, even the non-militant ones, is too great for such an approach to administration to flourish. Teacher association or union demands for master contracts and the legitimization of the term "participatory decision making" have all but precluded the effective functioning of the benevolent despot principal.

Inextricably intertwined with the changing authority role of the principal is the responsibility the principal bears for the successful operation of the school. Although the responsibility, and the requisite authority to meet it, for the more technical administrative tasks still remains securely in the domain of the principal, the more professional matters which deal with the teacher and his work are no longer conceded to be purely under the direction of the principal. As teaching becomes more complex, it becomes more apparent that the principal, acting by himself, is in a very difficult position should he desire to implement district curriculum plans in the school or, more significantly, take upon himself the responsibility for evaluating all aspects of an individual teacher's performance in the classroom. In point of fact, if a principal does not visit a given teacher's classroom on a regular basis and confer intelligently and frequently with the teacher about teaching—the objectives, the methods, the assessment of pupil progress—then principal evaluation of teachers is meaningless.

In addition to the problem of teacher evaluation, the principal is put into a difficult position if he indeed shares his traditional decision-making power with his faculty. While "participatory decision making," especially in the instructional aspects of the school program, is currently recognized as enlightened administration, the very term suggests that the principal gratuitously abdicates from his position of absolute power within the school to create a tolerable environment for his teachers. However, if the principal reserves for himself the right of veto over faculty decisions and works for consensus school governance—when the teachers' position on any given issue is in agreement with his—such a decision-making scheme is at best sham democracy. Unfortunately, most participatory decision-making plans fall into this category.

Often, by virtue of his traditional authority, the principal wishes to retain veto power over faculty decisions because, as he rightfully maintains, he is the one individual who is held accountable for shared decisions, regardless of their merit. If this is the case, however, accountability never has a real chance to enter the classroom, and the teacher can legitimately avoid responsibility for the consequences of the decisions that are made, whether they are made by the principal with the faculty or by the principal alone. On the other hand, if the instructional or administrative decisions within a school are made by the teacher and if they cannot be overruled by a principal, it becomes quite clear where the responsibility for the success or failure of a school program resides.

The Nonteaching Resocialization of the Principal

For the principal to provide effective leadership for the teachers in his school, and for him to utilize his authority and to bear his responsibility in a meaningful way, it is necessary that he have a strong bond of identification with teachers. This bond, even if the principal acknowledges it out of a sense of professional politeness, is nonexistent in most schools. The principal is not a teacher, and the gulf that separates the two groups is real and sometimes quite wide. As one critic has pointed out:

> The analogy between slaves and teachers [in the past and today] was a metaphorical attempt to capture the essence of being a teacher in most public school systems. Like most metaphors, there is slippage around the edges and the fit between the two is clumsy. Yet there is something to it. Anyone who has spent time in large urban schools can see its validity in teachers kowtowing to principals, in the plodding dependency of too many teachers, in the unmanly tone of so many schools, in the rumblings of resistance followed by runaways (called teacher attrition), or by petty obstructionism pursued by angered teachers.[4]

Although the analogy offered above may be an overstatement, most observers would probably agree that the principal is socialized to a nonteaching, more elite role in the school than are the teachers. Evidence of this nonsocialization to teaching is not hard to find. Not only does the principal typically earn a higher salary than most of the teachers in the school and usually enjoy the benefits of an unstructured working day (with time for sociable personal and community luncheons) but he also has his own office (a luxury rarely enjoyed by a teacher), his personal secretary (who sometimes functions as a palace guard), and numerous other small but cumulatively significant perquisites of power which alternately can impress or intimidate teachers.

As suggested earlier, the "administrative type" who becomes principal usually gears his career so that he can leave teaching as soon as possible. This principal's norms are generally the norms of other administrators in the district and reflect a prime loyalty to institutionalized bureaucracy rather than to specific activities needed in the classroom. In addition to the socialization of the aspirant principal to administrative norms, once he assumes this role, the principal quickly joins administrative associations which specifically exclude nonadministrators from membership even though as a principal he was welcome, often in an honored status, in most teachers' professional groups until recently. Teacher groups such as the AFT, however, have recognized that the principal is not a teacher and have followed the lead of administrative associations by practicing professional discrimination in admitting members. Even the relatively conservative NEA, particularly in its local affiliates, now questions whether or not principals really have the same problems and concerns as do teachers. As teacher militancy grows and as administrators, especially the principals who work daily with teachers, are forced into retreat from effective school leadership by the prestigious isolation of their position and their traditional authoritarian role, it may be that the time has come for the principal to consider stepping aside in the school and aiding teachers in establishing the school without a principal.

TOWARD A SCHOOL WITHOUT A PRINCIPAL

Once a school staff becomes convinced that establishing a school without a principal is its objective, how does it proceed? Obviously reaching such a decision is difficult enough, but achieving such a new administrative structure without descending into chaos requires extremely careful planning and prodigious effort. Moving toward a school without a principal is not a task to be taken lightly, and it is not a task which can be accomplished in a short period of time.

Before any reorganization of a school can take place, particularly a reorganization of the magnitude described above, it is imperative that any negative innovations and threatened recriminations be abandoned by all parties—teachers and principals—who are involved in this endeavor. It is highly unlikely, whatever the reasons one might have for wanting to establish a school without a principal, that any substantive progress toward this goal can be achieved if there is a high degree of conflict among those who are to establish this administrative reorganization. The idea behind the school without a principal should not be reconstruction after revolution; rather, it should reflect the responsible decision of the entire school staff—administrators and teachers—to cope with new educational realities.

To a certain extent, restructuring a school so that it can function without the traditional office of principal is a movement toward differentiated staffing which, while variously described, is essentially

> . . . a staff utilization pattern that offers (1) a career pattern in teaching that does not inevitably lead out of the classroom into counseling or administration; (2) a more manageable teaching assignment, with improved matching of qualifications and interests to responsibilities; (3) a structure for decision-making, goal-setting, and evaluation in which teachers play a leading part (a collegial structure); (4) a salary schedule emphasizing contributions rather than seniority and training; (5) a flexible instructional pattern open to innovation at the level of each of the

schools's working units; a pattern that readily accommodates consultants and paraprofessionals, a variety of student/teacher groupings, and a wider range of curricula.[5]

A school with differentiated staffing, however, is not necessarily a school without a principal, even though a school without a principal would utilize a differentiated staff. Most differentiated staffs function in schools with principals, not without them. True, differentiated staffing, once it is introduced into a school, tends to minimize the disharmony which so often characterizes relationships between administrators and teachers. This is usually done by elevating at least some teachers to visible status levels as well as by remunerating at least some teachers with salaries roughly approximate to lower and lower-middle administrative salaries. Even so, questions persist over matters of how new (especially high level) positions and their occupants would be determined as well as to what degree administrative superordinate prerogatives would remain in the school. Differentiated staffing cannot solve all the problems in raising the professional status of teachers, of expanding their base of responsibility and accountability, and of implementing participatory educational decision making. Although differentiated staffing is a significant compromise with the traditional pattern of administration in the schools, it is still a compromise with what might be—the school without a principal, a school in which teachers have ultimate and total responsibility and accountability for the educational program in their school.

Phases of Establishing a School Without a Principal

As suggested above, translating a desire to establish a school without a principal into reality involves much work and careful planning. Although there are, no doubt, many change strategies one could suggest for achieving this reality, the following six phases, sequentially undertaken over a period of roughly five years, provide a framework for restructuring an individual school administration so that it will no longer be dependent upon or support the traditional office of principal. The following phases reflect at least a partial response to the objections against having a school *with* a principal.

1 The principal accepts as his responsibility the need to allow the teaching staff to take on new activities involved with the administration of the school.

2   The teaching staff becomes involved in setting criteria and developing procedures for evaluating teachers and administrators.

3   The teaching staff develops and implements a differentiated staffing plan.

4   Teachers from the top ranks of the differentiated staff share administrative responsibilities with the principal.

5   The principal resigns, going into another educational setting or returning to the classroom according to his appropriate place in a differentiated staff.

6   The teaching staff elects from the top ranks of the differentiated staff a dean of studies who, even though he continues to do some teaching, serves as a visible administrative functionary for a specific period of time unless he is prematurely recalled from his office by the teachers in the school.

Phase 1: The Principal Involves the Staff   It is no doubt ironic that the principal is a key figure in establishing a school without a principal. If one considers the arguments in behalf of the attempt to restructure the school's administration, it would appear that involving the principal in the changeover process invalidates these arguments. The principal, it can be argued, is not an impediment to change, and in fact, a school cannot function without a principal. Both of these observations may be accurate; however, they should not be accepted as a conclusive rebuff to the proposal being developed here.

The importance of the principal in establishing a school without a principal rests on the fact that schools—even those which consider themselves most progressive on the issue under discussion—do have principals who generally exercise virtually all the ultimate power in them. Most principals, for example, do retain the veto power in shared decision-making operations. To deny this reality and at the same time encourage a teaching staff to develop such an administrative structure is to invite rebellion and the organizational chaos which could follow. As suggested earlier, establishing a school without a principal should be a gradual, evolutionary process in which old superordinate-subordinate roles must be adapted to the needs of the new objective. Thus it is imperative that the principal participate in the changeover process.

Any principal who would be involved in this type of administrative reorganization would be a magnanimous individual. Not only would he have to be aware that in a matter of a few years, at most, he no longer would hold his position, but also he would have to provide the leadership necessary to bring about his own demise. Hence, it is quite apparent that a plan to phase out the principalship in a school demands a uniquely qualified principal to facilitate its implementation.

The type of principal who would be able to cope with such a change would have to be an individual who is capable of understanding his role not in personal but organizational terms. He must be a person who has a firm understanding of organizational change and one who is not the typical product of empire-building schemes. Simply put, he must be a person who is psychologically and professionally capable to work himself out of a job. Perhaps such a requirement will necessitate the recruitment of a new breed of administrator, one in agreement with what some observers would call radical movements in education. On the other hand, there may very well be many principals already in the schools today who have a broad enough view of education and who possess the confidence that educational problems can be solved with nontraditional responses rather than merely maintained with status quo management.

A school where there has been teacher interest in taking a more active role in decision making is most likely the place to begin implementing a plan for a school without a principal. It is in such a school that a helpful principal is likely to be found. Thus, phase 1 amounts to getting a principal who is fully aware that he will not hold his position in the future, together with an involved teaching staff for the purpose of sharing in the administration of the school. In addition, it must be clear to the teachers from the outset, as it is to the principal, that as they and the principal work together in making and implementing decisions for the school, they must prepare themselves eventually to assume the full administrative power in the school.

Phase 2: Involving the Teaching Staff in the Evaluation Process   Once the staff of a school has decided that it wants a school without a principal and the principal has displayed his willingness to cooperate in such a venture, it is important that teachers begin to become involved in assessing not only the strengths and weaknesses of their school program but also their roles in implementing such a program. Teachers, then, must become active agents in the evaluation process.

The word "evaluation" generally conjures up negative images for teachers. Evaluation has traditionally described the annual or semiannual visit and rating form employed by principals to check up on nontenured (and in special cases tenured) teachers to be certain that orderly behavior, orderly instruction, and orderly learning are present in the classroom. Seen from the militant teacher's point of view, evaluation is an official act performed by the principal to keep teachers in line.

Everyone in the field of education should know that evaluation involves far more than is described above. With the accountability movement in full strength, evaluation includes needs assessment, behavioral objectives, goal setting, and PPBS, to suggest but a few of the terms spilling forth from the current cornucopia of educational jargon. Although all the concern about evaluation is on behalf of improved education for the children, the teacher sees evaluation as a threat. It is a way for the principal—now bolstered by the central administration, the board and its constituency of taxpayers, the county and state offices, and various political officials—to be certain that the teacher really earns his salary. Thus evaluation, despite the many platitudes and scholarly analyses offered in its behalf, is essentially a rather primitive tool in the average school.

It is at this primitive level that most teachers and principals must begin, regardless of their desire to professionalize or upgrade the education being provided for the children of America. A faculty—both teachers and principal—working toward establishing a school without a principal must face this primitive notion of evaluation as a critical impediment to be overcome. A working relationship between principal and teachers is essential at this point. The principal must, and probably has if the proposed administrative reorganization of the school has progressed this far, abandon any attempts to control teachers by supervision, and teachers must be willing to admit that, from his perspective, the principal does have some insight into what is and should be going on in the school.

When this working relationship has been established, then a total staff can begin to look critically at its specific educational tasks and to determine how to assess whether or not these tasks are being successfully accomplished. The technical intricacies and the "how to" suggestions of evaluation approaches have been thoroughly described elsewhere.[6] The important thing is that teachers take an active role in evaluation, both of themselves and of the principal. By developing and using criteria to assess the effectiveness of what goes on in the school, teachers will have taken a major step toward the day when they can, without acrimony, operate without a principal.

Phase 3: The Teaching Staff Develops and Implements a Differentiated Staffing Plan   As teachers begin to take on increased responsibility for a school's program and for activities that extend beyond their classroom doors, they have begun to move toward establishing a differentiated staff. Although setting evaluation criteria and participating in the evaluation process, as discussed in phase 2, do not directly turn the power in the school over to teachers, it does acknowledge the principle that teachers are capable of providing direction for a school; once this principle has been established, the next step in reorganizing the administrative structure of the school involves defining a new set of roles for teachers.

It has been pointed out above that differentiated staffing can be a compromise with having a school without a principal. In addition, since a differentiated staff is not, by general description, a staff without a principal, it should not be regarded as the ultimate that can be achieved in restructuring a school administration. This is not to say that differentiated staffing should not be attempted; on the contrary, it is a key step in institutionalizing a higher order of roles for teachers in the administrative structure of the school. In a sense, developing a differentiated staffing plan is a turning point in establishing a school without a principal.

Of course the critical factor involved in differentiated staffing is the determination of who does what and why. If this determination is made by the principal, then differentiated staffing is of little interest in terms of this chapter. However, if the determination and assignment of roles within a differentiated staff is made by the teachers in a school, with the advice and perhaps consent of the principal but not subject to his veto, then the benefits of such a faculty reorganization become obvious. What should result is a situation such as Dwight Allen describes:

> Taking educational policy making out of the hands of the administrative hierarchy and sharing it among the most talented teachers is just one major objective of the differentiated staff concept. In this, as in other respects, it has no educational precedent, a fact worth noting by those who think it will be easy.
>
> Professors and Senior Teachers, as members of a school cabinet chaired by the principal (also a Professor), would seek full authority from the school board and the superintendent to formulate new educational policy; to make decisions as to what educational functions should be served, how they should be served, and by whom they should be carried

out; and in general to govern the school as an autonomous body. This does not mean the cabinet would not seek outside help. On the contrary, it would seek and get the kind of help in introducing constructive change that schools have been cut off from up to now.[7]

Thus the third phase in a program to establish a school without a principal involves a major realignment of power within the school. Teachers would have defined roles and, assuming they are not subject to principal veto, collectively would have the authority and responsibility with which they could begin to phase out the office of principal and in so doing work toward the types of constructive change which education so desperately needs.

Phases 4 and 5: Teachers Take Over Administrative Tasks and the Principal Resigns   Once teachers have defined roles for themselves in a differentiated staffing program, it becomes relatively easy for some teachers, at least those from the higher ranks (perhaps "master teachers," as they are sometimes called) to share in the administration of the school. Those administrative tasks which most likely would be the initial concerns of teachers are in the area of curriculum, and if teachers have been recognized to have at least some expertise, they should with confidence take full responsibility for making the general curriculum decisions for the school. Through peer reinforcement, teachers should then see that these decisions are implemented in the classroom and that the consequences of these decisions are fully evaluated.

Exactly how the teaching staff is to take over the administrative responsibilities for the total school curriculum, of course, would depend on what direction the staff wishes to go—toward an elected supervisory committee of peers or toward full democracy. In either case, it is imperative that what is done is done by design of all the teachers in the school, not according to a principal's plan or, for that matter, by a power elite of master teachers. (In fact, one of the critical dangers that must be guarded against is creating a new power structure to replace the old. Whatever type of differentiated staffing arrangement is made, there must always be an opening for talent to rise to the level at which it can be fully used. The traditional bureaucratic structure of the schools which operates as a closed system, only rarely elevating a favored orthodox disciple to its hierarchy, must not be replicated as teachers, especially small groups of teachers, accede to power. Otherwise, all the effort expended to establish a school without a principal would be fruitless.)

In addition to giving teachers full responsibility for the curriculum
—which in the broad sense includes everything from teacher evaluation to textbook selection—there remain other administrative responsibilities to be considered; for example, who is to be responsible for
the buses, the cafeteria food, and attendance reporting? In other
words, how are managerial needs going to be met in a school without
a principal? Perhaps this is an administrative area best retained by the
principal. Although this suggestion is practical, it may not be compatible with the new roles that must be developed in the school without a principal. There is little doubt that managerial needs in a school
must be met. However, they require the attention of a person who is
a manager, not a principal.

The central point of an administrative restructuring such as is being discussed here is that all administrative power in the school ultimately should be in the hands of teachers, although it might be dis-
persed according to role assignments made to individuals by teachers.
Once the principalship has been phased out, so should the title "principal," and although new hierarchical functions such as school managers will inevitably arise, they must be subject to the collective will
of an entire teaching staff. Thus, when a teaching staff, with the help
of the principal, has developed a set of procedures and role definitions
for efficiently running a school and has taken over the major administrative tasks of the school, it is time for the principal to exit.

It is a legitimate question to ask what becomes of the principal
once the arduous sequence of events which allow for an orderly transition of power from principal to teaching staff takes place. Unquestion-
ably, any administrator who has the ability to work with a faculty to
bring itself to the point where it can assume responsibility for the total
school program is a valuable individual for any organization to have.
Certainly such a principal would be welcomed should he wish, as a
teacher, to join the faculty with which he has so recently worked. On
the other hand, once a faculty has reached the point at which it is
ready, through its procedures, to teach the children and administer the
school without a principal, it would probably be better if the principal
would leave the school lest he become overly involved in the problems related to his former position. Indeed, once a principal has been
voluntarily phased out of his position, it would appear that a logical
place for him to go is to another school which is ready for an administrator who is able to work with another set of teachers in such a
way that they too will be able to establish a school without a principal.
In other words, this magnanimous principal is really not in the tradi-

tional sense a principal at all; he is a professional change agent with a specialization in administrative reorganization.

Phase 6: The Teaching Staff Selects Its Leader   As the principal steps down and the teaching staff takes over full administrative responsibility for the school, it is necessary that some organizational structure be instituted so that the school will continue to operate smoothly. Although the administrative design to be used must be acceptable to the staff, the following plan is offered as a possible final step to be undertaken in establishing a school without a principal.

Since the staff has already defined differentiated teaching roles according to the various educational needs it has perceived, it has most likely identified a rank for teachers who are capable of providing leadership for the school. From this rank, a teacher would be elected for a term of three years as dean of studies (or some other title the faculty fancies) to serve as the chief visible representative of power in the school. Since this dean would continue to teach for at least a minimal part of each day, he would become a first among equals. He would not hold evaluative power over any aspect of the school program, since this function would be performed by the entire faculty or by its appropriately designated committees of teachers. Managerial functions would be the domain of a professional school manager who would be accountable to the total staff. The other school functions, such as counseling for example, would remain the job of professionals trained for this work. The performance of these other functions would of course be evaluated by the total staff or its designated representatives. Thus, the ultimate criterion in judging the performance of any activity in the school would not be its reflection of the status quo or its reputation as being "a stepping-stone to administration," but rather would be its contribution to the total educational program of the school.

In essence, the dean of studies would be the coordinator of the various administrative activities of the teachers, and he would be the representative of the faculty to the public. He would be the elected chairman of the faculty and in no way its direct administrative superior or its superordinate in the trappings of power and monetary reward. Plush personal offices would be abolished, and appropriate conference rooms, available to all faculty members according to need, could be used for meetings with parents or other community members. In fact, to insure that the dean would not attempt to install himself as a principal with a new title, he would be subject to recall by a simple vote of no confidence by the teachers, and he would not be allowed to serve in that position for more than one term, being eligible for re-election to the deanship only after he had returned to his primary occupation, teaching, for three years. Thus the deanship would be frequently open to a variety of qualified teachers, so ranked by teachers according to the criteria established in their differentiated staffing plan, and it would be a position which could reflect the current concerns of a staff. A subject matter specialist might be elected for one term only to be succeeded by a counseling or methodology specialist in a subsequent term.

A FINAL THOUGHT

Although there are no doubt many questions which are left unanswered in this chapter and some flaws in the suggested procedures, it has indicated that there is a need for planning a possible way of establishing a school without a principal. In a paper this short in which an idea so far-reaching is suggested, it is virtually impossible thoroughly to discuss all the countless details which must be attended to.

The point has been less one of specifying "how to do it" than of suggesting that there is an alternative to the traditional administrative structure. Under the proper circumstances and with highly professional attitudes on the part of teachers and principals, teachers can effectively govern schools. Although establishing a school without a principal will not solve all the educational problems with which a school is concerned, it can, by elevating the status, the authority, and the responsibility of teachers and by stressing the importance of their work, redirect attention away from concerns over maintenance and power so that more attention can be given to teaching and learning.

NOTES

1 For a discussion of the problems of the urban administrator, see Luvern Cunningham, "Hey Man, You Our Principal? Urban Education as I Saw It," *Phi Delta Kappan*, vol. 51, no. 3, November 1969, pp. 123–128.

2 For a discussion of principals' and teachers' attitudes toward change, see Richard C. Williams, Charles C. Wall, W. Michael Martin, and Arthur Berchin, *Effecting Organizational Renewal in Schools*, McGraw-Hill, 1973, Chapter 4.

3   *The Elementary Principalship in 1968,* Department of Elementary School Principals, NEA, Washington, 1968, p. 25.

4   Larry Cuban, "Teaching the Children: Does the System Help or Hinder?" in *Freedom, Bureaucracy and Schooling,* Association for Supervision and Curriculum Development, NEA, Washington, 1971, p. 160.

5   Peter Coleman and Herbert A. Wallin, "A Rationale for Differentiated Staffing," *Interchange,* vol. 2, no. 3, 1971, p. 29.

6   A practical approach to evaluation is provided by Samuel G. Christie, Adrianne Bank, Carmen M. Culver, Gretchen McCann, and Roger Rasmussen, *The Problem Solving School,* Institute for Development of Educational Activities, Dayton, 1972.

7   Dwight Allen, "Putting Teaching Talent to Work," in James L. Olivero and Edward G. Buffie (eds.), *Educational Manpower: From Aides to Differentiated Staff Patterns,* Indiana University Press, Bloomington, 1970, p. 171.

CHAPTER **9**

ACCOUNTABILITY:
FACT, FICTION, OR FARCE?

Jerrold M. Novotney

The controversy surrounding the accountability movement
is enormously complex. In this chapter, Jerrold Novotney
discusses the many facets of the movement by providing
a sample of the host of definitions of the term *accountability* as well as by attempting to clear up the many
misconceptions surrounding the various evaluative techniques which are often confused with the concept of
accountability. In addition, the author calls attention to
the uncertain future of the accountability movement by
posing the question as to whether it is a significant educational development or just another innovative fad.

Dr. Novotney serves as assistant director of the
|I|D|E|A| Research Division.

It is virtually impossible to answer the question posed by the title of
this chapter without crossing swords with someone. Armed camps
representing various views of the accountability question are on all
sides. The pros and cons are aired to such an extent in current educational literature that many of us are quite self-conscious about adding
to the extant verbiage. Yet one thing appears evident—confusion and
controversy abound.

FACT

In sorting through what has occurred in education and what has been
written about education over the last four or five years, it becomes
clear that the problem of educational accountability is not only with us
today but will very likely remain for some time to come. Although not
a new concept, the idea of accountability was undeniably accentuated
and thrust into the national limelight through the efforts of Leon

Lessinger while he was Associate United States Commissioner for Elementary and Secondary Education. In his testimony before the Subcommittee on Appropriations of the House of Representatives during May 1969, Lessinger described several new management concepts being used in the Bureau of Elementary and Secondary Education. Among them was the concept of accountability. In Lessinger's words, as he applied the concept to government-sponsored projects:

> Basically, accountability means that the grantee will be held responsible at any time during the project for accomplishing the objectives of the project which the grantee himself proposed within the time periods specified, within the budget limitations and according to the standards established. Thus, at any point in the life of the project there will be a benchmark against which to measure performance.[1]

Although Lessinger denies responsibility for fathering the concept, there is little doubt that he has been a prime mover with regard to its promulgation in the educational world. As he sees it:

> In the same way that our technological system is geared to produce a better product for the most economical expenditure of time, materials, space and machinery, we should be able to make education an increasingly more efficient and effective process. . . .
> Accountability is the name for a new movement in education which is designed to reach that goal.[2]

In another article, Lessinger describes accountability as a new process of "concrete practical activity" which we can use to confront some of our most critical educational dilemmas, including reestablishment of confidence in our educational system.[3]

Confusion of Definitions

In discussing the current status of accountability, Raymond Bernabei points out a major problem:

> Accountability seems to be taking on like an educational rorschach. It seems to be spreading in all directions. Many are talking about it; many are expounding its virtues. There is little doubt of its importance. Yet much confusion exists among the perceptions held by educators.[4]

This confusion is well exemplified by a glance at the varying interpretations of the accountability concept. Different meanings are attached to it by different people. Take, for example, the following definitions (italics added):

. . . Accountability is *a procedure* whereby resources and efforts are related to results in ways that are useful for policy-making, resource allocation, or compensation.[5]

Accountability is, in essence, *a statement of policy.* It states that educators will accept responsibility for their performance—or lack of it. It implies that there is a contract between school personnel and the public and that contract involves more than showing up for work on time.[6]

Accountability is *the product of a process* at its most basic level, . . . it means that an agent, public or private, entering into a contractual agreement to perform a service will be held answerable for performing according to agreed-upon terms, within an established time period, and with a stipulated use of resources and performance standards. This definition of accountability requires that the parties to the contract keep clear and complete records and that this information be available for outside review. It also suggests penalties and rewards; accountability without redress or incentive is mere rhetoric.[7]

Accountability is not performance contracting. Accountability is not program budgeting (P.P.B.S.). Accountability is not cost effectiveness. It is not testing nor is it merit pay for teachers, or a means of relieving teachers of their jobs. Accountability is *the guarantee that all students without respect to race, income, or social class will acquire the minimum school skills* necessary to take full advantage of the choices that accrue upon successful completion of public schooling.[8]

Accountability means to me a *continuous willingness to evaluate education, to explain and interpret the results with all candor,* to divulge the results to the publics or constituencies that need to know them, and to be personally and organizationally responsible for the weaknesses as well as the strengths revealed. . . . What it means is that school boards and local and state educators will face the responsibility of taking the public into full partnership—explaining the problems and limitations of testing and other means of evaluating education, welcoming assistance, and sharing the resulting information (after having done everything possible to assure that it will be properly interpreted and used).[9]

The variety of definitions seems to stem from what might be a confusion of accountability as a concept and accountability as a process. The former is much akin to responsibility; the latter understanding involves at least four components:

1   Specification of desired learner performance.

2   Specification of those processes which will be implemented in order to bring about the desired learner performance.

3   Establishment of procedures to monitor and audit the above processes to determine if they are in fact implemented.

4   Publication of a report relating student performance to the implemented educational program.[10]

Given either understanding of the term, however, the fact is that if accountability is to be a dominant theme in education, both the profession and the public will have to broaden their range of skills, change their attitudes, and upgrade their knowledge of the educational world and its phenomena. Accountability as only a professional exercise is unrealistic; accountability as a political exercise for community and educator is workable,[11] but we have a long way to go before smooth operation is achieved.

The scope and complexity of accountability perhaps explain why a myriad of questions about it remain unanswered. As Roger Lennon pointed out, we still have not clearly determined:

1   What are the schools to be accountable for? For student accomplishment and development of cognitive, affective and motor skills. This is taken to imply explicit and detailed statements of desired outcomes or goals will be presented and set forth in behavioral terms susceptible to observation or, preferably, measurement. In the absence of these statements, there can be no evaluation of an enterprise.

2   Who is accountable? Our senses of logic and justice tell us that each person whose task it is to influence learning—teacher, supervisor, principal, curriculum coordinator, counselor, whoever—should be accountable for precisely that part of the educational outcomes which he can effect directly through his own efforts.

3   How is accountability to be established? Clearly, there is a need for an accountability information system providing systematic information on output and input. Further, there is need for relating the elements of input, including staff efforts, instructional materials, support systems, etc., to outcomes, in a manner that will permit the attribution of the outcomes in proper measure to these various input elements.

4   By whom shall accountability be determined? There is substantial feeling that whatever a school or system may attempt in its own self-evaluative endeavors, independent auditors or accounting agencies are desirable.[12]

The Complexity of the Accountability Question

The many definitions of accountability and the multiplicity of suggestions for implementation offered are evidences of the complexity of the accountability question. This complexity is compounded by other factors as well. There are, for example, fairly diverse points of view concerning its usefulness. David Selden, president of the American Federation of Teachers AFL-CIO, gives his opinion that

> Accountability offers ready teacher scapegoats to amateur and professional school-haters, from the fellow who did not get along well with his eighth grade teacher to the corporate executive who judges schools by his company's property tax rate.[13]

In contrast, President Nixon said in his message to Congress on educational reform in February 1970, "We have as a nation too long avoided thinking of the productivity of schools." Shortly after the President's message, Congressman Albert Quie of Minnesota in an interview told *Nation's Schools* that in his opinion accountability would henceforth be required by Congress when making educational appropriations.

The conflict in viewpoints is especially evident in the dichotomy that exists between those who have been advocating the necessity of humanizing the schools to a greater degree and those who see teaching and learning as completely quantifiable tasks subject to explicit measurement. As Hencley points out, "On the one hand, there is resolute support among Silberman's many followers for making schools less grim, less mutilative of spontaneity, less destructive of creativity and less ruinous to the development of a healthy self-concept."[14] Certainly George Leonard, Ivan Illich, and John Holt are in this camp. However, there is an opponent camp headed by Leon Lessinger, with support from such people as W. James Popham and Robert Mager. Their drive toward accountability centers upon the clear delineation of objectives, the use of careful measurement procedures, and the full communication of student learning outcomes to the public. Unfortunately, the extremes of the educational dichotomy between the humanists and the behaviorists are most difficult, if not impossible, to bridge.

Finally, the complexity of the problem of accountability resides most evidently in its comprehensiveness and in its dependence upon the cooperation of decision makers at many levels. As Kenneth Tye has said:

> Education is a complex enterprise. It is not just a teacher in a classroom with 25 to 35 students. It involves government at all levels. It in-

volves literally millions of decisions made by the lay public, by administrators, and by the intermediate educational agents who influence what the teacher can and does do. All are accountable—to themselves, to the students they serve, and to the public.[15]

Indeed, it is a fact that responsibility for the ultimate success of educational programs really involves everyone in a particular district, region, or state system. But the problem is one of clarifying areas of responsibility, to avoid the round robin of instructors, administrators, and legislators each looking to the other for implementation of accountability.

A simple statement of the complexity of the problem of defining roles for accountability might be as follows: Accountability requires both a personal and a shared responsibility for each of the participants. Learners remain responsible for persisting in their studies in order to accomplish their school's objectives. Instructors remain responsible for developing, evaluating, and improving instructional programs. Local, district, regional, and state administrators remain responsible for establishing the conditions and procedures necessary for continuous school improvement. Legislators remain responsible for passing laws and appropriating money supportive of and consistent with the movement toward accountability in education. Thus, each of the above groups remains responsible for helping the others to perform their part of the accountability process.[16]

FICTION

As with any occurrence of major import, the trend toward accountability in education has generated more than its share of groundless fear and has, in addition, spawned a veil of fiction which tends to obscure its true worth. As was pointed out earlier, there is considerable latitude in the way accountability is defined; however, it also appears that most of what is taken for accountability is really not accountability but only a part of it.

Evaluation

There has been a tendency, for instance, to identify accountability with evaluation. They are not identical. Accountability is characterized by planning for and assessing educational outcomes. Evaluation, on the other hand, is a function of accountability by which one can determine how well goals have been met. Evaluation is more nearly identified with measurement in that it assesses performance against a set of expectations. Accountability, however, can be more broadly interpreted to encompass the description, explanation, or justification of one's behavior. It may, in fact, not necessitate accomplishing all of one's objectives. The accountable person therefore monitors, assesses, and evaluates what he does. As such, accountability and evaluation are separate and yet complementary processes.[17]

Performance Contracting

Another concern which flirts with the fictitious is the aura surrounding performance contracting. If Leon Lessinger is remembered at the U.S. Office of Education (USOE) for his push for accountability, he will also be known for his effort to apply the performance contracting concept to it.[18] Writing in *Nation's Business,* Lessinger says:

> We have the tools to make accountability both attractive and practical for schools . . . developmental capital and performance contracts. Together they link up spending to teacher performance and student achievement.[19]

Nevertheless, not all has proved tranquil where contracts have been used. An early contract project widely heralded as a prototype was that of the Texarkana, Arkansas, school district with Dorsett Educational Systems. Seeking a dropout prevention program for students in grades seven through twelve, Texarkana obtained a grant in May 1969, from the USOE under Title VIII of the 1965 Elementary and Secondary Education Act (ESEA). Subsequently, a performance contract was signed with Dorsett to pay $80 for each student who improved his academic achievement by one grade level after 80 hours of instruction. Payment was not to be made if this was not achieved after 168 hours of instruction, and greater amounts were to be paid if it was achieved in fewer than 80 hours. All appeared to proceed well and publicity abounded until May 1970, when pupils were tested for achievement. An independent auditor stated that students had been taught to the test. Lloyd Dorsett, the contractor, agreed that the experiment had been more interested in making money than in improving education.

As Helen Bain, then president of the National Education Association, pointed out in late 1970,

> As things stand now, we don't know whether the contracts are written to serve the needs of children or of special interest groups. We

don't know the extent, if any, to which contracts are written to meet their learning objectives—or, indeed, whether the objectives are consistent with sound educational policy.[20]

Clearly, serious questions are being raised about performance contracting by the teaching profession, but even the educational industry itself is aware of the tenuous position it occupies. Robert Locke of the McGraw-Hill Book Company, at an accountability conference sponsored by Educational Testing Service, pointed out that any contractor is first of all interested in money. He noted that several economic elements had to be considered, since a firm's materials and equipment would likely be higher priced in a performance contracting situation than if they were bought "off the shelf." Locke said that the only way a performance contract can cost less is if it fails.

Another major concern of the performance contractor, Locke indicated, is the role to be played in a contract situation by the regular teaching staff. In Locke's opinion, companies are not particularly interested in proving themselves more effective in teaching the basic academic skills than are regular teachers. The contractor's problem is to find school districts which are able to develop their own performance objectives and state them succinctly. In addition, companies are anxious to do business with school districts that have a thorough understanding of evaluation processes and techniques. Realistically, Locke criticized the short-term performance contracts like those funded by the Office of Economic Opportunity since, he said, they tend to create "the false expectations that an education company can set up, operate, and leave in good working order a new instructional system—all within the space of a year."[21]

Cost Effectiveness

Locke's comments lead quite logically to what may be another chapter in the fiction of accountability; namely, that once a school system has installed a carefully delineated process of accountability, it will be getting more for each educational dollar it spends. Few individuals, however, have taken a careful look at the costs involved in the installation of such a process. In terms of district administrator, principal, and teacher time alone, the cost would be high. Note, for example, the following procedures (abridged from a list of forty-eight) originally proposed as steps toward planning, developing, and implementing a program of accountability in a large metropolitan school district.

Action Step	Description of Action	Organization/Staff To Be Involved
1	Decide to establish an accountability program in specific areas and prepare broad policy objectives for it	Superintendent/ Executive Staff
2	Identify personnel in the school system technically competent to write objectives to assist program task forces	Executive Staff/ Designated Staff
3	Identify consultants who may aid in the development and finalization of objectives for program accountability	Superintendent/ Executive Staff
4	Constitute program task forces to develop comprehensive program of objectives and clearly specify their tasks	Executive Staff/ Designated Staff
5	Prepare assignments of technical assistance staff to program task forces	Division of Planning, Research, and Evaluation; Division of Budget and Executive Management
6	Spell out program intent, major features at every level of operation, target population it is to impact, anticipated outcomes to be derived from the program, and the level of achievement which will be expected in a one year time framework. Identify all organizational elements in the school system which will have specific roles and responsibilities in the operation of the program, and relate the major features of the program to these organizational elements	Program Task Forces
7	Develop organizational objectives for program objectives and identify characteristics of target populations—quantitative and qualitative	Program Task Forces; Division of Planning, Research, and Evaluation

Action Step	Description of Action	Organization/Staff To Be Involved
8	Develop learner objectives; specify levels of accomplishment for one year and then consolidate all objectives into a program objectives tier	Program Task Forces
9	Consolidate programs and objectives and submit to superintendent	Division of Planning, Research, and Evaluation
10	Review, discuss, modify; preliminary approval for programs and program objectives	Superintendent/ Executive Staff
11	Cost out programs with preliminary approval and inventory the resources available to implement the programs	Division of Budget and Executive Management
12	Determine program priorities and phasing operations necessary for implementation	Superintendent/ Executive Staff
13	Make necessary resource allocation shifts and make necessary changes in organization structure	Superintendent; Division of Budget and Executive Management
14	Develop and conduct training programs necessary to implement program activities	Program Managers/ School Staff
15	Develop assessment plans and instruments and analyze programs and objectives to determine information needs for program accountability and management	Departments of Research and Evaluation; Division of Budget and Executive Management; Division of Instruction; Department of Automated Information Service
16	Assess status of educational management information system as it relates to accountability needs	Division of Planning, Research, and Evaluation; Division of Instruction
17	Discuss information needs and determine priorities for development	Superintendent/ Executive Staff

Action Step	Description of Action	Organization/Staff To Be Involved
18	Work out information system co-ordination plan as to data generation, data storage, and data retrieval	Superintendent/ Executive Staff/ Division of Planning, Research, and Evaluation
19	Integrate program operations, information (accountability), and assessment	Designated Staff[22]

The time line proposed for covering these steps is conservatively estimated as eighteen months to two years. A lengthy explanation of the steps just enumerated is unnecessary; even an inexperienced person can quickly see that the amount of administrator and staff time required for meetings and preparation work will not be small. Given the fact that normal school operation must be maintained as the accountability program is created, released time obviously will have to be provided, and additional dollars must be allocated for district staff education and teacher inservice training. This tends to negate the belief that accountability will permit us to get greater educational value for our dollar and suggests that such a statement may contain more fiction than has generally been realized.

Tests and Measurement

As we talk about the fictions generated by the thrust toward accountability, we must turn to questions of tests and measurement. With great rationality and considerable logic, the accountability proponents point out that we need only to state measurable educational objectives and then test to see if they have been achieved. Yet, as Hulda Grobman recently stated, schools are multipurpose institutions.

In the context of a given school and grade level, the focus of accountability must be on short term and intermediate aims that may be measured readily during the school year. But we are seriously constrained because we do not know how to measure attainment of many things we are concerned with in education. There is no compelling evidence, furthermore, that shows a sufficient correlation between goals that can be measured and those that cannot, so that the former are an adequate indicator of the latter.

We blindly assume, for example, that mastery of a series of concepts is the natural and logical precursor of ability to reason out future problems, or that ability to parse a sentence enhances the individual's use of grammatical English. But substantial evidence makes these assumptions questionable. Several studies have found no positive correlation between scores on traditional knowledge-oriented tests and those on tests that simulate real life situations and require retrieving information, sorting it out, and applying it in a new complex situation. Yet most school tests, including those used for accountability purposes, reflect only a knowledge-oriented focus.[23]

Professor Grobman's comments open the question of what to do about elements of schooling, such as long-range learning outcomes, which seemingly cannot be measured. Perhaps even more important is the problem of measuring affective or social development. For example, a fair number of early childhood education experts tell us that the kindergarten experience is primarily intended to socialize the child.[24] But how is this to be measured? What, too, of the value orientation many schools are presumed to provide to students? With what instruments are they to be measured? Clearly, children and adults will upon occasion act contrary to their admitted value systems. Can testing really determine what has been learned? The answers to these questions are still being formulated.

Accountability is built upon the idea that inputs and outputs, vis-à-vis the teaching-learning process, can be accurately measured. "Because the evaluation of achievement is no better than the measurement instruments used, the identification of appropriate instruments to measure the attainment of the objectives specified . . . is essential.[25]

As Lennon has so succinctly stated, "The evaluation of performance contracts and the working out of the accountability concept can ultimately be no more secure than the measurement data upon which they depend. If these data are flawed by psychometric difficulties . . . we will never be able to assess properly the usefulness of this approach."[26]

But where does one begin to look for proper measurement instruments? Traditionally, we have turned to standardized tests. However, in studying the use of such tests in accountability programs, the Center for the Study of Evaluation (CSE) at UCLA points out that they have at least four limitations: (1) likelihood of poor overlap between the test's and the school's objectives and the priorities associated with these objectives; (2) inappropriate test designs and formats for the target populations; (3) difficult and confusing test instructions and administration procedures that introduce irrelevant factors into a student's score; and (4) low test validity in the sense that the tests do not really assess the kinds of student skills and abilities that their titles imply they do.[27] The CSE report concludes with a statement to the effect that a void exists between the demands of accountability and the present stock of standardized instruments.

As an alternative measurement, specialists are suggesting that criterion-referenced measures be used in accountability procedures. Such instruments are intended to provide an assessment of student performance as it relates to some criterion or standard of performance. This is in opposition to the standardized or "norm-referenced" tests which use the performance of other students or the norms of a hypothetical group as a measure. Criterion-referenced tests presuppose delineation of objective standards (which explains the current pressure upon schools to come up with succinct and individualized behavioral objectives). The use of such tests, experts suggest will insure that learners will not be competing with each other, but instead, will be working to meet impersonal goals.

Without taking a position on either side of the measurement question, it appears that the assumption that accountability will allow accurate cost/benefit analyses in all areas of school endeavor may be built upon a considerable amount of fiction. We seem to lack some very essential tools.

The "Teacher-Teaching" Problem

Finally, let us turn to what can be called the teacher-teaching problem. Much of the accountability furor lately has been centered upon the teacher and what he or she does in the classroom. (California's Stull Bill, mandating periodic evaluation of all teachers, tenured and non-tenured, in terms of instructional objectives, is an example of this.) Almost without question is the desire upon the part of the profession and the public to have excellent, highly productive teachers in all our schools. We are unanimous in our demand for good teaching. Yet, what constitutes good teaching? As Hencley notes, "Our knowledge about the teaching-learning processes is still relatively primitive. We do not know what educational processes best translate educational inputs into desired educational outputs."[28] One has only to look at the diversity of teacher-training programs offered from one institution to another across the land to note that no one has apparently sufficiently delineated the variables in the teaching art in order to provide a solid base for all teacher training. Perhaps these variables cannot be defined since teaching and learning result from human interaction that will be as varied in its quality as are the human beings involved. This is not to say that general principles cannot be used as guides in the teaching-learning process, but whether the utilization of these principles can be measured sufficiently at this point to provide a basis for sorting out the good teachers from the mediocre or the bad is still open to question. This situation exists, according to Hencley, because

1 The knowledge base undergirding education is relatively weak—great expansions in basic knowledge appear necessary.

2 Specialized roles in the areas of research, development, and diffusion are relatively undefined—training programs for specialized roles require extensive development.

3 Provisions for experimental innovation in education are scanty—the development of effective linkages among specialized change roles requires intensive attention.

4 Since developmental activities lack system, educational inventions often remain invisible, undocumented, and inaccessible.

5 There is a lack of a professional network of trained and competent change agents and communicators in education and, consequently, dissemination activities lack effectiveness.

6 Specialists in education lack extensive creative working relationships with social scientists—the disciplinary base of participation in educational research has typically been narrow and has often been restricted to educational psychology.

7 The research roles of various educational agencies at local, state, regional, and national levels have tended to remain unclear.[29]

Quite obviously, to remedy our lack of knowledge we will have to make a substantial commitment of money and time for educational research and development.

How, then, shall we in our present state proceed to hold the teacher accountable? Henry Dyer, in providing guidelines for drawing teacher accountability boundaries, says that

At an absolute minimum, a teacher should be expected to: limit his absences from the classroom and the school to unavoidable sickness and unforeseen accidents; keep physically fit to teach; and avoid physically injuring any student, stealing, encouraging a student to cheat, or making invidious distinctions in the treatment of students.

Beyond these minimum requirements exists a multitude of "good works" for which a teacher is to be held accountable provided he is given the chance to perform them. They fall into three interrelated categories: knowing his subject, knowing his students, and acting in such a way as to maximize the probability that his students will learn what he is supposed to teach.[30]

Strangely, these boundaries have a familiar ring. They are, in fact, little different from what most school districts of the country already demand of teachers in order to keep their jobs. If these are to be the guidelines for accountability, there truly is more fiction than threat in the saga of accountability.

Behavioral Objectives

However, not all guidelines are of Dyer's kind. UCLA's W. James Popham, a proponent of the behavioral objective approach, has outlined a procedure to appraise teacher achievement in the classroom. His approach is to give a teacher an explicit instructional objective along with a sample measurement item showing how the achievement will be judged. The teacher is then given a specified amount of time to teach a class that has been pretested. Immediately following the instruction, students are tested with regard to attitude and content. These measures of pupil cognitive and affective results are used as an index of teacher effectiveness. Presumably, a teacher who fails to teach effectively on the basis of several short performance tests can be considered ineffective in a regular teaching situation. Given our already stated lack of knowledge regarding good teaching and the apparently nonvalidated assumption that the students are always eagerly waiting to be taught or anxious to achieve a stated objective during each test situation, it appears that serious questions can be raised about the procedure. Popham himself says, "Talk is cheap. While everyone's talking about the merits of educational accountability, few mention the fact that practical procedures for making accountability work have not been devised."[31] And Myron Lieberman points out:

> . . . it is easier to evaluate outcomes than the processes leading to them. For example, it is easier to give an achievement test to students

than to judge whether the teacher in the classroom acted with professional skill and judgment. This is why we can so easily be persuaded that "results" are the proper basis of evaluation and of accountability. "Results" are relevant to a decision concerning what to do in like situations; the test of whether a professional is performing creditably is whether he does what maximizes the chances of success. To know this, we must look to the past and find out what worked and what did not in certain situations. Only in this way can we evaluate professional behavior. The conventional wisdom tells us to look at the "result" to achieve accountability, but unless the advice takes into account the complexities of evaluation, it will lead us into one untenable situation after another.[32]

From these brief references to evaluation, performance contracting, cost effectiveness, tests and measurement, the teacher-teaching problem, and behavioral objectives, it seems that accountability as a whole may carry with it more smoke than fire. None of the above *is* accountability, but all clearly are related to it. Since all these areas are plagued with deficiencies in information and technique, it will assuredly be some time before adequate implementation catches up with the accountability rhetoric. In the meantime, serious efforts will have to be made to keep the accountability fiction from undermining the efforts of those dedicated individuals desiring to see better utilization of our educational resources, both human and financial.

FARCE

Whether or not the current stress on accountability is a farce is a matter of personal judgment. Obviously, the interest it has generated indicates that it must be taken seriously. On the other hand, the controversy and the lack of data and technical expertise evident in certain areas seem to indicate that the educational world may simply be on another binge which will only result in a devastating hangover! Support for the latter point of view seems to come from at least one representative of those now involved in performance contract work.

Three years from now [says Lewis D. Eizen of Educational Design, Inc.] over one third of the initial batch of performance contracts left will be in the courts or in some other stage of litigation. Approximately 100 school systems will have attempted performance contracting and found that they "learned a lot from the experience" but are not doing any more of it. . . . The general consensus of the educational community on performance contracting will be that it is something with potential benefits but too many risks.[33]

Program Planning and Budgeting Systems

California's stress on a Program Planning and Budgeting System (PPBS) for education together with the state's recently passed Stull Bill, appears to lend further credence to the accusation of farce. In 1968, the California State Board of Education adopted a plan prepared by the Advisory Commission on School District Budgeting and Accounting for the implementation of PPBS in every school district of the state by 1972–1973. Educational administrators were thrown off guard. Not only did few know what PPBS was, but hardly any had an idea of what skills were required to carry out a successful implementation program. A flurry of activity resulted. A considerable amount of verbiage was exchanged in the profession and in the press over the pros and cons of the system. Consulting firms were employed to study ways and means of implementing the law in the various districts. Inservice training programs were hastily thrown together at the state and district levels. The names of the game became "behavioral objectives" and "cost/effectiveness." But even with all this effort and dialogue, it soon became obvious that, practically speaking, implementation of accountability systems could not be achieved in time to meet the prescribed deadline. Subsequently, the deadline was extended. Whether the new deadline is realistic remains to be seen. In some quarters, there is real doubt that it ever will be implemented.

The Stull Bill: Accountability Legislation

The Stull Bill is another attempt to make teachers accountable. Mandating implementation in the fall of 1972, this legislation demands, among other things, that each principal sit down by October 15 of each year with his individual teachers to determine, mutually, specific objectives to be achieved during the course of the year and against which the teacher's proficiency would be measured. The fear and threat that this legislation has caused only can be surmised; however, the number of workshops for teachers and administrators and the accompanying flurry of materials indicates that more than a little effort is being invested in its implementation. The eyes of the country are turned to California to observe the outcome.

What all of this actually means for children is not clear. Perhaps no judgment can be made until the smoke clears and the magnitude of the accountability impact is defined. However, if, the present concern with accountability is only a screen behind which the lawmakers and the community at large can escape from their own obligations to educate the young, then the accountability movement truly is a farce —a farce intended to make educators the scapegoats, as David Selden has indicated. Such a situation would tend to disregard the truth that the school at this point is only one of a number of educative devices and is utterly incapable of providing a total educative experience for any child. If, on the other hand, the current interest in accountability is the beginning of constructive dialogue involving the profession and all segments of the community and aimed at clearly laying out what teachers can be held responsible for and what they realistically can achieve, then the trend would appear to be of substance. The eventual result will hopefully see accountability broadly recast to embrace not only educators but parents, students, and legislators as well.

THE QUESTION

Is the accountability trend fact, fiction, or farce? At present, it appears to be a mixture of all three. The question is really whether, by combined national effort, we can change this highly volatile and somewhat cloudy mixture into a clear educational solution.

Our national heritage has always stressed responsibility and accountability. By vote, the people have been responsible for government; by law, parents have been responsible for their children; by custom, individuals have been responsible for their own support and individual behavior. In time of neglect or transgression, each has historically been asked to account. All of this provides a basis for optimism.

As we move into an era which will see education as a lifelong process, beginning at birth and ending with death, additional resources in terms of people and money will have to be provided. The base of responsibility will have to be enlarged, and time will have to be provided for research and development of new educational devices and techniques not only to do better what must be done, but also to measure the effects. Presumably, only then will the fiction and farce be removed to leave accountability as an effective tool for use in improving education.

NOTES

1 Leon M. Lessinger, "A Historical Note on Accountability in Education," *Journal of Research and Development in Education,* vol. 5, no. 1, Fall 1971, College of Education, University of Georgia, Athens, 1971.

2 Leon M. Lessinger, "It's Time for Accountability in Education," *Nation's Business,* August 1971, pp. 54ff.

3 Leon M. Lessinger, "Accountability in Public Education," *Today's Education,* vol. 59, no. 5, May 1970, pp. 52ff.

4 Raymond Bernabei, "Instructional Accountability." Paper presented to the Mid-Atlantic Interstate Project Conference on Educational Accountability, New York, Feb. 10, 1972.

5 Myron Lieberman, as quoted in *Accountability: Review of Literature and Recommendations for Implementation,* North Carolina Department of Public Instruction, Divisions of Planning, Research, and Development, May 1972, p. 3.

6 Nolan Estes and Donald R. Waldrip, as quoted in ibid., p. 3.

7 Leon Lessinger, as quoted in ibid., p. 3.

8 John W. Porter, as quoted in ibid., pp. 3–4.

9 Ewald B. Nyquist, as quoted in ibid., p. 4.

10 Terry D. Cornell, *Performance and Process Objectives,* Educational Innovators Press, Tucson, Ariz., 1970, p. 16.

11 Conrad Briner, "Administrators and Accountability," *Theory into Practice,* vol. 8, Oct. 1969, pp. 203–207.

12 Roger T. Lennon, "To Perform and to Account," *Journal of Research and Development in Education,* vol. 5, no. 1, Fall 1971, published by College of Education, University of Georgia, Athens, Ga., p. 5.

13 David Selden, "Productivity, Yes. Accountability, No.," *Nation's Schools,* vol. 89, no. 5, May 1972, pp. 50ff.

14 Stephen P. Hencley, "Impediments to Accountability," *Administrator's Notebook,* vol. 20, no. 4, Dec. 1971.

15 Kenneth A. Tye, "Educational Accountability in an Era of Change," paper presented to the White House Conference on Education, St. Louis, Feb. 1970.

16 James Quinn, "Planning for Accountability in Education: Issues, Problems, Directions," unpublished paper, Insgroup, Inc., 5855 Naples Plaza, Long Beach, Calif. 90803.

17 For a more complete discussion, see ibid.

18 Ron Schwartz, "Accountability, Special Report," *Nation's Schools,* vol. 85, no. 6, June 1970, pp. 31ff.

19   Leon M. Lessinger, "It's Time for Accountability in Education," op. cit.

20 |I|D|E|A| *Reporter,* Winter Quarter 1971, p. 3. This issue has an extensive discussion of performance contracting.

21   From a speech prepared for presentation at the Conference on Educational Accountability, held under the sponsorship of Educational Testing Service in Washington on Mar. 22, 1971, and in Hollywood, on Mar. 29, 1971.

22   From a proposal by Thomas White submitted to the District of Columbia Public Schools under the auspices of Instructional Systems Group (Insgroup, Inc.) of Long Beach, Calif.

23   Hulda Grobman, "Accountability for What?: The Unanswered Question," *Nation's Schools,* vol. 89, no. 5, May 1972, pp. 65ff.

24   See, for example, John I. Goodlad, M. Frances Klein, Jerrold M. Novotney, and Associates, *Early Schooling in the United States,* McGraw-Hill, 1973.

25   James R. Forsberg, "Accountability and Performance Contracting," ERIC Clearinghouse on Educational Management, Eugene, Ore., 1971, pp. 4ff.

26   Lennon, op. cit., p. 12.

27   Stephen P. Klein, "The Uses and Limitations of Standardized Tests in Meeting the Demands for Accountability," *UCLA Evaluation Comment,* vol. 2, no. 4, Jan. 1971.

28   Hencley, op. cit.

29   Stephen P. Hencley, "Procedures in Effecting Change," in Edgar L. Morphet and Charles Ryan (eds.), *Planning and Effecting Needed Change in Education,* Citation Press, New York, 1967, p. 57.

30   Henry S. Dyer, "Guidelines for Drawing Accountability Boundaries," *Nation's Schools,* vol. 89, no. 5, May 1972, pp. 63ff.

31   W. James Popham, "Found: A Practical Procedure to Appraise Teacher Achievement in the Classroom," *Nation's Schools,* vol. 89, no. 5, May 1972, pp. 59ff.

32   Myron Lieberman, "Education and Accountability." Paper presented to the Mid-Atlantic Interstate Project Conference on Educational Accountability, New York, February 1972.

33   Ben Brodinski (ed.), *Education Summary,* vol. 23, no. 24, Feb. 19, 1971, p. 8.

CHAPTER 10

TOWARD A DEFINITION OF TEACHER ACCOUNTABILITY

Kenneth A. Tye

In this chapter, Kenneth Tye defines and discusses the limits and scope of the teacher's responsibility and accountability. Instead of the simplistic approaches which define accountability merely in terms of student scores on an achievement test, it is suggested here that there are decisions and actions which must be taken at all levels of the system in order to make it plausible to ask the teacher to assume responsibility for specific accomplishments of pupils. If the teacher is to be held accountable, then the public and its representatives, school boards, district personnel, and principals have responsibilities for which they, too, must be held accountable.

Dr. Tye is program officer and assistant director of the Research Division of |I|D|E|A|.

Recently in the Los Angeles Unified School District a program was instituted which sought to eliminate the reading deficiencies of children in innercity schools. The plan called for teachers to state explicit behavioral objectives for the reading program, based upon which both instructional strategies and criterion-based tests were to be designed. The theory was that if student learning did not improve, teachers would be held accountable for the failure. The fact is that after three years, and despite some limited success, the reading scores in most of the schools involved did *not* improve significantly.

The Los Angeles story is not unique. It has been and is being repeated in district after district across the country. Who is to blame for these failures? Who is accountable? It is tempting to blame only the teachers, for it is their duty to state objectives and to carry out programs, but such an answer is too simple. It fails to take into account the complexity of the educational system, and it adds to the "confusion and controversy" about accountability noted by Jerrold Novotney in the preceding chapter.

WHY TEACHER ACCOUNTABILITY IN THE SEVENTIES?

There are many reasons why we have turned our attention to making teachers more accountable for what they do in the classroom. One reason is that we are faced with great social problems such as class and racial segregation, poverty, violence, and conflicting values. Yet we seem unable and/or unwilling to cope with these problems as a society and thus tend to expect and even to demand that our visible and vulnerable social institutions, particularly schooling, will somehow cope with them. At the same time we distrust and even fear allowing these institutions to function as anything more than mirrors of society. In such an ambiguous situation, we tend, however irrational it may be, to focus attention on social servants such as teachers, asking questions like "Why can't they do their jobs better?" "Why aren't they accountable?" The implied meaning of such questions, of course, is that somehow social servants like teachers should solve our problems for us; they should be accountable while we avoid our individual and collective responsibilities. But teachers cannot be singly accountable for that which they only mirror and for those things for which we are all responsible.

Another reason for the stress on teacher accountability is the business orientation of our society. We have become so used to reliance upon this orientation that it has permeated our thinking about all our institutions, including schools. We have adopted words such as "management," "systems," "efficiency," "performance," "cost-benefit," "program budget," "contract," "voucher," "input," "output," and "accountability" to describe the operation of our schools. We have gone so far in this direction in the twentieth century that we have developed an almost mystical faith in the scientific management techniques of business and industry as the means for solving our problems.[1] It is as if we believe that teachers have only to think of students as products and learning as profit, and schooling will improve. But students are not products and teachers are not assembly-line workers to be paid on the basis of quantity produced.

A third reason for the stress on teacher accountability is that we have come to rely almost totally upon the use of authority as the means for bringing about change and improvement in schools. Thus, we see state authorities telling boards of education what to do, boards telling school district personnel, school district officials telling principals, and principals telling teachers (Figure 10.1). The teachers, at the bottom of the ladder, end up being accountable. Although this may be an improvement upon blaming the students for school failures, it simply does not go far enough.

FIGURE 10.1.   THE USE OF AUTHORITY IN BRINGING ABOUT EDUCATIONAL CHANGE.

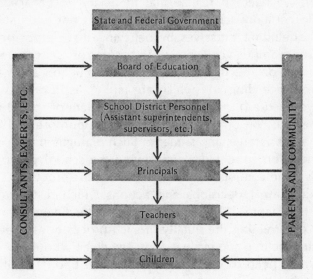

SORTING OUT ACCOUNTABILITY

Our complex social problems *do* need to be remedied, and the schools and teachers have a role in that process. Tools of scientific management can certainly be utilized to assist school improvement. There is a place for authoritative leadership in the change process. But education is a complex enterprise. It involves decisions made by literally thousands of people, all of whom influence what the teacher is able to do. It is not enough to pass the buck to the teachers, holding them solely accountable for schooling. *All the actors in the educational drama are accountable—to the students, to the public, and to themselves.*

Perhaps we can begin to sort out the matter of accountability by reexamining the reasons for its being stressed. First, we need to commit ourselves to the notion that our schools are part of a much greater sociopolitical system and not independent. Therefore, we need to spend a good deal of time clarifying the societal role we expect the schools to play, the value base from which our schools are to operate, and the means and resources for supporting that operation. It is this value base which serves as the data source for educational goals to guide teachers. It is not the role of teachers to determine our societal values.

Second, we need to realize that there are no panaceas for our schools, and certainly scientific management is not our only answer. Rather than deluding ourselves by believing that output or product measures (for example, achievement test scores or criterion-referenced measures based on specified objectives) will somehow show us which teachers are succeeding and which are failing, as in our Los Angeles example, we need a broader view of the problem of school improvement. There must be time for dialogue about purpose and direction among the staff, parents, and students. Such dialogue must lead to decisions and actions directed at improving the school program. Also, there needs to be continual evaluation of both the processes employed and the educational decisions and actions which result from these processes. In Chapter 12 of this volume, Bette Overman sets forth criteria for determining the quality of such processes as dialogue, decision making, action, and evaluation in any given school.

Finally, we need to overcome our reliance upon authority as the model for educational improvement. Possibly we can begin by committing ourselves to the notion that within a complex social system, the school is the single most important unit for educational improvement. Change will not originate in the state, the district, or even the classroom, because it is the school which is the one complete unit that is close to the learner. It has a staff, a designated leader, facilities, equipment, and students. If we assume that the school is the critical unit, we can also assume that other educational agencies—the state, the school board, the district—exist to serve and support the activities of the school.

At the local level, state educational authority is vested in the school board, which, supporting the school, is responsible for the formulation of educational policies. Such policies incorporate the values clarified by the legislature. Further, such policies give direction to the institutional goals set throughout the school district.

One problem which frequently confuses the matter of accountability is that school boards sometimes go beyond the bounds of policy decisions. At times, they define subject matter and methods of teaching. When they do this, they must be willing to accept direct responsibility. For example, if a board of education were to *tell* teachers that they should use one reading program to the exclusion of all others, it would be the board which would have to be accountable for the outcome of reading instruction. On the other hand, a board which sets a policy that reading-skill mastery is of major importance in the primary phase of schooling can hold the district personnel and teachers accountable for implementation as long as the board also provides the necessary human and material resources to get the job done.

School district personnel have had almost unlimited power over teachers in the form of decisions they make or the rewards and punishments they mete out. By assuming that the school is the single most important unit of educational change, we also assume that school district personnel will give up some of their power through the decentralization of many decisions to the local level. That does not mean that district jobs such as administrator, coordinator, or supervisor will be easier. On the contrary, it is much more difficult to play a facilitating and supporting role for others than it is to make the decisions. Those who already have attempted to decentralize know this full well. Personnel at the school district level will have new responsibilities and will be accountable for new behaviors. School district personnel must be responsible and accountable for translating board policy into manageable and measurable goals for the schools. They must establish a climate of freedom and set norms for change in the district. They must provide for the updating of staff skills. They must be responsible for allocating human, fiscal, and physical resources to the schools, including a sizable amount directly to teachers for their use. They must facilitate communication among the school board, community, and staff. They must adopt procedures to monitor the accomplishment of district-wide goals. Most importantly, they have the responsibility to establish in their schools those processes which can be referred to as institutional renewal processes, one of which is described in Chapter 12. School district personnel's accountability includes the implementation of district-wide and school-wide needs assessment and goal-setting procedures, the encouragement of innovative instructional programs, the involvement of teachers in decisions about staffing patterns, the formation of community advisory councils, the provision of release time for teacher inservice education, and the implementation of district-wide evaluation systems.

Before we can begin a discussion of teacher accountability, another factor must be discussed: There must be leadership in the school which promotes the kind of processes being described here. Such leadership, in general, is provided by the principal, who is accountable for it, and who establishes a climate for change, deals with conflict, monitors decisions and actions without directing them, is supportive of the efforts of others, opens communication channels, and the like. At present, most principals are not equipped to work as leaders. Rather, they are trained to respond or to behave as directors, as authorities, as people who make sure that teachers carry out decisions made for them by others. School principals, then, must be responsible and accountable for their own behaviors as educational leaders. The kinds of behaviors discussed by this writer in Chapter 2 are those for which the principal becomes accountable.

TEACHER ACCOUNTABILITY

For what, then, can teachers legitimately be held accountable? Let us assume for a moment that the public and its legislators have clarified our societal values and provided adequate support to education; that school boards have set policy which gives direction to educational goals; that the school district has set goals and provided the necessary support systems for schools; and that principals have provided the necessary leadership for their schools. We can now turn to teachers and talk of their accountability for instruction (see Figure 10.2).

FIGURE 10.2. SHARED ACCOUNTABILITY.

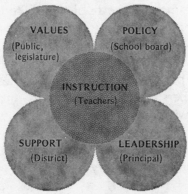

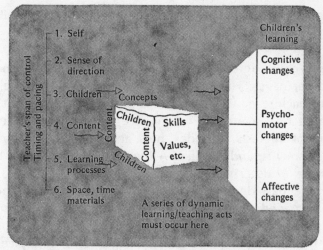

FIGURE 10.3. THE TEACHER'S SPAN OF CONTROL. (From John I. Goodlad, "Three Dimensions in Organizing the Curriculum for Learning and Teaching," *Frontiers of Elementary Education III,* Syracuse University Press, Syracuse, N.Y., 1956.)

As long ago as 1956, John Goodlad attempted to set forth the teacher's "span of control."[2] The dimensions of this span of control, somewhat updated, are (1) insight into and management of self in the instructional setting; (2) a sense of direction; (3) a knowledge of the children with whom the teacher works; (4) a knowledge of the content of instruction; (5) an understanding of human growth and development; and (6) an ability to employ learning resources including space, time, and materials (see Figure 10. 3).

If the teacher is to be accountable for his own behavior, he must understand himself in the instructional setting and be able to view his teaching behavior objectively. Such understanding is built through interaction with others. Teachers should plan, teach, and evaluate together.[3] For this they need time.

Teachers should know their goals. It is here that we can put the behavioral objectives movement into proper perspective, as Novotney suggests in the previous chapter. It is *not* a panacea for all the ills of education. If the goals of the district and the school are clear and if they have resulted from dialogue about purpose, then teachers can be expected to have objectives clearly in mind. In those areas of instruction which lend themselves to specificity—skill development, for example—teachers should be able (or learn) to state behavioral objectives. In other areas which do not lend themselves to such specificity—

value formation, for example—teachers may not wish to utilize such objectives, but they still will want a sense of direction.

Long ago, we educators agreed to the notion that each student is unique. We also agreed to the idea that we need to diagnose individual learner needs. However, we do not always adequately gather data about each student. Teachers not only need data about skill development, achievement, and intelligence, but they also should know about student interests, attitudes, peer and sibling relationships, cultural environments, and the like. A hungry child may need breakfast more than he needs a spelling lesson.

Over the past decade, the content of schooling has been dramatically upgraded: there is "new" math, science, English, and social studies. Unfortunately, many of these new curricula have not filtered down to the classroom level. Inadequate time for inservice training accounts for much of this gap. With such training, teachers should be accountable for implementation.

Much of what teachers do, or are required to do, is contrary to what we know about human physical, social, intellectual, and emotional growth and development. For example, grade-level requirements are based upon the outmoded notion that all children develop at about the same rate. A knowledge of human development would soon lead teachers toward more rational decisions about school organization and away from arbitrary grade-level standards.

Teachers should be free to decide upon instructional materials, physical and human resources, and time and space. Such decisions, accompanied by the financial wherewithal to supply the necessary resources, would lead to such things as the use of a wide array of materials and equipment, differentiated staff, and utilization of community resources. Certainly, it would open the door to more creative learning environments than are now typical.

Teachers are responsible and accountable for those things which fall within their span of control. It is the manner in which they bring these things into play to create dynamic teaching and learning which will, in the end, create improved intellectual, physical, and emotional learning for students.

CONCLUSION

As stated earlier, it will not be easy to change our views on the matter of accountability. The use of authority backed up by the scientific management tools at our disposal is deeply imbedded in our educational thinking. The idea that the legislator is as accountable as the teacher for what happens in our schools is not an easy one for some people to deal with. Nevertheless, until we can accept such a position and until we can begin to sort out who is accountable for what, there will be many more improvement efforts which end in failure. Are we really ready for accountability? Given the right support and an appropriate voice in decision making, teachers may be. It's worth a try.

NOTES

1 For a documentation of the growth and failure of scientific management in education, see Raymond E. Callahan, *Education and the Cult of Efficiency,* University of Chicago Press, Chicago, 1962.

2 John I. Goodlad, "Three Dimensions in Organizing the Curriculum for Learning and Teaching," in *Frontiers of Elementary Education III,* Syracuse University Press, Syracuse, 1956.

3 Teachers working together is discussed in depth by Robert H. Anderson, *Teaching in a World of Change,* Harcourt, Brace & World, New York, 1966.

CHAPTER 11

AN INSTITUTIONAL EVALUATION SYSTEM

Irene Frieze

This chapter presents a model for evaluation of the single school by those most intimately involved in the school— the staff, the parents, and the students. The use of a variety of techniques for determining goals, assessing student progress, and establishing a continuous system of evaluation is discussed.

As a member of |I|D|E|A|'s Elementary School Appraisal Study staff, Dr. Frieze helped to develop a variety of instruments for measuring student attitudes, self-concepts, and peer relations. Dr. Frieze is presently at the University of Pittsburgh, with a joint appointment in psychology and women's studies.

All too often innovation in the schools becomes change for the sake of change. If meaningful change is to occur, care must be taken that innovations are instituted where change is needed. Not only must educators determine what is to be changed, but they must also decide how it is to be changed. These issues are the substance of a topic which has alternately reassured and frightened educators. That topic is evaluation.

Today, evaluation is an important concern not only at higher levels of educational practice such as federal agencies which wish to assess the effectiveness of federally funded programs, but also those closest to students, personnel in both district offices and local schools, who need information to help them determine which programs they wish to continue and which programs are not producing the expected results. It is to aid both of these groups—the higher levels and the local levels—that an |I|D|E|A| team has been developing an institutional evaluation system.

The development of models for evaluation has received a good deal of attention in recent years. The evaluation system presented here has elements in common with various of the models which have been derived. The reader is referred in particular to the work of Robert Stake,[1] Ralph Tyler,[2] and Daniel Stufflebeam.[3]

The complete evaluation system involves collecting data regarding the effects of various school programs so that educational decisions may be based on objective information. The system also becomes an integral part of the planning of new programs which are designed to improve student performance in those areas which the entire school community—teachers, administrators, students, and parents—has determined to be important. In effect, the system focuses upon determining appropriate goals for the school as well as measuring the effectiveness of various instructional programs.

USING THE SINGLE SCHOOL IN EVALUATION

Our experience has shown us that the most useful level at which to conduct any kind of evaluation of the educational process is within the single school. The community served by a single school experiences a common identification with that school and with its problems. Often, the community served by that school is relatively homogeneous, and the members of that community have relatively few difficulties in determining what they feel to be important goals for the school. The single school itself comprises a group of people—teachers, administrators, students, and parents—who interact frequently and can easily meet together to make decisions about their school. These advantages are not available when evaluation includes several schools or an entire district as a unit, nor are they available for evaluating conditions within the isolated classroom. Multischool evaluation is difficult to coordinate, and the problems inherent in arriving at meaningful goals are multiplied. On the other hand, the isolated classroom is often too small a unit to permit the effective measurement of meaningful change, since special occurrences unique to a particular classroom may distort any of the findings which might be obtained.

School personnel who are concerned with change in their school may feel the need for support from others outside the school. This need may be filled in part by the involvement of parents in the surrounding community. In addition, the special need to discuss problems with other school staff members may be met by forming cooperative arrangements with other schools for the purpose of sharing experi-

ences, of gaining new ideas, and of obtaining informal help with problems.[4] However, even if such a cooperative arrangement is desired
and is established, the evaluation process itself is most meaningfully
conducted within a single school.

THE EVALUATION MODEL

The evaluation model which we developed involves several phases
that form a continuous process in which results from previous evalua-
tions can be used for determining new goals and for making decisions
concerning the programs which will be utilized in achieving these
goals. The remainder of this chapter will discuss each of the steps in
the evaluation model and the techniques we have found to be of most
use in helping individual schools evaluate their various programs. Our
evaluation model, which is outlined in Figure 11.1, includes these components:

1 The entire school community (teachers, administrators, parents, and
   students) determines what educational goals it wishes to achieve. Decision is aided by the use of the Delphi, ANOVA, and JAN techniques
   (see below).
2 The current status of the school in relationship to desired future outcomes is assessed.

FIGURE 11.1. THE SINGLE-SCHOOL EVALUATION MODEL.

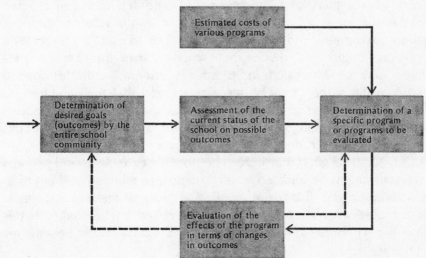

3 Information relevant to the current status of the school and its various programs is combined with data regarding costs of new programs which might be instituted to achieve desired goals; based on this combined information, determination is made of a specific program or programs to be evaluated.

4 After new programs are adopted, their effects are evaluated in terms of changes in outcomes.

5 The entire process is repeated to provide an ongoing evaluation system in which results from earlier years are used in helping determine programs in subsequent years.

Determining Goals

The determination of goals is one of the most important aspects of any school evaluation program. No matter how effectively each successive stage of the evaluation process is carried out, without adequate goal determination, the resultant cognitive or attitudinal changes, if they occur, may well be either meaningless or negative for the school community.

No matter what procedure is used to determine school goals, it is important that representatives of the entire school community be involved in this essential first step in evaluation. The effects of schooling are significant not only for teachers and school administrators but also for auxiliary school staff, students, and parents. Each of these groups contributes in its unique way to determining a school's goals and to helping bring about desired changes once the goals have been established. In fact, their formal involvement in the determination of goals may be one means of insuring their cooperation in future projects as well as adding new and important dimensions to establishing realistic and meaningful objectives for their school. For example, school personnel may be interested in improving students' attitudes toward school, while parents may be more concerned that their children be adequately prepared in basic skills such as mathematics and reading. The students themselves, however, might wish to have more freedom and responsibility in determining what their school environment will be like. All these goals may indeed be possible to achieve, and perhaps a program might be initiated which attempts to meet all of them to at least some degree. If it is not possible to meet all these perhaps conflicting objectives, discussion by all interested parties might better allow the school to set its priorities in a way which insures benefits for everyone.

A second issue to be considered when a school determines its goals is that these goals must be stated in quantitative terms so that they can be assessed or measured. Our evaluation model involves testing whatever programs a school initiates in order to identify any measurable changes in desired outcomes. Such testing is not possible if there is no clear-cut way to know the previous achievement or attitudinal level of the school and if there is no way to know its new levels for these variables after experiencing a change program.

There are several ways in which goals may be quantified. Goals may be stated in terms of outcomes for which there are existing standardized tests or for which tests might be developed. Tests presently exist for many kinds of achievement measures as well as for various affective outcomes. These instruments are available from many of the major test development companies.[5] A school might also develop its own assessment instruments. This procedure, however, may be complicated and time consuming unless very specific outcomes are involved. For example, it would be easier to create a measure of a student's grasp of topics covered in a class on American history than to attempt to measure his attitudes toward the United States or his potential for becoming an active and contributing citizen. Although each of these possible measures would necessitate some agreement on the definition of the concept or outcome to be measured, the latter two outcomes are more vague and therefore more difficult to assess with written test items. This is especially true when the consensus of many people—in this case, the entire school community—concerning the definition of outcomes is needed before an evaluative instrument can be developed by a school. Such problems are technically known as validation procedures and have usually been adequately handled by those who publish standardized tests. Rather than developing written tests, a school may use specific, observable measures as quantifiable outcomes. For example, a readily measurable outcome could be improved school attendance or decreased vandalism in the school. Either of these might be an outcome which the school community determines as an important goal.

Formal Techniques for Determining Goals

Although goals can be determined by members of the school staff and community meeting together and informally agreeing on goals for the coming year, there are a number of formal techniques which may help a school and community to determine the goals which are most desired by everyone. These techniques not only provide a means for structuring goal-setting procedures, but they are also often useful in aiding the group to discover goals they might otherwise overlook. Thus, the utilization of structured procedures to determine goals can help the school community to select those changes which would actually be meaningful to them.

Delphi Technique   The Delphi technique for determining goals is a way of ascertaining and combining the opinions of a number of people about the goals which they individually feel would be appropriate for the school. In essence, the Delphi technique provides a means through which each member of the goal-setting group can participate in group decision making while allowing the school principal or some other key individual or administrative committee (such as senior staff members) to have a central position in the decision-making process through their administration of the technique.

Briefly, the Delphi technique is a decision-making process which involves a number of people who meet together to resolve some complex problem. In our situation the complex problem is the determination of goals for the school. Each of the people who meet together under the direction of the principal or administrative committee is given a series of questionnaires, the exact number reflecting the complexity of the problem to be solved. In the first questionnaire each person is asked to list all the goals he believes the group should consider to be essential in any final list of objectives they might prepare. Suggestions from each member of the group are then collected and compiled into a general list by the administering committee, which also edits and supplements the list before returning it to the group members. Then a second, combined list which contains a number of possible school goals, some of which were suggested by several people and others which were original suggestions of only one person, is given to each group member. Each group member then rates each of the goals on this second list in terms of how strongly he feels it to be an important goal for the school. Then, once again the administering committee combines the various ratings and makes these composite ratings available to the group for discussion. After this discussion, group members may then rerate the various goals until a final consensus is reached. The rating and discussion cycle may be performed as many times as desired by the group.

The final rankings of the goals compiled in the last composite list are then used to assign priorities for the establishment of the various goals. Exact weights are then assigned these goals on the basis of other considerations such as cost and results of pretesting.

A feature of the Delphi technique is its capability to include suggestions about goals from people who are not directly participating in the process but who might have important suggestions. Their suggestions are incorporated into the first compiled list of goal possibilities. Such outside opinions might be obtained through reading by members of the group or through formal questionnaires sent to people who do not belong to the group. For example, questionnaires might be sent to all parents and students affiliated with a school (since not everyone is part of the formal goals determination group) or to district and state offices for additional recommendations.

Another aspect of the Delphi technique to be considered is the potentially strong control which can be exercised by the administering committee. This group edits and combines suggestions and may eliminate unimportant or irrelevant suggestions. Since the determination of goals is to include the entire school community, the administering committee must use care to avoid showing undue bias toward their own desired goals. However, since the ultimate goals decided upon will be the responsibility of only a few people in the school, perhaps it is beneficial for these people to have a special place in the determination procedure.[6]

ANOVA and JAN Techniques Once a set of possible goals has been established for a school, either through a formal procedure such as the Delphi technique or informally through group discussion, the question immediately arises concerning which of these goals are more or less important. Assuming that limitations in resources prohibit a school from achieving all its goals, there must be some selection of those goals which deserve the largest allocations of personnel, time, and money. Although simple rankings based on a Delphi technique or upon ratings assigned by the principal or some other group of decision makers could easily be used to assign priorities, there are several reasons why this type of approach might be inadequate. As has been shown in studies of how people make decisions or judgments, people often do not realize what information they actually use to make their final decision.[7] For example, a principal might say that he attaches a very high value to improved self-concepts in his students and less importance to high academic performance. However, if this same principal were asked to evaluate a series of schools in terms of how good he felt they were, he might consistently rate those schools as highest which had high academic performance. This distortion might occur for a number of reasons. The principal might be satisfied with the current academic performance of his school and therefore not consider it as a goal, even though he would be highly disappointed if his school dropped in this area, or he might not realize just how important he felt traditional academic values were. This importance might only be evident to him when asked to evaluate schools other than his own.

Fortunately, several alternative techniques have been developed to avoid this difficulty by statistically determining weights or priorities on the basis of how people make actual ratings of hypothetical schools. Thus, rather than asking people to rank such goals as academic values, self-concepts of students, good peer relations for students and staff, and winning athletic teams, people would rate the following sample schools:

> School A has a high academic ranking and the students have high self-concepts. However, the relationships between students are poor, and the staff has a low level of interaction. The school has winning athletic teams.
>
> School B has a low academic ranking and losing athletic teams. However, the students have high self-concepts and good peer relations. The staff members have good relationships with one another.
>
> School C has a low academic ranking, and the staff relates poorly with each other. However, students have high self-concepts and good peer relations. The school has winning athletic teams.
>
> School D has a high academic ranking and winning athletic teams. The students have good peer relations. However, the students have low self-concepts, and staff relations are poor.

After a person rates a number of such hypothetical schools, it is possible to determine which of the five values (academic ranking, student self-concepts, student peer relations, staff relations, and winning or losing athletic teams) are more important and the weight or importance which is assigned to each either through linear regression (JAN technique) or through analysis of variance (ANOVA technique). Both of these are mathematical ways of showing how changes in one variable are related to changes in another variable. These mathematical techniques would show, for example, that if a person rated schools A and *D* higher than *B* or *C*, he was using academic ranking as the most important consideration. On the other hand, if a person rated schools *B, C,* and *D* high but rated *A* low, he would be basing his weighting on student peer relations.

In addition to providing more accurate analysis of what people consider important in a school, these techniques also allow different decision makers to compare the priorities they individually assign to various suggested goals. Often people cannot discuss their discrepant judgments or differing priorities because of their own lack of awareness of what goals they actually value. Insight obtained through these mathematical techniques might make this process much easier.

JAN and ANOVA techniques take relatively little time to complete, and they do provide significant help to participants in determining goals both through aiding discussion and through giving accurate priorities to various goals. However, because they involve rather sophisticated mathematical techniques for scoring, a computer would probably have to be used. Therefore, their more precise ranking of goals and shorter time for administration would have to be balanced against the longer but cheaper Delphi technique.[8]

Combined Techniques   Since there are advantages to both the Delphi and the JAN and ANOVA techniques (hereafter referred to as ANOVA techniques), a school might choose to combine these methodologies. In Table 11.1 the advantages and disadvantages of the separate and combined techniques are compared, and in Figure 11.2 the advantages of utilizing the hypothesized combined process are presented.

In this combination procedure, group members meet as they do when using the Delphi technique to make suggestions about possible school goals. These goals are then compiled into one list which is re-circulated to the group for ranking. Once each group member ranks all the goals, the rankings for each goal are averaged. The ten goals which have the highest average rankings are then restated as characteristics in hypothetical schools which are then used for an ANOVA analysis. Next, each group member rates the hypothetical schools, after which group analysis of variance is done to determine the actual weights for each of these ten highest goals.

The combined procedure weds the advantages of the Delphi technique in considering many possible goals to the accurate and speedy determination of exact weighting of possible goals through ANOVA techniques.

TABLE 11.1   COMPARISON OF DELPHI, JAN AND ANOVA TECHNIQUES FOR DETERMINATION OF SCHOOL GOALS

Bases for Comparison	Delphi	JAN and ANOVA	Combined
Time	A Minimum of Several Hours	One Hour Maximum	One Hour to Several Hours
Cost Factors	Minimal	Computer Costing—Coding and Preparation of Data	Like JAN and ANOVA
Special Role for Administrators in Determining Goals	Key Role in Editing and Combining Various Suggestions	No More than Other Group Members	Flexible. Can Be As Much As Delphi or As Little As JAN and ANOVA
Number of Goals to be Considered	No Maximum	A Maximum of Ten Discrete Goals May Be Judged at One Time	No Maximum At First but with Narrowing of List To No More Than Ten Discrete Goals
Preselection of Goals	None	Necessary	None
Outside Suggestions Incorporated	In Original Compilation of Group Suggestions	Only If Done in Preselection Phase	In Original Compilation of Group Suggestions

FIGURE 11.2. A COMBINED PROCEDURE FOR DETERMINING GROUP PRIORITIES FOR POSSIBLE SCHOOL GOALS.

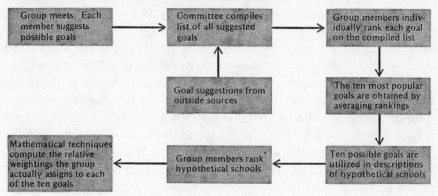

Choosing a Change Program

While the determination of school goals is one of the most important steps in deciding what educational programs will continue or will be dropped in the school, most procedures for determining goals often ignore several other important factors essential to making final decisions about programs. These factors include the reassessment of goals based on information about current achievement or attitudinal levels for desired outcomes as well as cost considerations of all kinds. These factors might meaningfully be included in the goals determination process if they are provided as information for the individuals who are setting group goals, or they can be applied to goals chosen in advance of using either the Delphi or ANOVA techniques by administrators or others who have final decision-making power. The importance of this procedure is obvious. If as many members of the school community as possible are to be meaningfully involved in goal setting, they should be given such information so that they can intelligently decide on final goals and the programs necessary to achieve these goals.

Pretesting Information   Information about the current status of the school in terms of many desired outcomes and about cost factors is helpful in setting goals as well as in deciding upon specific programs. Such information will automatically be available once an ongoing evaluation program is established, particularly when follow-up data on the results of the previous year's programs are analyzed. Thus, if improved student peer relations were a goal the previous year, and if pre- and posttesting had been done to determine whether peer relations had improved, the posttests could then be used as pretest data the following year.

However, as is often the case, new goals may be generated for the school which have never before been assessed. Even so, the present level of the school in terms of these new goals should be determined through questionnaires or rating forms of some kind. This information can then serve as pretest data to be compared with results of measures used at the end of the year in order to see if improvement has occurred. Secondly, this information about the current status of the school in terms of a new outcome may show unexpected strengths and weaknesses in the school which were not apparent when the goals were originally ranked. Thus, if the achievement or attitudinal level of the school is already high for the desired new goal, the individuals setting goals may feel no need to institute special programs to bring about the improvement which giving this goal a high priority may have encouraged; instead, they may decide to concentrate upon achievement of other goals. On the other hand, if pretesting should indicate that the level of goal attainment was even lower than anticipated for a particular goal, the need for improvement would cause this goal to assume a higher priority than it would have without the pretest information.

Cost Considerations   There are several types of cost factors which also affect the decision of whether or not to initiate specific educational programs in the school. One basic consideration concerns existing, established programs which could help achieve desired goals. If such programs do exist, using them is easier than having to develop new programs. However, the inability to design good programs to change students or the larger school environment in directions in which the school has high priorities has been a continuing difficulty for all educators. In many cases, no adequate program is available, and the school is forced to do its best to develop its own, especially when new goals are selected for emphasis.

If there are already existing educational programs directed toward attaining new goals the choice can be based upon the following criteria:

1   Is the program relatively easy and inexpensive to administer? If not, perhaps the inconvenience of the program will make it unattractive in terms of aiding the school to reach many of its goals.

2   Has the program brought about meaningful changes in the past at

the specific school which wants to use it or at schools similar to this school? Have there been any negative or positive side effects of the program? Studies have shown that sometimes a program intending to and actually accomplishing one type of change may at the same time precipitate other types of unwanted outcomes. For example, if both improved student self-concepts and high academic standards are desired goals, it may be impossible to find programs which can positively affect both these characteristics, since increases in one may cause decreases in the other. On the other hand, changes in student self-concepts may also lead to improved student peer relations. If the necessary information is available, these positive and negative interactive effects need to be considered in choosing a program.

Assessing the Effectiveness of School Programs

Once goals have been established and programs have been selected to achieve these goals in the school, the final step in the evaluation process is to assess how effective these programs are.

Setting Criteria for Improvement   One aspect of goal setting is the determination of minimal standards deemed appropriate for assessing the attainment of each goal. The goal may be to achieve at or above national norms, using a standardized test as a measure for a particular outcome, or the goal may be to show improvement within the school on a particular score over a semester or over a year. In situations in which scores typically decrease from year to year (for example, reading scores for minority students), the goal may be simply to stop this decrease and show normal progress from year to year. Whatever criteria are decided upon should be stated explicitly before assessment procedures are begun so that posttest measures can be assessed against these criteria. Setting these standards might be beneficially included as part of the goal-setting procedures, thus involving the entire school community.

Experimental Design for Assessing Change   There are many possible ways to measure for the desired changes implicit in stated goals. Because these are discussed in detail in available works by Campbell and Stanley[9] and by Isaac and Michael,[10] they will be mentioned only briefly in this chapter.

One of the simplest procedures which allows for adequate testing is to assign classes in a school to experimental and control groups without telling classes which group they are in. These assignments should be made randomly so that there are no basic differences in the experimental and control groups. Then the new program or programs should be administered to the experimental group for only half the school year. The control group, of course, follows whatever procedures have been previously established in the school. Then, midway through the year, both groups should be tested for change by comparing scores, separately for the experimental and control groups, from pre- to posttesting. The experimental group should have higher scores than the control group at the time of posttesting and should also show greater improvement from pre- to posttesting. If this improvement meets the previously established standards for the goal, the program has been a success. If the program has been successful, the control group should be exposed to the program for the remainder of the year so that it, too, can now share its benefits.

Some objections to this procedure might be raised. For example, people closely involved with the students in the school may feel that letting only half the school experience the new program is very unfair to the control group. However, this splitting of the groups is of key importance if the benefits of the program are to be assessed. Without the control group, teachers, principals, and parents can never know if the program actually did any good or if the school would have shown improvement without any expensive new programs. Also, if the program really had no effect, the control group certainly did not suffer and may have benefited from not experiencing the program. Thus, experimentation is possible without subjecting the entire school to untried programs. Also, everyone will eventually benefit, since valuable programs can be identified while others are eliminated.

A second reason for a control group is based on personal experiences we have had in studies of change at |I|D|E|A|. We have found many situations in which all posttest scores—for both experimental and control groups—have decreased from their pretest levels. Without a control group it would have been impossible to know that, for example, even though all scores in the school decreased from October to May, the experimental group showed *less* decrease. Thus, the program was effective in slowing down the apparently normal drop in attitudes occurring near the end of the school year.

In addition to the use of a control group in assessing a new program, a school must also be sure to allow sufficient time between pre-

and posttesting for change to occur. Although it is not recommended that testing be done late in the school year because of the typical drops in scores as in the situation mentioned above, several months usually are needed to make any great changes toward achieving major goals. Thus, testing in September and January or February is usually ideal, especially if time is to be allowed for the control group to experience successful programs for at least one-half of a school year.

Continuing Evaluation

Once the school has completed one evaluation phase, subsequent evaluation procedures can then draw upon previous knowledge. Posttest scores can be used as pretest data in following years. Also, the posttest information may be highly valuable for setting goals for the following year. Additionally, information about which programs work and which do not work will begin to be available. This will facilitate the planning of future programs. Finally, once teachers, parents, and students have accepted the idea of a continuing evaluation process, there may be less difficulty in convincing part of the school to serve as a control group each year.

SUMMARY

The evaluation model presented here is a model for determining goals for a single school, establishing programs to attain these goals, and then assessing the effects of these programs to decide if change did occur. The setting of goals is seen as a key part of the evaluation process, and it is recommended that the entire school community—teachers, principal, auxiliary staff, students, and parents—be involved in goal setting. Several techniques are outlined to aid in this process of helping the school community agree on goals.

Evaluation can be an exciting, meaningful process within the school. It can bring various members of the school community together for discussion about the school, creating a fruitful dialogue. It can help bring about an environment which is open and receptive to innovation. Also, of course, it provides information about which programs are beneficial for the school. Teachers and school administrators need not fear evaluation and may instead find that they enjoy participating in the evaluation process.

NOTES

1 Robert E. Stake, "The Countenance of Educational Evaluation," *Teachers College Record*, vol. 68, 1967, pp. 523–540.

2 Ralph W. Tyler, "General Statement on Evaluation," *Journal of Educational Research*, 1942, pp. 492–501.

3 Daniel L. Stufflebeam, "Evaluation as Enlightenment for Decision-Making," in W. H. Beatty (ed.), *Improving Educational Assessment and an Inventory of Measures of Affective Behavior*, NEA, Washington, 1969.

4 A more complete description of the possibilities inherent in these cooperative arrangements can be found in discussions of the League of Cooperating Schools in "Working Together: The Peer Group Strategy," Chapter 5 in this volume and in Mary M. Bentzen and Associates, *Changing Schools: The Magic Feather Principle*, McGraw-Hill, New York, in press.

5 Our work has involved assessment with affective measures such as student attitude toward learning, toward school, and toward technology, as well as students' self-concepts and peer relations. These instruments, designed primarily for sixth graders, are entitled *School and Learning Attitude Scales*. They are available through Educational Testing Service's Experimental Series. For further information contact Educational Testing Service, Princeton, N.J.

6 Further information concerning the Delphi technique is provided in M. Abelson et al., "Planning Education for the Future: Comments on a Pilot Study," *American Behavioral Scientist*, 1967, p. 10, and in Olaf Helmar, *Social Technology*, Basic Books, New York, 1966.

7 R. N. Shepard, "On Subjectively Optimum Selections Among Multi-Attribute Alternatives," in Maynard W. Shelley and G. L. Bryan (eds.), *Human Judgments and Optimality*, Wiley, New York, 1964, pp. 257–281.

8 The ANOVA technique is discussed more fully in P. J. Hoffman, P. Slovic, and L. G. Rorer, "An Analysis of Variance Model for the Assessment of Configural Cue Utilization in Clinical Judgments," *Psychological Bulletin*, vol. 69, 1968, pp. 338–349; and in P. Slovic, "Analyzing the Expert Judge: A Descriptive Study of a Stockbroker's Decision Process," *Journal of Applied Psychology*, vol. 53, 1969, pp. 255–263. Further information about the JAN technique may be found in D. Gag, "Judgment Analysis for Assessing Doctoral Admission Policies," *Journal of Experimental Education*, vol. 38, 1969, pp. 92–96.

9 D. T. Campbell and J. C. C. Stanley, *Experimental and Quasi-experimental Designs for Research*, Rand McNally, Chicago, 1967.

10 S. Isaac and W. B. Michael, *Handbook in Research and Evaluation,*

CHAPTER 12

CRITERIA FOR A GOOD SCHOOL

Bette Overman

As a research associate with the |I|D|E|A| Research Division's League of Cooperating Schools project, Bette Overman assumed a major responsibility in the research design, the development of instruments, and the co-ordination of data processing and analysis. In this chapter, Mrs. Overman draws upon her background in psychology and measurement to present an instrument designed to assess the school in terms of a variety of staff activities and role characteristics. Formulated with the cooperation of League school principals and teachers, the CRITERIA instrument is discussed as a tool which can be used by a staff to provide indices of the extent to which it is engaging in the processes necessary to the self-renewing school.

What is a good school? What are the criteria people use when they say one school is "better" than another? How does a school staff, aware that they have a morale problem, go about determining the factors that have brought about such a situation?

These are some of the questions which plagued principals and teachers in the early years of their association in |I|D|E|A|'s League of Cooperating Schools, a group of eighteen schools, each from a different district in California, selected to participate in a study of educational change. Since there was considerable variation among the eighteen schools in regard to size of pupil enrollment, location of the school (that is, whether it was urban, suburban, or rural), ethnic background of the student population, age and experience of the principals and teachers, and instructional programs, it seems reasonable to think of these schools as a microcosm of schools throughout the country. A more detailed discussion of the League and the nature of this study is presented in the introduction of this book.

The principals of these League schools were committed to improving the quality of education offered by their staffs, and their primary focus was the everyday business of education in their own buildings. Some of these principals felt that their schools were better than some of the other schools in their district; others expressed the need for greater improvements in their schools; but all of them realized that their opinions were based on subjective impressions, perhaps quite valid but less useful for evaluative purposes than an objective analysis of the quality of their schools. These principals wanted some reliable means of verifying their impressions or determining what educational changes should be made; however, none of the existing assessment techniques was comprehensive enough to serve these needs.

The principals of the League schools decided, therefore, to undertake the task of developing an evaluation instrument which could be used in their own schools and which could be used by any school staff interested in the same kinds of questions. The development of this instrument involved several meetings and discussions in which the eighteen principals exchanged ideas and extracted evaluation questions from the multitude of behaviors and interactions which are a part of everyday school activity, those things which they agreed to be most valuable for the attainment of a well-functioning school. They compiled a comprehensive list of statements which could be used as criteria for evaluation. The principals then consulted with the teachers at their respective schools to determine the extent to which, from the teachers' point of view, these criteria were not only useful but also essential in evaluating a school. Before a final instrument was developed, teachers in each of the eighteen schools were encouraged to add statements which they thought should be included. As a result, valuable additions and modifications to the instrument were made.

The |I|D|E|A| research staff assisted the principals and teachers in formulating the items and in presenting them in a questionnaire format which could be tried out in the League schools. All the principals and teachers were then asked to rate their own schools using these criteria items. After the initial administration and analysis of results, a few items found to have common high correlations were deleted and the wording of some items was changed to increase clarity.

The development of any measuring device includes a process of design, administration, and revision which is often repeated several times. The fact that all the principals and teachers in all the League schools had the opportunity to participate in this process makes it reasonable to assume that the items which finally remained in the present form of the CRITERIA instrument (as we at |I|D|E|A| call it), represent the views of many teachers and principals—the people who are most intimately involved in the business of education.

THE CRITERIA INSTRUMENT

The final form of the CRITERIA instrument consists of sixty-eight items which describe six major categories of school activities and role characteristics: *Dialogue, Decision Making, Action, Meetings, Principal,* and *Teachers*. The first three of these six categories include items most relevant for what we at |I|D|E|A| called the DDA (Dialogue, Decision Making, Action) process. The concept of DDA was developed during the early years of the research project when the staff at |I|D|E|A| was searching for a way to study the process of change as it occurs when a school is trying out new programs, different methods, or alternate forms of organization. Since the content of change could be different for each school—perhaps one school starting a team-teaching program and another wanting to work out a different way of reporting pupil progress to parents—it was necessary for the research staff to determine just what it was that all these various programs had in common, something that could be measured, would be applicable to all schools, and would be directly related to the process of change. It was agreed that any innovation requires some *dialogue* among those persons involved, some *decisions* to be made, and some *action* to be taken in order to implement the decisions. The DDA concept was used extensively throughout our study of change in the League of Cooperating Schools. (Evaluation was added as a separate component of the process later in the project, so that DDA became DDAE. A measure of evaluation is included in the CRITERIA instrument as part of the Action dimension.)

Many of the items which the teachers and the principals had included in the CRITERIA instrument described this process. They agreed that good *Dialogue* depends on the degree to which all of the staff have the opportunity to participate in discussions and how well informed they are, the degree to which a variety of persons is allowed to assume leadership positions, and the degree to which content of the discussion is relevant to the total school program and includes issues suggested by teachers, parents, and students as well as by the principal. *Dialogue* items are

In my school:

- Discussions include contributions by most of the members present (item 1).
- Many persons assume the leadership positions during group discussions, depending upon the function to be performed (item 20).
- Issues and programs discussed by the staff are suggested by both teachers and principal (item 24).
- Dialogue is appropriate to the problem confronted, for example, brainstorming when seeking new and imaginative ideas and task orientation when attempting to solve a particular problem (item 25).
- Issues and programs discussed by the staff can be suggested by parents (item 31).
- Dialogue has a purpose (item 35).
- Dialogue allows for in-depth discussion of issues that are pertinent to the education of children (item 37).
- Issues and programs discussed by the staff can be suggested by the students (item 41).
- Persons read what scholars and informed practitioners have written on the subject and bring relevant ideas from their reading into the dialogue (item 60).

The second category, *Decision Making,* measures the extent to which the total school staff participates in the decision-making process, the extent to which decisions are clearly communicated to all persons affected by the decision, the extent to which alternatives are examined, and the extent to which there is staff consensus (or a high level of agreement) on the decisions made. Items in the *Decision Making* category are

In my school:

- Decisions are clearly communicated to all persons who are affected by the decision (item 3).
- Persons examine and/or experiment with several approaches before making a decision (item 9).
- Both principal and teachers participate in making decisions which affect the school (item 21).
- Persons become familiar with the experiences of other schools before making a decision (item 26).

- Group decisions are reached by consensus (item 34).
- Decisions are made on the basis of school goals (item 38).
- Decisions are carried out with enthusiasm and good will (item 46).
- When appropriate, the advice of district personnel is sought before a decision is made (item 49).
- Group decisions are reached by voting (item 55).

CRITERIA items which describe the *Action* stage of the process refer to the appropriateness of the action taken relative to the decision made, the commitment of persons responsible for implementation, the efficiency with which action is carried out, the degree to which action is modifiable in meeting unanticipated situations, and the evaluation of the completed action relative to its proposed goal. Items in the *Action* category are

In my school:

- When a decision is made, action is taken to implement it (item 6).
- Anyone who is interested is encouraged to take the responsibility for implementing decisions (item 12).
- Actions can be modified to handle unanticipated situations (item 30).
- Responsibilities for carrying out actions are assumed by many different people on the staff (item 44).
- Actions are carried out with a high degree of organization and efficiency (item 48).
- Before a decision is made, the implications of alternative actions are thoroughly explored (item 53).
- There is a high degree of commitment on the part of people responsible for putting decisions into action (item 54).
- Appropriate actions are taken based on the decisions made (item 57).
- After an action has been taken, it is evaluated (item 65).

The fourth category, *Meetings,* measures the climate and effectiveness of staff meetings by rating the importance of content, the degree to which all teachers have the opportunity to contribute to the agenda and participate in the discussions, the openness and frankness which characterize the meetings, and the practice of providing written summaries of staff meetings. Items in the *Meetings* category are

In my school:

- Staff meetings are generally reserved for matters concerned with curriculum, instruction, and school organization—not administrivia (item 2).
- Meetings are on time (item 4).
- Meetings are such that members listen to each other (item 15).
- Each meeting is followed by a written memorandum that summarizes the proceedings of the meeting (item 17).
- Meetings have an agenda composed of items that any member of the staff can suggest (item 22).
- Meetings involve only persons who need to be involved (item 28).
- Meetings are such that persons can engage in an open and frank discussion of issues (item 45).
- Meetings are such that there is an interaction of teachers (item 58).
- Meetings can be called by both teachers and principal (item 66).

The fifth category, *Principal*, contains items pertaining to the role of the principal, including his interaction and communication with teachers, students, and community members. Items in the *Principal* category include

In my school:

- The principal has the respect and good will of the students (item 8).
- The principal respects the teachers (item 14).
- The principal knows his staff well (item 18).
- The principal encourages others to provide leadership (item 27).
- The principal encourages and assists the staff in developing goals for the school (item 29).
- The principal communicates effectively with students (item 32).
- The principal utilizes resource persons from the district to help teachers (item 39).
- The principal builds the status of his staff (item 40).
- The principal shows that he appreciates his staff (item 43).
- The principal communicates effectively with teachers (item 47).
- The principal encourages the staff to visit other classrooms (item 51).
- The principal has the respect and good will of the teachers (item 52).
- The principal respects the opinions and beliefs of teachers (item 56).
- The principal communicates effectively with the community (item 59).
- The principal provides fair and equitable treatment for all (item 61).
- The principal promotes openness in his staff (item 63).

- The principal attends conferences relative to his professional growth (item 67).

The sixth and last category, *Teachers,* consists of several items which describe the professional role of the teacher. This category examines the degree to which teachers engage in discussions defining school goals, make instructional decisions, read professional educational material, experiment with new materials, respect the opinions and beliefs of students and other teachers, and evaluate their teaching in terms of achieving school goals. *Teachers* items are

In my school:

- The staff engages in discussions aimed at defining school goals (item 5).
- Teachers make instructional decisions (item 7).
- Teachers visit other schools (item 10).
- Teachers read professional educational material (item 11).
- Teachers periodically visit other classrooms in the school (item 13).
- Teachers can arrange to have their teaching critiqued by other teachers (item 16).
- Teachers attend conferences relative to their professional growth (item 19).
- Teachers try to evaluate the extent to which school goals have been realized (item 23).
- Teachers work to implement the goals of the school (item 33).
- Teachers critique each other's teaching (item 36).
- Teachers attend courses at colleges and universities (item 42).
- Teachers experiment with new materials (item 50).
- Teachers respect the opinions and beliefs of students (item 62).
- Teachers evaluate their teaching in terms of achieving school goals (item 64).
- Teachers respect the opinions and beliefs of other teachers (item 68).

USING CRITERIA

There are several ways in which any school staff can use the CRITERIA instrument in a self-evaluation program. The simplest way, and the way used in our study, is to ask the principal and each teacher to fill out the questionnaire (a copy of the CRITERIA instrument is included in Appendix B). When the school staff has completed the questionnaire, their responses and those of the principal are then tallied, and the frequency of each response for every item can be entered on a blank form of the questionnaire. In this way the staff can see to what extent there is agreement among them relative to each item as well as the modal response for the school. If it is desirable to know whether or not the principal perceives the school in a way similar to the majority of the staff, the principal's scores can be excluded from the tally and recorded on the frequency form by a line or X in an appropriate box on the rating scale.

Table 12.1 is an example of how, in a school with twenty teachers, the responses on the first ten items might look. In this illustration the principal's scores are not included in the tally, but his score on each item is indicated by a line in the box he selected for his rating.

Scores on each of the six major categories—*Dialogue, Decision Making, Action, Meetings, Principal, and Teachers*—can be obtained by consulting the Category Item Key (Table 12.2) which lists the items, by number, contained in each dimension. Table 12.3 shows an example of how the school score on the *Dialogue* dimension can be determined.

The frequency of response is listed for each item in the *Dialogue* category. In Table 12.3, no teachers checked "never" for item 1, two teachers checked "seldom," four teachers checked "sometimes," six teachers checked "frequently," etc. The frequencies for each type of response are totaled for all items in the category. In our illustration the sum of the frequencies for "never" is 11, the sum of the frequencies for "seldom" is 28, "sometimes" is 36, "frequently" is 46, etc.

The sum of the frequencies for each response is multiplied by its appropriate response weight. Each item is rated on a six-point scale from "never" to "always" and the responses are scored as follows: Never = 1, seldom = 2, sometimes = 3, frequently = 4, usually = 5, and always = 6. In our example the sum of the frequencies for "never" is 11. This is multiplied by the response weight of 1, which equals 11. The sum of the frequencies for "seldom" is 28 and is multiplied by the response weight of 2, which equals 56, etc. The sum of these products (in the example, $11 + 56 + 108 + 184 + 210 + 102 = 671$) is then divided by the number of items in the category (9 items in *Dialogue*) and the number of teachers who have completed the questionnaire (20 in our example) to obtain the average score for the teachers in the school on the *Dialogue* category.

School scores on each category provide a useful index for an indi-

TABLE 12.1.   EXAMPLE OF ITEM FREQUENCY FOR A TOTAL OF TWENTY TEACHERS

	Never	Seldom	Sometimes	Frequently	Usually	Always
In my school:						
1 Discussions include contributions by most of the members present.	0	2	4	6	8*	0
2 Staff meetings are generally reserved for matters concerned with curriculum, instruction, and school organization—not administrivia.	1	2	8	6	3	0
3 Decisions are clearly communicated to all persons who are affected by the decision.	0	0	7	10	3	0
4 Meetings are on time.	0	0	3	5	10	2
5 The staff engages in discussions aimed at defining school goals.	0	9	6	3	2	0
6 When a decision is made, action is taken to implement it.	0	1	2	10	6	1
7 Teachers make instructional decisions.	4	6	0	1	9	0
8 The principal has the respect and good will of the students.	0	2	8	6	4	0
9 Persons examine and/or experiment with several approaches before making a decision.	1	3	8	5	2	1
10 Teachers visit other schools.	0	3	10	7	0	0

* Principal's rating is indicated by horizontal line in appropriate box.

SUMMARY: In this example, the modal response on item 1 is "usually," as is the principal's score. On item 2 the modal response is "sometimes," but the principal has checked the box "usually." On six of the ten items illustrated, the principal's perception of the situations described is the same as the modal response of the teachers. However, on items 2, 5, 6, and 8 his perception is different from that of the majority. The distribution of teachers' ratings on each item suggests that they do vary in their perception of the described situations, but only on item 7 is there striking disagreement. This item may warrant some discussion by this particular staff. For some reason, ten of the teachers indicate that they rarely make instructional decisions, whereas ten other teachers indicate that they usually or frequently do so, and the principal has given this item a high rating. Perhaps it can be explained by the organization at the school, district policy, etc., and will pose no problem. On the other hand, it could be a source of discord previously unidentified.

TABLE 12.2   CATEGORY ITEM KEY

	Dialogue	Decision	Action	Meetings	Principal	Teachers
item	1	3	6	2	8	5
	20	9	12	4	14	7
	24	21	30	15	18	10
	25	26	44	17	27	11
	31	34	48	22	29	13
	35	38	53	28	32	16
	37	46	54	45	39	19
	41	49	57	58	40	23
	60	55	65	66	43	33
					47	36
					51	42
					52	50
					56	62
					59	64
					61	68
					63	
					67	
Total Categories	9	9	9	9	17	15

vidual school when using the CRITERIA instrument to measure change over a period of time. They are also useful for making comparisons across two or more schools.

THE USEFULNESS OF CRITERIA

The CRITERIA instrument can be used as a diagnostic tool to assess the present level of a school in the six major categories and as a measure of agreement among the staff on individual items. It provides an objective method of locating areas in which there is disagreement within a staff and provides a basis for further discussion should there be attempts to resolve these problems. The effectiveness of solutions adopted can be evaluated by readministering the CRITERIA instrument (or relevant portions of it) at a later date to determine whether or not the staff has reached a desirable degree of consensus on the issue.

The use of the CRITERIA instrument is not, of course, limited to the eighteen League schools. Although it was designed by principals and teachers who were League members, it was their intention that the

TABLE 12.3. EXAMPLE OF SCORING PROCEDURE FOR DIALOGUE CATEGORY

Dialogue Item	Never	Seldom	Sometimes	Frequently	Usually	Always
1	0	2	4	6	8	0
20	3	8	6	3	0	0
24	0	1	3	9	5	2
25	0	0	1	4	10	5
31	4	6	8	2	0	0
35	0	0	2	6	8	4
37	0	0	3	5	8	4
41	3	8	5	4	0	0
60	1	3	4	7	3	2
Sum of Frequencies:	11	28	36	46	42	17
Response Weight:	$\times 1$	$\times 2$	$\times 3$	$\times 4$	$\times 5$	$\times 6$
	11 +	56 +	108 +	184	+ 210 +	102 = 671

Divide by number of items in category—9: $671 \div 9 = 74.56$
Divide by number of teachers—20: $74.56 \div 20 = 3.73$ School Score on
Dialogue

instrument would be made available to any school which desired to use it. In fact, since its development, it has been administered to eighteen other schools on two separate occasions. Used as a periodic assessment tool, the CRITERIA instrument enables any staff to measure objectively the changes which have occurred during the intervening time.

Several examples can be cited to demonstrate the applicability of the CRITERIA instrument to various school situations. A school which had several new teachers had been vaguely aware that there seemed to be less cooperation and lower staff morale than during the previous year. Analysis of their responses on the CRITERIA instrument revealed extremely low scores on all the items which made any reference to "goals" of the school. A systematic effort by the principal and teachers to discuss openly the subject of school goals and come to some agreement on the identification of goals and their application to teaching practices resulted in a greater degree of cooperation and higher morale throughout the school.

Frequently, a school will have high scores on *Dialogue* and *Decision Making* but lower scores on the *Action* dimension. Analysis of the individual items which make up the *Action* subtest will provide the staff with the information they need if they wish to reduce this discrepancy. It may be that responsibility for carrying out the action always falls on the same few people; perhaps alternative actions need to be explored, thereby adding flexibility and the increased likelihood that some appropriate action will be implemented.

An obvious problem exists if the principal's ratings on a majority of the items are widely divergent from the teachers' ratings. If this is the first time the principal has had objective evidence of these discrepancies, the awareness of their existence can lead to better communication and greater mutual understanding.

With the ever-increasing pressures associated with the business of education, techniques for improving the quality of communication and reducing misunderstandings among school personnel can have a wide range of positive influence from increased staff morale to improved quality of schooling for all concerned.

CHAPTER **13**

A PLAN FOR AN ACCOUNTABLE ELEMENTARY SCHOOL DISTRICT

Richard C. Williams

Richard Williams is an associate professor of educational administration in the UCLA Graduate School of Education. As a consultant to the League of Cooperating Schools project, he worked with principals for over a year in developing the plan for accountability described in this chapter. The plan involves a strategy to establish, on a district-wide basis, an organizational model in which individual schools are free to develop innovative programs appropriate to their particular educational problems. Within the context of this model, what is to be changed in the individual schools is determined by the principal and his staff in cooperation with the students and parents which the school serves. The individual school is held accountable to its clientele, and those students and parents who do not believe the changes produce better educational results or who do not desire to participate in the school's program are free to choose other schools in the same district which have different programs.

There is widespread public concern over the effectiveness of America's schools. Both the popular and professional press have reflected these concerns, noting a decline in the effectiveness of schools as educational institutions. This literature has attracted a sizable public audience. For example, Charles Silberman's recent *Crisis in the Classroom* was on the best-seller list for many weeks and stirred considerable public debate.

As one might expect, these various examinations of the schools have not been of one mind in their diagnoses of the causes for the schools' limitations. It follows that their prescriptions for recovery are also dissimilar. Diagnoses and recommendations range from replacing inept teachers and administrators with more qualified people, to employing some particular technical device or plan so as to increase the rate of pupil learning or improve the efficiency of the schools' operation, to getting rid of the whole present school organization and moving toward a "deschooled society." However, few of the proposals for school reform have had much of a lasting impact on the schools. There are several reasons for this, perhaps the most important one being that many of the plans have been too limited in their definition of the problem and too piecemeal in their proposed solutions.

A major purpose of this chapter, then, is to present a *comprehensive* plan for accountability that incorporates, as appropriate, the various ideas and schemes that have been suggested as a means of improving the schools' effectiveness. The chapter is divided into the following sections:

1   A brief review of various accountability proposals for those readers who are perhaps not totally acquainted with all of them.

2   A brief description of the authors of this plan, their background, and their unique qualifications to develop the plan.

3   A presentation of the basic assumptions that guided the authors' thinking as they developed the plan.

4   A description of the plan.

5   A discussion of ways in which the plan can be implemented, including a description of the responsibilities of and relationships among the various parties to the implementation process (educators, school board members, parents).

A REVIEW OF ACCOUNTABILITY PROPOSALS

The major portion of the accountability literature has been devoted to plans and technical programs designed to enhance the ability of schools to be more effective in the utilization of their resources and to enable them to monitor more adequately and report more completely on their success in attaining instructional objectives. The adoption of these plans, it is argued, would enable schools to be responsive to their clients, hence more accountable. The following is a brief description of some of the major accountability schemes and plans that have been suggested.[1]

Use of Modern Management Techniques

Advocates of modern management techniques believe that the schools could operate more efficiently and effectively if they would utilize some of the planning and problem-solving techniques that have been developed in business, industry, and government.[2] Among the techniques suggested are:

Program Planning Budgeting Systems (PPBS) PPBS is a system whereby budgets and subsequent expenditures are related to specific plans and the achievement of specified and quantifiable objectives. Those who advocate the use of PPBS in the schools assert that monies could be more effectively accounted for and educators would have a far more valid basis for assessing alternative decision strategies if such a system were adopted.

Systems Analysis This technique involves the use of quantitative analysis of the many facets of a problem in an attempt to determine relationships and assess probable outcomes of alternate decision routes. Systems analysts argue that since many of the problems that confront schools are very complex, simple one-dimensional approaches to the problems cannot possibly result in significant solutions. They assert that systems analysis techniques will greatly improve educational planning.

Management by Objectives Proponents of management by objectives argue that administrators cannot hope to make much progress unless they think hard about what their school is trying to accomplish, translate the school's proposed activities into measurable objectives, and then evaluate, after a predetermined time, whether the school has achieved them. By utilizing the techniques of management by objectives, school administrators will have a firmer "fix" on where they are going and whether or not they are successful.

Accurate Measurement of Pupil Achievement

A major tenet of those who subscribe to this approach to accountability is that a fundamental function of the schools is the education of pupils, and one cannot begin to determine the degree to which schools are successful until accurate measures of pupil learning or growth are developed and utilized. There are several approaches to the measurement of pupil growth:

Norm-Referenced Tests   This is the traditional measurement approach to school achievement testing. Pupil success is determined by comparing the individual student's scores with the achievement scores of other pupils of a similar age or grade. A pupil's performance is always expressed in terms of how he ranks in a comparable norm group.

Criterion-Referenced Tests   Advocates of criterion-referenced tests argue that rather than compare the pupil with a norm group, one should look at the degree to which the pupil has mastered the material to which he has been exposed.[3] If instruction is successful, all pupils will achieve at a given level of performance; the comparison of one pupil with another is of little or no value.

Behavioral Objectives   Adherents of this procedure emphasize that learning is largely the changing of pupil behavior. Accordingly, the appropriate way to plan and conduct an instructional program is to define objectives, determine the criteria for measuring the objectives in behavioral terms, evaluate the pupil's behavior after the completion of instruction, and redesign the instructional program if the level of attainment is unsatisfactory.[4]

Expansion of Schooling Responsibility beyond the Public Schools

Adherents of this point of view state that the public schools have had their chance to provide educational services and the quality of the services has proven to be unsatisfactory. Thus it is time, they argue, to allow outside agencies to share in public investments in education. Among the proposals that have been made are:

Voucher System   Basically this plan would allow parents to receive a voucher for each school-age child.[5] The parents could then use the voucher to send their child to the school of their choice. The parents could choose from among the public schools and schools run by independent entrepreneurs, churches, and other groups. Two of the main arguments used by voucher system proponents are that parents will have a greater selection of educational alternatives and that the resulting competitiveness of the system will drive out ineffective schools.

Performance Contracting Under this plan, the schools would contract with independent agencies or businesses to carry out certain instructional activities for them.[6] A feature of some of these contracts is that the agencies or businesses guarantee results; that is, they will not be paid unless at the end of instruction the pupils meet preestablished performance criteria.

Public Support of Private and Parochial Schools Another subgroup that can be included under this approach includes those who for many years have been asking that public monies be given to established private and parochial schools.[7] Their argument is based heavily on the concept that the responsibility for educating the child rests with parents, and they should have an opportunity to send their child to a private school without having also to support the public education system. They further argue that many private and parochial schools are in financial difficulty, and if they are forced to close for lack of money, a very heavy additional burden will be placed on the taxpayer as the private school pupils flood into the public schools. The education of everyone would be better served, they maintain, if help were extended to keep the private and parochial system intact or even to expand it.

Some Dissenting Views

A number of criticisms of these various approaches to accountability have been made. The use of modern management techniques has been questioned on several grounds. First, many of the techniques are built on the assumption that the various subcomponents of the system can be quantified. In education, however, it is unlikely that many important variables, such as teacher morale, the social system of a classroom, or the child's home environment, can be reduced to quantifiable measures. Without such precision, these systems have very limited application. In addition, many of the modern management techniques are based on static systems; that is, the parts of the system do not interact with the system once it is established. Human systems are more dynamic; the human members of the system tend to be in continuous interaction. This factor tends to complicate considerably the problem of applying systems analysis to the schools.[8]

The difficulty of quantifying is also a main objection to the reliance on the measurement of pupil achievement for evidence of accountability. In an attempt to maximize the ability of the school to be accountable, some schools may place greater emphasis on the more easily quantified instructional activities (such as mathematics) while ignoring other "softer" activities (such as the appreciation of literature). Also, questions can be raised as to whether those behaviors that are measured immediately after instruction are the most important learning outcomes and whether such changes in behavior will persist through time after a week, a month, a year, or five years.

In addition, many fear that the expansion of public spending on education to nonpublic agencies and organizations may result in the development of segregated schools. Yet another problem emerges in terms of monitoring the expenditure of public funds to a large variety of private organizations. It is possible that a number of unqualified, even unscrupulous persons could appropriate public monies for questionable purposes and practices.

Finally, a general criticism of the plans discussed above is that they lack comprehensiveness. Although each plan might improve the particular malady for which it is designed, none of the plans approaches the achievement of a coordinated system that would allow for total accountability. What is needed is a system that will provide for accountability on such various factors as pupil achievement, fiscal planning, teacher performance, and parental satisfaction, and the system has to be so designed that it maximizes the amount of freedom and innovation that is allowed in the schools. To put it another way, what is needed is a system that will utilize the advantages of the various accountability techniques in a comprehensive manner and in such a way so as to allow schools to grow and change and meet competing demands.

Such questions and concerns regarding the various proposals for accountability have received attention in many quarters. Indeed, some who suggest such schemes are often well aware of the limitations of their proposals and the problems they face in implementation.

THE AUTHORS OF THIS PLAN

One group that has completed a systematic review of the various proposals for accountability comprises the principals of schools that compose the |I|D|E|A| League of Cooperating Schools. The League of Cooperating Schools consisted of eighteen elementary schools, each from a separate school district in Southern California. The League was formed in 1966 as part of an |I|D|E|A| research project on the study of change. Each school was charged with the task of exploring ways in which it could develop and implement an improved educational program. Most of the schools were freed from some of the curricular policies that governed the other elementary schools in the district. The principals of the schools met periodically during each school year to share experiences and ideas about the process of change. At the beginning of the fourth year of the project, the principals began extensive discussions of the various accountability proposals that have been suggested. During their review they searched in vain for a comprehensive, workable accountability scheme that could be implemented in elementary schools, a scheme that drew upon the most desirable features of the plans while at the same time not limiting the freedom of the school to be creative and innovative. Failing to find such a scheme, they developed their own, which they termed a *plan for an accountable elementary school district.*[9]

The principals brought to this task diverse and unique backgrounds. They varied widely in terms of age, experience in education, level of educational preparation, and views toward schooling and politics. Their school districts differed in many ways as well. Some were large, others small. They represented urban, suburban, and rural areas. Their student bodies ranged from racially mixed to all white; their communities ranged from liberal to conservative. Most of the principals had been in the same school throughout the duration of the League, although some had replaced the original League principal.

Each principal also brought to the task the unique and impressive experience he had gained in administering a school that stood alone in its district. Each had experienced the frustration, anxiety, fatigue, and exhilaration of trying to bring about change in his school. Thus, the plan that is described in the following pages is not the vision of abstract theorists or academic dreamers. Rather, it is the product of the considered judgment of experienced administrators who have been deeply involved in the change process in real schools. The principals are convinced that the plan is workable and that it can provide a way to maximize accountability without limiting innovation and choice.

ASSUMPTIONS UNDERLYING THE PLAN

As an initial task in designing the model, the principals stated the basic assumptions they held about education and schooling:

Parents differ in their opinions of what are preferred educational programs.

Some parents prefer a more structured program; others seek more freedom for their child in the school. Some prefer a curriculum based on the three R's; others would like to have a curriculum that focuses on the child's emotional and social development. Some adhere to the necessity of grouping students into ability tracks within grades; others prefer a multigrade or multiaged approach.[10]

The response of the school to mixed clientele preferences has often been to compromise, to offer a program that is politically and educationally neutral, a program that will offend no one. However, too often the result of this strategy is that the school program pleases no one—the schools are judged to be too conservative, or too liberal, or too neutral. As a consequence, the schools are in a constant state of battle with a minority of parents who are deeply disturbed about some phase of the program.[11] Experience has shown that a small number of parents can be startlingly effective in forcing the schools to conform to a neutral program or to abandon some new program.

The League principals often found this to be a serious problem in their attempts to innovate in their schools. The innovation would be developed on the basis of some particular pedagogical approach, while the students who attended the school were selected on a geographical basis. Inevitably, a certain percentage of the school's parents would disagree with the pedagogical assumptions and would bring pressure to alter the school to their way of thinking. Thus many of the League schools never realized their potential because so much of the staff's energy was spent in dealing with a minority of disgruntled parents.

There is no one school organization or educational program that will be appropriate for all children or all parents.

Rather than continue to seek some perfect compromise in schools, it would be far more productive to begin to identify different kinds of school models, each of which would satisfy some particular group of clients. The schools could differ in a variety of ways, namely, organization (graded, nongraded, track), pedagogical approach (open schools, preparatory, comprehensive traditional elementary schools), or some combination of these various structures and pedagogical approaches.

Parents should be allowed to choose, from among several alternative schooling models, the school model(s) they prefer for their children.

The participation of parents in selecting the schooling model for their children should greatly enhance the likelihood of the school achieving its goals. The amount of parental interference that is based on fundamental (and usually unchangeable) differences in pedagogical assumptions would be reduced significantly.

An interesting comparison can be drawn between this problem and that which was faced by the motion picture industry. Prior to the adoption of the present rating system (G, PG, R, X), movies were subject to censorship by various religious and civic groups. As a consequence, the industry was unable to deal very realistically with many important topics such as sex, corruption, crime, narcotics, mental illness. The result was the familiar Hollywood nonrealism that characterized so many movies. Like the schools, the movies had dealt with the problem of differing publics by compromising and offering little that was offensive to anyone.

Since the adoption of the rating systems, movies have been able to deal far more forthrightly with controversial topics. Those who are judged too young or immature to see some films are denied admission; what is more important, through the rating system the public can get an approximate indication of the kind of film they will be seeing. If someone objects to a certain type of film, he is warned, and he can choose not to see it.[12]

Thus, if parents were given a greater choice in the schooling of their children, a similar phenomenon would take place in public education. Educators would be freer to innovate, and parents would have a greater, more direct hand in determining their children's educational program. Those who objected to a particular pedagogical model could send their children, at public expense, to schools which offered a program more compatible with their views. But the dissenting parents would not have the need, nor the right, to deny other parents their choice.

A school district can tolerate and indeed will prosper from the existence of two or more different schooling models.

The League of Cooperating Schools offers ample proof of this assertion. Each of the districts has been able to tolerate a school which significantly differs from other schools in the district. Indeed, often the League school has stimulated the development of other "League-type" schools in its district. In some cases, dissenting parents have been allowed to transfer their children out of the League school, and other more sympathetic parents have been allowed to transfer their children into the League school. In many instances, the individual

League school has provided a multiple educational program within the same building; for example, some rooms are self-contained, some are multiaged, and some are based on the British primary school model. Parental preferences are considered when pupils are assigned to the different programs.

All professional staff members whose personal and professional lives will be affected must participate, in some way, in those decisions that form the structure and operation of the individual schools.

It is well known that anyone who is attempting to accomplish fundamental changes in an organization must rely on the cooperation of those who will be affected by those changes. The innovator is not likely to get very far unless those so affected are consulted in a truly meaningful way.[13] Not only will the change agent be blunted by a wall of resistance so often constructed by those who view themselves as change "victims," but also, the change agent will be denied the creative force that is unleashed when concerned professionals are asked to contribute to the formation of the proposed change. A change agent simply cannot predict and counter all the problems that will challenge his plans. He must have the creative input from concerned and talented colleagues.

The degree of client and educator involvement in decision making will differ with the kind of decision to be made.

Progress will be made more rapidly and smoothly if the various parties to educational decision making play a predominant part in those decisions for which they are most qualified and responsible. Roughly, these spheres of decision making are as follows:

Parents   Traditionally in American education, parents (society) have been given the major responsibility for determining the ends of education for the elementary school child. In many instances, they have influenced the means as well.[14] For purposes of this plan, it is assumed that the determination of the appropriate ends of education will continue to rest with parents (society).

Principals and Teachers   Educators are best qualified to make decisions regarding the educational program, the means of education, that will achieve the ends of education that have been decided upon by parents.

Superintendent and Central Administration   The function of the top administrators should be to design and implement ways of measuring whether the educators are achieving the ends they have agreed to attain. In addition, they are responsible for reporting to the schools' clients on the success the schools are experiencing in achieving agreed upon goals (accountability function).

School Boards   The responsibility of school boards is to develop the policies that will enable the accountability system to operate. *No accountable educational system can violate the constitutional guidelines that have been developed by the U.S. Supreme Court.*

For example, no school can advocate the violent overthrow of the government, breach the wall between church and state, or be maintained for the purpose of perpetuating racially segregated schools.

DESCRIPTION OF THE PLAN

The plan that follows should be considered as the framework for a workable accountability scheme for an elementary school district or the elementary schools in a unified district. It should not be considered prescriptive (the only way to do it) or exhaustive (all possible problems have been solved). School districts differ from one another in many ways, such as size, geography, racial composition, socioeconomic level of the community, and political persuasions. Each district brings a unique set of characteristics to the model, and thus each district needs to derive its own plan for implementation. The plan does assume, however, that a district be small enough or administratively subdivided in such a way that all elementary students are in reasonable proximity to the school of their parents' choice and that the district can provide transportation for all children who need it.

The plan is quite simple. It calls for the schools in a district to cluster around different pedagogical or schooling models, designed to meet different parental preferences concerning structure (graded, nongraded, multigraded), and school types (open schools, classical grammar schools, British primary schools, traditional comprehensive elementary schools). Perhaps some are combinations of various structures and types. For example, some parents might prefer the nongraded classical grammar school or the multiaged open elementary schools. Some parents might emphasize affective learning, some might focus more on cognitive skills, and still others might strive for a program that balances these two emphases.

When the different schooling models are selected (a discussion of how this might be accomplished appears in a following section), parents are to be given considerable information about the different schooling models and their implications for the schools' structure, orientation, and goals. Parents are then asked to select the school model they think will benefit their child. (It is not necessary for a family with more than one child to send all its children to the same school).

The budgets of the different schools are determined largely by the student enrollment, that is, so many dollars per student enrolled or ADA, although means may be developed to augment individual school budgets where warranted.

When the enrollment and budget are set, the administration and staff of each school design and implement the school programs to accomplish the educational goals of their schooling models. They also devise methods whereby the schools' success in achieving the educational goals are to be evaluated.

The central administration is responsible for implementing the entire system, from establishing the ways in which the different school models are developed, to assisting parents in the selection of their children's school, to devising a scheme whereby each school's success is monitored and reported to the school board.

The school board develops policies to assure the likelihood of the plan's success and to minimize the misuse of the plan by parents who may wish to propagate racial, religious, economic, or social separatism. The board is responsible for reporting to the public on the effectiveness of the schools.

IMPLEMENTING THE PLAN

It is very difficult to move from an established system to one that differs significantly from the norm.[15] Such an effort involves redirecting human and material resources and changing human behavior that in many instances has been built on years of experience and accustomed ways of doing things. The number of problems involved and the amounts of time required to make such changes cannot be overestimated. Yet such changes can be made if the plan for moving from one system to another is designed to occur in separate but interrelated steps.

The following discussion, then, presents the various actions necessary to establish an accountable elementary school district. The actions are presented in a rough chronological order, although the suggested order is subject to change. Indeed, several of the actions could well go on simultaneously. What is important is that careful planning go into each of these stages of development. A delineation of the advising and decision responsibilities of all parties to the accountability plan appears in Table 13.1.

Developing Potential Schooling Models

Before beginning the actual development of the schooling models, the school board should establish policies regarding two important aspects of the schools:

1   Policies which define the constraints in the development of the school models—particularly in terms of the kinds of school models that cannot be established. Initial guidelines can be taken from decisions of the U.S. Supreme Court discussed above.

2   Policies regarding how pupils are to be selected for the schools. The guidelines developed by Christopher Jencks to govern the implementation of voucher systems are one source for ideas on how to minimize the possibility of establishing a system which results in the separation of students in terms of racial or religious or socioeconomic characteristics.[16]

Once these policies are established, there are a number of ways in which the models themselves can be developed. The most efficient way is probably for the central administration to take primary responsibility. Sources which the administration might use for the development of the models include the curriculum literature, discussions with or reviews of the writings of those who have experience with different models, and conferences with parent groups who have expressed schooling preferences. Also, as a means of determining public views toward education, the administration might poll parents on the educational objectives they most prefer for their children.[17]

When the schooling models are developed, they are then presented to the parents for their consideration. It is suggested that each parent be asked to indicate first and second preferences and the relative importance they attach to their child attending a neighborhood school or a particular schooling model if such a model means their child must be transported out of the neighborhood. Once the school administration receives this information, it has a fairly good "fix" on the kinds of schooling models that are preferred, the approximate enroll-

TABLE 13.1. SUGGESTED DECISION-MAKING AND ADVISORY RESPONSIBILITIES IN DESIGNING AND OPERATING AN ACCOUNTABLE ELEMENTARY SCHOOL DISTRICT

	School Board	Central Administrative Staff Super-intendent	Principals	Total School Professional Staff Including Principal	Parents	Pupils
POLICIES						
Policies Regarding Kinds of Schools To Be Considered	Decision	Advisory	Consulted	Consulted	Consulted	Consulted
Policies Governing Assignment of School Staff	Decision	Advisory	Advisory	Advisory	Consulted	Consulted
Policies Governing Location of Schools	Decision	Advisory	Advisory	Advisory	Advisory	Advisory
Policies Regarding Determination of School Building	Decision	Advisory	Advisory	Advisory	Consulted	Consulted
Policy Governing Student Transfers	Decision	Advisory	Advisory	Advisory	Advisory	Advisory
Policies Regarding Accountability Contract	Decision	Advisory	Advisory	Advisory	Advisory	Advisory
OPERATION AND ADMINISTRATION						
Determining School Models To Be Implemented	Decision	Advisory	Advisory	Advisory	Advisory	Consulted
Assignment of School Staffs		Decision	Advisory	Advisory	Consulted	Consulted
Locating Schools		Decision	Advisory	Advisory	Advisory	
Determination of School Budgets		Decision	Advisory	Advisory		
Developing Educational Programs of Schools		Advisory	Advisory	Decision	Consulted	Consulted
Selection of School to be Attended by Pupils		Advisory	Advisory	Advisory	Decision	Decision
Final Decisions of Student Transfers		Decision	Advisory	Advisory	Advisory	Consulted
Administering Accountability Contract		Decision	Advisory	Advisory	Advisory	Advisory

KEY:

Decision: Primary *decision* responsibility*
Advisory: Serve in a major advisory capacity
Consulted: *Consulted* regarding their opinion

* Legally the board has ultimate responsibility for the entire range of decisions to be made. What is suggested by the Table is that the board can most effectively carry out its responsibility by delegating some decisions to others. It is understood that such decisions are always subject to board review.

ment in each, and the residential locations of pupils whose parents prefer the various models. Those models which receive an adequate level of parental support are then eligible for further development by the district.

Staffing the Schools

When the various schooling models to be offered are established, the school board develops policies to govern the assignment of teachers and administrators to the various models. Two considerations must underlie such policies:

1 The advisability of minimizing the possibility of assigning any teacher or administrator to a school model with which he disagrees. Teachers and administrators should be given an opportunity to express their preferences for the school models in which they desire placement, and such preferences must be part of the considerations when assignments are made.

2 The potential need for and advantages of providing inservice training for the staffs of the different school models. It is recommended that the amount and kind of inservice training be based largely on the expressed needs of the staff.

With these policies as a backdrop, a specific decision-making model for determining initial placement of school staffs and for considering requests for staff transfers must be developed. Some of the components of this decision model are the order in which the requests are received, the individual's expressed preferences, the individual's training and experience in relation to the school model of his choice, seniority, and the need to maintain a balance within the staff of each school model in terms of age, sex, race, and experience.

Establishing the Number and Location of the Schooling Models

The school board next makes decisions, based on recommendations of the central administration, on the number and location of the various school models. These decisions involve balancing a number of factors:

1 The number of pupils who have expressed a preference for each model. A consequent consideration is the maximum and minimum

enrollments in each school. The board might consider the possibility of having two or more models in the same school building if the projected enrollment for some models does not meet the minimum enrollment standards for a separate school.

2   The number of faculty members who are interested in and qualified to teach in the various models. In all likelihood, there will not be a perfect match between the teaching staff needed and the pool of talent available. Accordingly, personnel recruitment and development should be planned so as to provide the necessary resources. Upon developing projections of personnel needs, and upon determining the present staff talent (including the degree of staff turnover), the district is in a position to recruit new teachers who possess the needed talents. In addition, the talent pool can be enriched by the provision of inservice programs (for those who desire them) to upgrade the qualifications of the staff of a new schooling model.

3   The residential patterns of the pupils. Wherever possible, schooling models should be located so as to minimize the distance to be traveled by students in order that they can attend the model of their choice.

A linear programming scheme could be used to help in making decisions that account for the factors discussed above. The use of such a sophisticated tool depends, of course, on the size and complexity of the problem.

School Budgeting

Additional policies are necessary in order to determine the budgets of each school. A basic foundation in budgeting is the allocation to each school of a certain amount of money per child enrolled. It may be, however, that the schooling models of some schools require more money per child to implement fully the programs involved; or if the school models represent a radical departure from more traditional practices, it may be necessary to provide developmental funds. Such funds may not be needed by schools operating a traditional program with which they have had considerable experience.[18]

Another consideration is for the district to set aside a fund each year for innovation. Individual schools can then submit proposals for special projects, and those judged as most promising will receive funding by the district. This allows those schools with a desire to experiment with new approaches the funds to develop such activities.

Developing the Educational Programs in the Schooling Models

Once the staff has been selected for each school, they begin the task of developing the educational program to achieve the goals of the schooling model. The instructional programs of the schools will differ from schooling model to schooling model. Indeed, individual schools within schooling models might design different instructional activities to achieve similar goals. The reason for this is that the schools will differ in the characteristics of the teaching staff and the pupils. Some school staffs will feel more confident with one approach, and other school staffs may be more successful with a different instructional program.

What is vital is that the central administration establish a mechanism for the communication of ideas and sharing of experiences among the schools. This could take the form of regularly scheduled meetings of administrators and teachers from the different schooling models for the purpose of exploring ways of improving the schools and gaining an understanding of the goals and practices in other schools.

The success of the instructional program in the attainment of instructional goals lies at the heart of this accountability plan. Thus, concurrently with the development of the instructional program, the staff should begin exploring ways in which it will measure its success in achieving the goals of its school model.

Handling Transfer Requests

Just as parents will express preferences for one schooling model over another, it follows that they may change their minds about a particular model or a particular school and subsequently want their child transferred. Thus, a policy to govern transfer requests is necessary. Although the specifics of transfer problems may vary from district to district, the board might consider the following guidelines in developing a transfer policy.

1 It is undesirable to transfer a large percentage of the pupil enrollment of a single school within a short period of time. Thus, developed policy should determine the maximum percentage of student enrollment that can be transferred out of a given school during a given time period.

2   Although provisions may be necessary for emergency transfers, the transfer policy should establish a specific schedule for decisions on most transfer requests. It is suggested that such requests can receive the most complete review if decisions are scheduled to be made in the spring with the actual transfer to occur in the fall. This allows the district sufficient time to make decisions that optimize the possibility of maintaining enrollment balances and minimizing transportation distances.

3   A decision-making structure which defines clearly who will make what decisions in administering the transfer policy must be established. Because each transfer affects more than one principal, it is suggested that final transfer decisions be made by the central administration after appropriate conferences with the principals involved.

4   The transfer policy should also determine the decision-making model by which the variety of factors which might be considered in making individual transfer decisions are to be balanced. Suggested components of such a model include the order in which transfer requests are received, the number of previous transfers allowed the requesting parent, the reason for the transfer request (for example, convenience, displeasure with staff, or change of opinion concerning appropriate pedagogical model for child).

It can be expected that the transfer policy will be a very sensitive factor in the accountability plan. One anticipated source of difficulty will be those parents who are continually discontented with their children's schools and seek transfer after transfer. Hopefully such parents will be small in number. However, the transfer decision system should insure that the requests of such parents can be identified and dealt with separately from the requests of parents who seek only an occasional transfer, presumably after careful consideration. However, if a sufficiently large number of parents wish to transfer their children from a particular school, this may be indicative of some serious problem in the school. In such cases, the central administration should investigate the causes of discontent and determine what changes are necessary.

The Accountability Contract

The accountability contract is drawn up between the individual schools and the central administration. As the schools differ from one another in school models, so will the specifics of the individual accountability contracts. Nonetheless, each contract should specify:

1 The specific goals the school hopes to achieve. These goals can be both short term and long term. They can be in the form of substantive goals (for example, the pupils can read at given grade level) or process goals (for example, the pupils will have spent N hours in reading instruction).[19] They should include both activities and accomplishments of pupils, teachers, and administrators.

2 The ways the staff will determine if the goals have been achieved. The measuring devices should be both comprehensive and appropriate to the objectives. A variety of methods should be used. For example, standardized tests,[20] criterion-referenced tests,[21] and behavioral objectives[22] may be useful for determining pupil performance and growth. Attendance and tardiness records may be indicative of student attitudes and morale. Pupil-teacher classroom interaction patterns[23] may indicate both teaching style and student participation. Parental support, teacher attitudes, and a host of other success indicators may be examined through unobtrusive measures.[24]

3 A clear delineation of who will make the overall assessment of the school's success. Hopefully, each contract will include internal assessment (by teachers and administrators) and external assessment (by the central office, administrators and teachers from other schools or districts, parents, and outside experts).

The accountability contract for each school is negotiated with the central administration. It reviews each contract, and when both parties are satisfied, the contracts are submitted to the board for final approval. It is the responsibility of the central administration to monitor the individual contracts and to submit periodic progress reports to the board for its information. In turn, at specified times the board reports to the public on the schools' success in achieving their goals, as outlined in the accountability contracts.

Recycling

This accountability plan requires a continuing recycling of its various components. As some schools grow and demonstrate they are accountable, parents may seek to have their children enrolled in them or in similar programs. Other school models may go out of existence or be reduced in size as parental preferences change or as the schools fail to achieve specific goals.

This constant pulsating of school sizes in the district is the essence of a truly responsive and accountable school district. Individual school administrators and teachers will be in competition, not so much with other schools, but with themselves and their ability to achieve specified goals. Their success will rest on their ability to demonstrate that their school is seeking worthwhile educational goals, that the school has the means to achieve those goals, and that they, the school staff, can present proof of their success. The ultimate judge of their success will be the schools' clients—the parents. This is the essence of an accountable elementary school district.

ACKNOWLEDGMENTS

The material that appears in this chapter is the result of a series of discussions the author held with several of those who served as principals of the schools that constituted the |I|D|E|A| League of Cooperating Schools. In a very real sense this chapter is theirs. My role in this was to translate their discussions into a written document. I wish to express my thanks to them for their willingness to answer my persistent questions and to clarify my thinking about many things. The principals who were involved in these discussions and the schools they served were:

Mr. Henry Behrens
Edison Elementary School
Santa Monica Unified School District
Santa Monica, California 90401

Mr. Jarratt L. Brunson
Jefferson Elementary School
Pasadena City Schools
Pasadena, California 91106

Mr. Al Chudler
Sherman Oaks Elementary School
Los Angeles City Schools
Los Angeles, California 90054

Mr. Jack Conley
El Marino Elementary School
Culver City Unified School District
Culver City, California 90230

Mr. George Dearmin
McKinley Elementary School
Santa Barbara City Schools
Santa Barbara, California 93105

Mr. Lawrence S. Gritz
Chesterton Elementary School
San Diego City Schools
San Diego, California 92103

Mr. Harold Howarth, Jr.
Banyan Elementary School
Timber School District
Newbury Park, California 91320

Mr. William Johnson
Park View Elementary School
Simi Valley Unified School District
Simi, California 93065

Mr. Edmond A. Krucli
Stephen Foster Elementary School
Bellflower Unified School District
Bellflower, California 90706

Mr. Robert Lindstrom
Andres Arevalos Elementary School
Fountain Valley School District
Fountain Valley, California 92708

Mr. Monte McMurray
Oak Street Elementary School
Inglewood Unified School District
Inglewood, California 90301

Mr. Tom Phillian
Palm Elementary School
Riverside Unified School District
Riverside, California 92501

Mr. Hugh Ryan
Washington Elementary School
Corona Unified School District
Corona, California 91720

Mr. Earl W. Schauland
Fremont Elementary School
Delano Union School District
Delano, California 93215

Dr. Sol Spears
El Marino Elementary School
Culver City Unified School District
Culver City, California 90230

Mr. Maynard Strong
Loma Vista Elementary School
Lompoc Unified School District
Lompoc, California 93436

Mr. John Tate
Cucamonga Junior High School
Central School District
Cucamonga, California 91730

NOTES

1 The literature on accountability is very large and rapidly expanding. Many journals that specialize in education have devoted entire issues to the topic. Four comprehensive references are "8 Articles on Accountability," *Phi Delta Kappan*, December 1970; Leslie H. Browder, Jr., *Emerging Patterns of Administrative Accountability*, McCutchan Publishing, Berkeley, 1971; *Proceedings of the Conference on Educational Accountability*, Chicago, June 1971, sponsored by Educational Testing Service; Leon M. Lessinger, *Every Kid a Winner: Accountability in Education*, Simon and Schuster, New York, 1970.

2 For a comprehensive review of the present status of the use of these techniques in education, see M. C. Alkin and J. E. Bruno, "Systems Approaches to Educational Planning," in Philip K. Piele and Terry Eidell (eds.), *Social and Technological Change: Implication for Education*, The Center for the Advanced Study of Education, Eugene, Ore., 1970, pp. 191–244.

3 W. James Popham, *Criterion-Referenced Measurement*, Educational Technology Publications, Englewood Cliffs, New Jersey, 1971; Jason Millman, "Reporting Student Progress: A Case for a Criterion-Referenced Marking System," *Phi Delta Kappan*, December 1970.

4 This, too, has a large, growing literature. For some background on this topic see Robert Mager, *Preparing Instructional Objectives*, Fearon Publishers, Palo Alto, Calif., 1962; Paul D. Plowman, *Behavioral Objectives*, Science Research Associates, Chicago, 1971. For a very good review, see the entire issue of *Social Education*, May 1971.

5 See Christopher Jencks, "Giving Parents Money for Schooling," *Phi Delta Kappan*, September 1970, pp. 49–54; "Education Vouchers: Peril or Panacea," (Symposium) *Teachers College Record*, February 1971, pp. 327–404.

6 See J. Stenner, "Four Approaches to Education Performance Con-

tracts," *Educational Leadership,* April 1971, pp. 721–5; R. Martin and C. Blasche, "Contracting for Educational Reforms," *Phi Delta Kappan,* March 1971, pp. 403–6.

7   G. A. Killen, "Federal Aid to Private and Parochial Schools: An Analysis," *NASSP Bulletin,* September 1970, pp. 88–100; R. J. Huff, "Parochiaid: The Cry for Help Gets Louder," *Nation's Schools,* September 1969, pp. 16–24.

8   For a detailed discussion of this problem, see Anthony G. Oettinger, *Run, Computer, Run, The Mythology of Educational Innovation,* Harvard University Press, Cambridge, Mass., 1970; for a humorous but not farfetched discussion of one example of this problem, see Gary Saretsky, "Every Kid a Hustler," *Phi Delta Kappan,* June 1971, pp. 595–596.

9   Late in the 1970–71 school year, the outline of a plan somewhat similar to the one proposed in this chapter was published. See Mario Fantini, "Options for Students, Parents, and Teachers: Public Schools of Choice," *Phi Delta Kappan,* May 1971, pp. 541–543.

10   For a lucid discussion of the goals dilemma facing the schools, see Thomas F. Green, "Schools and Communities: A Look Forward," *Harvard Educational Review,* Spring 1969, pp. 221–252.

11   The controversy over sex education is a good example. There are many examples of school districts that have either dropped or substantially altered proposed sex education plans as a result of pressure from an outspoken minority of objecting parents.

12   This is not to say that the adoption of the rating system is the only force at work in bringing about change in movies; for example, technical developments in movie equipment have freed producers and directors from heavy reliance on the giant studio system and the compliance these studios demanded. With the development of independent studios, directors have been given flexibility and freedom to create.

13   For a detailed, excellent discussion of the relationship between school structure and change see Seymour B. Sarason, *The Culture of the Schools and the Problem of Change,* Allyn and Bacon, Boston, 1971.

14   Some may wish that it were otherwise; that is, the child is the client of the school, as has been more the case in British schools. For a discussion of the differences between the clientele in British and American schools, see Frank Musgrove and Philip H. Taylor, *Society and the Teacher's Role,* Routledge & Kegan Paul, London, 1969.

15   Sarason, op. cit. This volume contains a valuable discussion of the difficulties of changing systems that are already in existence.

16 Jencks, op. cit.

17 A technique such as the needs assessment KIT developed by the UCLA Center for the Study of Evaluation (CSE) would be very useful in assessing the kinds of schools described. For a description of the KIT, see *Evaluation Comment,* vol. 2, no. 3, September 1970.

18 Here the district may wish to utilize Program Planning and Budgeting Techniques (PPBS) as a means of assessing the relative costs of the school programs. Based on such data, an individualized budgeting system for each schooling model could be developed.

19 E. L. Lindman presents a cogent argument for the use of process goals rather than learning goals in adapting PPBS to the public schools. He asserts that the school should be accountable for the "scope and quality" of the educational services it offers. See B1–B8 in Educational Testing Services' *Proceedings of the Conference on Accountability,* op. cit.

20 For a particularly useful guide for schools seeking standardized tests to measure student achievement, see Center for the Study of Evaluation, *CSE Elementary School Test Evaluation,* UCLA Graduate School of Education, Los Angeles, Calif., 1970.

21 Popham, op. cit.

22 Mager, Plowman, op. cit.

23 Edmund J. Amidon and John B. Hough, *Interaction Analysis: Theory, Research, and Application,* Addison-Wesley, Reading, Mass., 1967.

24 Eugene Webb et al., *Unobtrusive Measures, Nonreactive Research in the Social Sciences,* Rand McNally, Chicago, 1966.

A BIBLIOGRAPHY ON THE PROCESS OF CHANGE

Lillian K. Drag

The current literature of change, as indicated in the following bibliography, is replete with "action" words: planning, strategies, models, roles, receptivity, resistance, innovating, facilitating, disseminating, decision making. It is hoped that this bibliography will encourage those who wish to take part in the change effort—to study the process of change and to plan for change in schools.

The bibliography has been arranged in three parts. Part I lists books and pamphlets, and Part II lists magazine articles and the League of Cooperating Schools films. Part III, which is not annotated, compiles additional references from the text.

Lillian Drag serves as curriculum and materials specialist to the Research Division of |I|D|E|A|.

* The first edition of this bibliography was published by the Institute for Development of Educational Activities, Inc., July, 1968.

PART I. BOOKS AND PAMPHLETS

Abbott, Max G., and John T. Lowell (eds.): *Change Perspectives in Educational Administration*, School of Education, Auburn University, Auburn, Ala., 1965.
Abbott's "Hierarchical Impediments to Innovation in Educational Organization" and Matthew Miles' "Education and Innovation: The Organization as a Context" are fruitful contributions.

Bennis, Warren G.: *Changing Organizations: Essay on the Development and Evolution of Human Organization*, McGraw-Hill, New York, 1966.
A significant contribution to the literature of change, bringing the reader up to date on action, writings, and thinking in this field. Chapter 3, "Toward a 'Truly' Scientific Management: The Concept of Organizational Health," offers a helpful analysis applicable to any organization. Part 2 describes attempts by behavioral scientists to apply their sociological and psychological knowledge toward improvement of organizations through planning and controlling organizational change. Includes discussion of planned change and "operations research," change agents, change programs, and strategies. Though emphasis is on industrial management, implications are obvious. Clarity of presentation makes the text easy to follow.

Bennis, Warren G., Kenneth D. Benne, and Robert Chin (eds.): *The Planning of Change*, Holt, Rinehart and Winston, New York, 1961.
A volume of readings stressing two aspects of planned change: the change agents and the clients' systems. The relationship established between the giver and receiver of help is considered basic to the outcome. "How well the process is understood by each and what degree of openness for examination and for possible reconstruction exists for both parties are, therefore, of central importance."

————: *The Planning of Change*, 2d ed., Holt, Rinehart and Winston, New York, 1969.
"Brings together some of the best current conceptualizations of different aspects of application and change process." Discusses and evaluates a growing body of change technologies. About nine-tenths of the readings in this edition are new.

Bennis, Warren G., and P. E. Slater: *The Temporary Society*, Harper & Row, New York, 1968.
Arguing that "democracy is inevitable" because it is the only system that can cope with changing demands of contemporary civilization, the authors see the tasks of education as teaching how to live with ambiguity, identifying the adaptive process, making a virtue out of contingency, and being self-directing. Especially valuable to administrators is Chapter 5, "New Patterns of Leadership for Adaptive Organi-

zations," with its emphasis on the concern for interpersonal relationships.

Bentzen, Mary M.: "A Comparison of Principals' and Teachers' Perceptions of Various Organizational Characteristics of Their Schools." Paper presented at the Annual Meeting of American Educational Research Association, Minneapolis, March 1970.

————: "A Peer Group Strategy for Intervention in Schools," Institute for Development of Educational Activities, Research Division, Los Angeles, July 1970 (mimeographed paper).

Both of these reports are based on the data derived from a cooperative research–school improvement project, the League of Cooperating Schools, in which eighteen elementary and intermediate schools were affiliated with the |I|D|E|A| Research Division, Los Angeles. The researchers studied processes of change in the school and intervened to encourage change.

Bentzen, Mary M., and Kenneth A. Tye: "Change: Problems and Prospects," The Elementary School in the United States, 72d Yearbook, Part II, National Society for the Study of Education, John I. Goodlad and Harold G. Shane (eds.), University of Chicago Press, Chicago, 1973, Chapter 14.

A review and synthesis of the accumulation of knowledge about the nature and use of change strategies. Despite these developments, the authors find few satisfying solutions to the problem of changing schools. Propose that schools be viewed as a social system, that they become self-renewing and that they "will either do it themselves or it won't get done."

Bhola, Harbans S.: Innovation Research and Theory, Ohio State University Press, Columbus, 1965.

Indicates that individuals and organizations show different characteristics as innovators and as adopters. In discussing educational change, terms are clarified, such as change agent, innovator, inventor, and adopter.

Brickell, Henry M.: "Two Change Strategies for Local School Systems," Rational Planning of Curriculum and Instruction, NEA Center for the Study of Instruction, Washington, 1967, pp. 135–153.

Elaborates on two strategies, one based on decision to invent a new instructional process, the other to adopt one invented elsewhere. Delineates conditions for each strategy which are practical enough to put into use in any school system committed to change.

Bridges, Edwin: The Role of the Elementary Principal in Innovation, Central Midwestern Regional Educational Laboratory, St. Ann, Mo., 1966.

Discusses the plan of action, rationale underlying this plan, what occurred during the seminar project, and the consequences.

Carlson, Richard O.: *Adoption of Educational Innovations,* Center for the Advanced Study of Educational Administration, University of Oregon, Eugene, 1965.
Sets forth three criteria affecting adoption: (1) the characteristics of the unit, (2) the way the adopting unit is joined to communication channels, and (3) the position the adopting unit holds in the social structure of like units. Interesting data are given on characteristics of innovators and unanticipated consequences associated with adoptions of educational innovations.

————: *Change Processes in the Public Schools,* Center for the Advanced Study of Educational Administration, University of Oregon, Eugene, 1965.
Report of a seminar of school officials and social scientists. Contains "Barriers to Change in Public Schools," by R. O. Carlson, "Planned Change and Organizational Health: Figure and Ground," by Matthew Miles, "The Place of Research in Planned Change," by R. J. Pellegrin, and "Directed Change in Formal Organizations: The School System," by Art Gallaher. Clinic sessions give attention to specific change problems encountered by school officials.

————: "Environmental Constraints and Organizational Consequences: The Public School and Its Clients," *Behavioral Science and Educational Administration,* Sixty-third Yearbook, Part II, National Society for the Study of Education, University of Chicago Press, Chicago, 1964, pp. 262–276.
A scholarly presentation which develops a typology of organization-client relationships in service organizations and then suggests some of the consequences and implications of the type of relationships clients have with public schools. Develops the notions of wild and domesticated organizations, proposing a method of dealing with change in them. Attends to the question "What mechanisms are used by public school systems to adapt to an unselected clientele?"

————: *Executive Succession and Organizational Change,* Midwest Administration Center, University of Chicago, Chicago, 1962.
Shows that insiders or place-bound successors are more limited in their influence on organizational change than are outsiders or career-bound successors. Points out characteristics of administrators who do and those who do not promote change.

Center for Coordinated Education: *Synergetics and the School: Strategies for School Improvement,* The Center, University of California, Santa Barbara, 1966.
Characterizes synergetics as cooperative interaction of various elements of a system. Takes the position that coordinated, participative action results in greater gains than separate unit efforts.

Charters, W. W., Jr., et al.: *Contrasts in the Process of Planned Change of the School's Instructional Organization,* program 20. The Center for the Advanced Study of Educational Administration, University of Oregon, Eugene, Ore., 1973.

A symposium prepared for the 1973 AERA Annual Meeting in New Orleans. Summarizes some of the findings of attempts made to implement staff organization plans at the "grass-root" level of school and school district. Identifies factors that served to hinder or facilitate implementation of innovations. Process view of change emphasized.

Chesler, Mark A. et al.: *Planning Educational Change, vol. 2, Human Resources in School Desegregation,* Department of Health, Education and Welfare (HEW), Washington, 1969.

Though addressing a specific problem (desegregation) and specific personnel (school superintendents), this manual outlines a process using planned steps: identification of goals, diagnosis of the situation, development of plans, feedback and evaluation, and a recycling step in which further goals are established for continuing change efforts. *Planning Educational Change, vol. 3, Integrating the Desegregated School,* Department of Health, Education and Welfare (HEW), Washington, 1970, discusses the principal as leader in the change process, Chapters 6–9.

Chin, Robert: "Models of and Ideas About Changing," *Media and Educational Innovation,* edited by Wesley C. Meierhenry, University of Nebraska, Lincoln, 1963, pp. 1–22.

Projects a five-category classification of change: substitution, alteration, perturbation and variation, restructuring, and value orientation change. Chin suggests three general change strategies: (1) the empirical-rational types, based on reason utilization; (2) the normative-reeducative types, based on attitude change; and (3) the power types, based on compliance.

Clark, David L.: "The Engineering of Change in Education," *Proceedings of the Conference on the Implementation of Educational Innovations,* Systems Development Corporation, Santa Monica, Calif., 1964, pp. 10–13.

Proposes a common terminology relating to processes necessary for change. Charts "Change in a Social Process Field," using defined vocabularly.

Clark, David L., and E. G. Guba: *Effecting Change in Institutions of Higher Education,* University Council of Educational Administration International Inter-Visitation Program, Columbus, Ohio, 1966.

Develops a logical structure describing the change process applicable to all levels of education. Identifies functions which appear to be necessary in effecting a program of planned change from development through diffusion.

————: "An Examination of Potential Change Roles in Education," *Rational Planning in Curriculum and Instruction,* National Education Association Center for the Study of Instruction, Washington, 1967, pp. 111–133.
Develops a logical structure for examining change roles in education. Divides the innovation process in four parts: research, development, diffusion, and adoption. Describes each stage in detail with recommendations for action.

Coffey, Hubert, and William Golden: "Psychology of Change Within an Institution," *In-Service Education for Teachers, Supervisors and Administrators,* Fifty-sixth Yearbook, Part I, National Society for the Study of Education, University of Chicago Press, Chicago, 1957, pp. 67–102. Looks at the person in relation to tension systems, differentiation, and isolation, as well as in direct communication with his environment. Discusses change in social systems, the concept of role, and characteristics of institutional groups. Cites major principles of institutional changes: two-way communication with continuous participation and feedback, and role differences between levels which create barriers to problem solving within a group and resistance to change within the individual.

Colgate University, Kettering Colgate Project: *A Study of Innovation and Change in Education: The Regional University-Schools Research and Development Program.* An Action-Research Project sponsored by the Charles F. Kettering Foundation and Colgate University, 1967–1971, Office of Educational Research, Colgate University, Hamilton, N.Y., 1971.
A detailed description of the action and the research elements of the project. Appendix E compares |I|D|E|A|'s League of Cooperating Schools, directed by John I. Goodlad, with this project.

Committee for Economic Development: *Innovation in Education: New Directions for the American School,* The Committee, 477 Madison Avenue, New York 10022, 1968.
A policy statement recommends (1) better organization of the schools for innovation and change; (2) increased emphasis on both basic and applied research and on dissemination of it; (3) utilization by school systems of cost-benefit and cost-effectiveness analysis; and (4) creation of a "National Commission on Research, Innovation, and Evaluation in Education." *The Schools and the Challenge of Change,* The Committee, New York, 1969, collects the papers from foremost educators which led to the recommendations cited above.

Congreve, Willard J.: "Implementing and Evaluating the Use of Innovations," *Innovation and Change in Reading Instruction,* Sixty-seventh Yearbook, Part II, National Society for the Study of Education, University of Chicago Press, Chicago, 1968, pp. 291–319.
Offers a "five-point rationale" for instituting desirable change: faculty commitment, resistance to current fads, continuous institutional self-study, awareness of innovative alternatives, responding sensibly to (sometimes resisting) outside pressure. Uses a case study in reading as an example of innovation and change.

Cooperative Project for Educational Development: See Goodwin Watson (ed.) in this section.

Corey, Stephen M.: *Helping Other People Change,* Ohio State University Press, Columbus, 1966 (Kappa Delta Pi Lecture Series).
Describes in personal style the role of the consultant in approaching the problem of producing desirable changes in the educational system in both the United States and India.

Cronbach, Lee J., and Patrick Suppes (eds.): *Research for Tomorrow's Schools: Disciplined Inquiry for Education,* Macmillan, New York, 1969.
Spells out the way to overcome the unproductiveness of present-day research with specific recommendations for research designed to result in genuine school improvement. Participants: the editors, James S. Coleman, Lawrence A. Cremin, John I. Goodlad, Calvin Gross, David M. Jackson, and Israel Scheffler.

Culbertson, Jack A.: *Organizational Strategies for Planned Change in Education,* University Council of Educational Administration, Columbus, Ohio, 1965.
Paper presented at the Conference on Strategies for Educational Change, Washington, November 1965. Proposes the creation of special organizational settings for stimulating and conducting programs of planned change.

Designing Education for the Future, An Eight-State Project: *Planning and Effecting Needed Changes in Education.* Reports Prepared for the Third Area Conference, The Project, Denver, 1967.
Available from Citation Press, New York. (See Edgar Morphet for annotation.)

Dill, William R.: "Decision-Making," *Behavioral Science and Educational Administration,* Sixty-third Yearbook, Part II, National Society for the Study of Education, University of Chicago Press, Chicago, 1964, pp. 199–222.
Pertinent discussion of the organizational environment, individuals as decision makers, and groups as decision makers. Suggests educators

take the lead in reporting new knowledge and innovations rather than relying on industry and government to provide ideas for action.

Eidell, Terry L., and Joanne M. Kitchel (eds.): *Knowledge Production and Utilization in Educational Administration,* University Council for Educational Administration and Center for the Advanced Study of Educational Administration, University of Oregon, Eugene, 1968.

Contributing authors Goldhammer, Guba, Havelock, and Schmuck focus on strategies for implementing change in educational organizations.

Fantini, Mario, and Gerald Weinstein: *Strategies for Initiating Educational Change in Large Bureaucratic School Systems,* Teachers College Press, Columbia University, New York, 1963.

A paper presented to Public Policy Institute, Teachers College, Columbia University, April 1963. Step-by-step description of change in a junior high school where two outside change agents worked with principals and teachers.

Goldhammer, Keith: *Issues and Strategies in the Public Acceptance of Educational Change,* Center for the Advanced Study of Educational Administration, University of Oregon, Eugene, 1965.

Delineates the factors affecting the public acceptance of change. Categories of factors are (1) the public's image of the advocate of change; (2) the public's image of the organization and the ends which it serves; (3) the public's view of the proposed changes; (4) the consequences of the proposed change with generally accepted values and recognized social needs; and (5) situational factors which facilitate or impede the acceptance of change.

Goodlad, John I.: "Educational Leadership—Meeting the Challenge of Change in Education," *Eleventh State-Wide Conference on Educational Leadership,* October 1966, Ohio State Department of Education, Columbus, 1967.

Poses questions about state educational bodies in reference to mechanisms for systematically examining education: to determine the "kinds of human beings" we wish to develop through the schools; to determine responsibilities at local, state, and federal levels; to study curricular innovations to determine how "projects" became "programs"; to develop viable innovations; to create and test previously untried innovations; and to assess the progress of education in the state.

Goodson, Max R.: "Nine Postulates Concerning Planned Educational Change." Reprinted from Occasional Paper No. 3, *Project MODELS,* Wisconsin Research and Development Center for Cognitive Learning, University of Wisconsin, Madison, 1966.

Uses diagrams to illustrate a conceptualization of the process of change. Figure 1 shows elevating and depressing factors affecting the level of educational opportunity. Figure 2 depicts centralized authority required for initiating change and decentralized authority for trying and evaluating innovations. Figure 3, "Three dimensions of planned educational change," and Figure 4, "Models for educational develop-ment," use remaining postulates in graphic way.

Griffiths, Daniel E.: *Administrative Theory*, Appleton-Century-Crofts, New York, 1959, pp. 98–102.
Describes a taxonomy of decision making to help executives initiate more creative decisions concerning change instead of simply respond-ing to pressure for change from others.

Gross, Neal, Joseph B. Giacquinta, and Marilyn Bernstein: *Implementing Organizational Innovations: A Sociological Analysis of Planned Educa-tional Change*, Basic Books, New York, 1971.
A telling account of an attempt to effect change in a school setting, with a searching analysis of factors which spelled success and failure.

Gross, Neal, and R. E. Herriott: *Staff Leadership in Public Schools: A Sociological Inquiry*, Wiley, New York, 1965.
Report a significant study on the efforts of elementary school prin-cipals to influence the behavior of teachers. Attempts to isolate de-terminants of the leadership efforts of elementary school principals. The principal as a change agent is also discussed.

Guba, Egon G.: *Methodological Strategies for Educational Change*, Uni-versity Council for Educational Administration, Columbus, Ohio, 1965.
Paper presented at the Conference on Strategies for Educational Change, Washington, November 1965. Author sees two general stra-tegies as available to an investigator: the experimental, manipulative, and interventionist; and the aexperimental, observational, and laissez-faire. He favors the latter for inquiry into educational change and ex-plains why. Same ideas are described in *SEC Newsletter*, vol. 1, July 1966, published by Ohio State University.

Guest, R. H.: *Organizational Change: The Effect of Successful Leadership*, Dorsey Press, Homewood, Ill., 1962.
Regular, judicious use of temporary systems (meetings, training ses-sions, and diagnostic conferences) brought about striking improve-ments in organizational effectiveness in this study.

Havelock, Ronald G., Janet C. Huber, and Shaindel Zimmerman: *A Guide to Innovation in Education*, Center for Research on the Utilization of Scientific Knowledge, University of Michigan, Ann Arbor, 1970.
Well-organized presentation of the development of the change pro-cess, delineating the steps clearly for the novice or practicing change agent in schools, with illustrative cases. May be useful at any level of

education. See also their *Major Works on Change in Education: An Annotated Bibliography with Author and Subject Indices,* The Center, Ann Arbor, 1969.

Havelock, Ronald G., and Alan Guskin: *Planning for Innovation through the Dissemination and Utilization of Knowledge,* Center for Research on the Utilization of Scientific Knowledge, University of Michigan, Ann Arbor, 1969.
A comprehensive analysis of the literature in the fields of mental health, agriculture, medicine, public health, law, business, and especially education. The authors draw upon social psychology, sociology, and communications science for their analytic framework, concluding with implications for further research and development.

Heathers, Glen: "Guidelines for Reorganizing the School and the Classroom," *Rational Planning in Curriculum and Instruction,* National Education Association Center for the Study of Instruction, Washington, 1967, pp. 63–86.
A section of this essay sketches out the steps a school system should take in preparing itself to design and conduct its own educational change programs.

Hemphill, John K., D. E. Griffiths, and N. Frederiksen: *Administrative Performance and Personality: A Study of the Principal in a Simulated Elementary School,* Bureau of Publications, Teachers College, Columbia University, New York, 1962.
Focus on administrative styles of 232 elementary-school principals, whose personal qualities were also studied. Chapter 8 describes a measure called "Organizational Change" which was developed as part of a scoring procedure in the study.

Hencley, Stephen P.: "Procedures in Effecting Change; Supplementary Statement," *Planning and Effecting Needed Changes in Education,* 3rd Area Conference Report of Designing Education for the Future; an Eight-State Project, Edgar L. Morphet and Charles O. Ryan (eds.), The Project, Denver, 1967, pp. 57–64.
Elaborates on Chin's three general change strategies as they relate to education: (1) empirical-rational, (2) normative-reeducative, and (3) power. Proposes appropriate recommendations for promoting educational change in the light of these.

Horvat, John J.: *Content and Strategies of Communication in Current Educational Change Efforts,* National Institute for the Study of Educational Change, Bloomington, Ind., 1967.
Presents a two-dimensional scheme for consideration of five content categories and five communication strategies. Finds that there is need to communicate more of the "hows" of educational change. Other

methods than the written word (such as training and involvement) are more effective in bringing about change.

Husén, Torsten: *Strategies of Educational Innovation*. Paper presented at the international conference on "The Changing Role of the Teacher" at the Padagogisches Zentrum in Berlin, Oct. 30, 1968 (mimeographed). Discusses how to bring basic research to general adoption, listing four ways to accomplish this. Feels that significant innovations and persisting changes in education ought to represent adequate responses to fundamental changes in culture and society. See also his *Educational Research and Educational Change*, Wiley, New York, 1967.

Institute for Development of Educational Activities: *The Principal and the Challenge of Change*, edited by Jerrold M. Novotney, |I|D|E|A|, Dayton, Ohio, 1968.
Examines problems reported by a group of elementary school principals when they attempted to initiate change in their schools. Discusses educational change in a systems framework, leadership behavior, dynamics of group interaction, and the role of the principal.

————: *Tell Us What to Do! But Don't Tell Me What to Do!*, |I|D|E|A|, Dayton, Ohio, 1971.
"Changing teachers talk about themselves" as participants in the League of Cooperating Schools' Study of Educational Change conducted by the |I|D|E|A| Research Division. Frustrations and feelings of accomplishment are spelled out from the planning stages, through the five years of the project, to the final stages.

Jasinski, Frank: "The Change Process," *Proceedings of the Conference on the Implementation of Educational Innovations*, Systems Development Corporation, Santa Monica, Calif., 1964, pp. 13–15.
Outlines common elements in innovational situations, summarizes six points for planned change. Also succinctly states necessary personal understandings and behaviors basic to innovation.

Katz, Daniel, and R. L. Kahn: *The Social Psychology of Organizations*, Wiley, New York, 1966.
Discuss the behavior of people in organizations based on "open-system theory," which is carefully defined. In Chapter 13, seven approaches to organizational change are considered: information, individual counseling and therapy, peer-group influence, sensitivity training, group therapy, survey feedback, and direct systematic change. Very readable.

Kimbrough, Ralph B.: *Administering Elementary Schools: Concepts and Practices*, Macmillan, New York, 1968.
The author thinks that many principals do not feel that the consequences of initiating instructional change are worth the effort because

of difficult social problems. He proposes a mode of thinking about human behavior that is fused with knowledge of operational management. He sees each elementary school as a social system that is unique and suggests ways of thinking about particular administrative setups, describing types of community power structures, organizational climates of individual schools, and varying personnel characteristics.

————: "Community Power Structure and Curriculum Change," *Strategy for Curriculum Change*, Robert R. Leeper (ed.), Association for Supervision and Curriculum Development, NEA, Washington, 1965, pp. 55–71.

What is the nature of power structures in local school districts? Who is likely to wield power affecting innovations? Why do power wielders make decisions? Kimbrough attacks these questions to encourage educators to use the local power structure in innovation.

————: "Power Structures and Educational Change," *Planning and Effecting Needed Changes in Education*, Third Area Conference Report of Designing Education for the Future: An Eight-State Project, edited by Edgar L. Morphet and Charles O. Ryan, The Project, Denver, 1967, pp. 115–136.

More detailed presentation than previous article. See also the author's book, *Political Power and Educational Decision-Making*, Rand McNally, Chicago, 1964.

Klein, Donald C.: *Dynamics of Resistance to Change: The Defender Role*, Boston University Human Relations Center, Boston, 1966.

Points out that the resistor role in change situations has the positive function of testing and evaluating the proposed change in terms of the accepted values of the system.

Kreitlow, Burton W., and Teresa MacNeil: *Evaluation of the Model for Educational Improvement as an Analytical Tool for Describing the Change Process*, Wisconsin Research and Development Center for Cognitive Learning, University of Wisconsin, Madison, 1969.

Report from the Project on Models for Effecting Planned Educational Change.

Lipham, James M.: "Leadership and Administration," *Behavioral Science and Educational Administration*, Sixty-third Yearbook, Part II, National Society for the Study of Education, University of Chicago Press, Chicago, 1964, pp. 119–141.

Sees leadership as the initiation of new structure for accomplishing an organization's goals and administration as utilizing existing structures to achieve an existing goal.

Lippitt, Ronald: "Roles and Processes in Curriculum Development and Change," *Strategy for Curriculum Change*, edited by Robert R. Leeper,

Association for Supervision and Curriculum Development, NEA, Washington, 1965, pp. 11–28.

Identifies five models of curriculum development process, particularly sources of influence toward change. Looks at professional roles and teamwork needed, as well as the ferment in education today.

Lippitt, Ronald, Jeanne Watson, and Bruce Westley: *Dynamics of Planned Change,* Harcourt, Brace & World, New York, 1958.

Discuss aspects of change and various types of professional workers concerned with it: change agents, the client system, change forces, phases of change, and methods of change.

Lonsdale, Richard C.: "Maintaining the Organization in Dynamic Equilibrium: Organizational Change," *Behavioral Science and Educational Administration,* Sixty-third Yearbook, Part II, National Society for the Study of Education, University of Chicago Press, Chicago, 1964, pp. 174–176.

A few pages which make the important point that organizations should strive to develop a favorable orientation toward change, a willingness to change, and a readiness for change.

Loomis, Charles P.: *Social Systems; Essays on Their Persistence and Change,* Van Nostrand, Princeton, 1960.

The author developed the conceptualized social system as a basic research model for the analysis of social phenomena possessing extreme change potentials. He applies the research model to variously derived data in a series of essays (case studies).

Macdonald, James B.: "Helping Teachers Change," *Eleventh Curriculum Research Institute,* Association for Supervision and Curriculum Development, NEA, Washington, 1966, pp. 1–10.

Points out the effect of the social system upon individual behavior, indicating that "the administrator symbolizes the setting and is the focal point for teacher observation and perception of the system." Notes that the knowledge about and enthusiasm for new practices on the part of the leadership personnel are probably the most significant factors in the environment. Delineates other conditions for change: developing supporting climate, providing reality testing procedures, developing ways of thinking with values throughout the "clarification" process.

March, James G. (ed.): *Handbook of Organizations,* Rand McNally, Chicago, 1965.

A comprehensive reference work which examines specific institutions such as schools in their organizational context. Chapters also deal with "Decision Making and Problem Solving," "Influence, Leadership, Control," and "Changing Interpersonal and Intergroup Relationships in Organizations."

McClelland, William A.: *The Process of Effecting Change,* Human Resources Research Office, The George Washington University, Alexandria, Va., 1968.
A helpful overview of definitions, what we know about change, problems in educational change, and change strategies. Summarizes some of the relevant literature.

Meierhenry, W. C. (ed.): *Media and Educational Innovation,* University of Nebraska Press, Lincoln, 1964.
A symposium on identifying techniques and principles for gaining acceptance of research results. It includes contributions by Art Gallaher, "The Role of the Advocate and Directed Change"; Paul Meadows, "Novelty and Acceptors: A Sociological Consideration of the Acceptance of Change"; Wayman Crow, "Characteristics of Leaders Who Are Able to Promote Change"; et al.

Miles, Matthew B. (ed.): *Innovation in Education,* Bureau of Publications, Teachers College, Columbia University, New York, 1964.
A basic reference for the study of change, especially these chapters: "Educational Innovation: The Nature of the Problem" by Matthew Miles; "Title III and the Dynamics of Educational Change in California" by Donald W. Johnson; "Curricular Change: Participants, Power, and Processes" by Gordon Mackenzie; "Administrative Theory and Change in Organizations" by Daniel E. Griffiths; "On Temporary Systems" and "Innovation in Education: Some Generalizations" by Matthew Miles.

Miller, Richard I. (ed.): *Perspectives on Educational Change,* Appleton-Century-Crofts, New York, 1967.
Focuses on the process of change proceeding from the general to the specific, looking at the theoretical and research aspects with case studies on actual situations. Chapter 10, "How the Lulu Walker School Came About," by Evelyn Carswell; Chapter 11, "Garden Springs Elementary School," by Raymond Wilkie; and Chapter 12, by Ruth Chadwick and Robert Anderson, "The School Reorganization Project in Newton, Mass." reveal graphically how change came about in specific elementary schools. Glen Heather's chapter on "Influencing Change at the Elementary Level" examines in a more general, but extremely useful, way how well innovations are being used to serve new educational aims.

Morphet, Edgar L., and Charles O. Ryan (eds.): *Planning and Effecting Needed Changes in Education,* Third Area Conference Report of Designing Education for the Future: An Eight-State Project, The Project, Denver, 1967.
Useful papers include Kenneth Hansen's "Planning for Changes in

Education," Robert Chin's "Basic Strategies and Procedures in Effecting Change," Robert Howsam's "Effecting Needed Change in Education," Ralph Kimbrough's "Power Structures and Educational Change," Don Glines' "Planning and Effecting Needed Changes in Individual Schools."

Novotney, Jerrold M., and Kenneth A. Tye: *The Dynamics of Educational Leadership,* 2d ed., Educational Resource Associates, Inc., Los Angeles, 1973.

Discuss the concept of leadership, its dimensions, various styles of leaders, the tools of leadership and relationships in working with groups. Develop the conceptual framework for such work emphasizing the importance of knowledge of human beings and principle of human interaction.

O'Connell, Jeremiah: *Managing Organizational Innovation,* Richard D. Irwin, Homewood, Ill., 1968.

Although written about insurance company organization, this study is applicable to making effective change agents out of principals. Chapter 7, "The Planning of Change," discusses role, focus, and intervention strategy as well as key elements and deviation in plans. Chapter 8, "The Control of Change," points up the need for behavior and performance measures, diagnosis of the existing situation, a monitoring system, and data to express validity of changed behavior.

Owens, Robert G.: *Organizational Behavior in Schools,* Prentice-Hall, Englewood Cliffs, N.J., 1970.

Attempts to provide the school administrator with information to enable him to gain new behavioral knowledge and use it in coping with professional problems; Chapter 5, "Decision Making"; Chapter 6, "Leadership in the School"; Chapter 7, "Change in an Organizational Setting."

Pellegrin, Roland J.: "An Analysis of Sources and Processes of Innovation in Education," Center for the Advanced Study of Educational Administration, University of Oregon, Eugene, 1966.

A paper presented at the Conference on Educational Change, Allerton Park, Ill., February 1966, which discusses the existing and potential sources of educational innovations, the conditions under which innovations can occur, and the changes that must be made in order to tie together knowledge and practice.

Peterson, Barbara et al.: "Innovation in Education." Unpublished paper prepared for the Education 246B, Administration of Elementary Education, Graduate School of Education, University of California, Los Angeles, 1966.

A valuable presentation on change if you see innovation as the idea and the acceptance of the idea of change. Paper compiles data relative to the ability of the innovator to bring about change: Chapter 1, "Institutional and Organizational Change"; Chapter 2, "Environment for Change"; Chapter 3, "Problems of Implementation"; Chapter 4, "Innovators and Change Agents."

Rogers, Everett M.: *Diffusion of Innovations,* Free Press of Glencoe, New York, 1962.

Shows that traditional versus modern orientations in a particular community or subculture affect adoption rates markedly. Greater personal innovativeness is associated with "cosmopoliteness" (the result of experience in more than one social system). Emphasizes the characteristics of inventions that made them more or less acceptable, such as relative advantage, compatibility, complexity, divisibility, and communicability. Lists stages in adoption: awareness, interest, evaluation, trial, and adoption.

————: "Toward a New Model for Educational Change," University Council for Educational Administration, Columbus, Ohio, 1965.

Paper presented at the Conference on Strategies for Educational Change, Washington, November 1965.

Rogers, Everett M., and F. Floyd Shoemaker: *Communication of Innovations: A Cross-Cultural Approach,* Free Press, New York, 1971.

In this second edition of Rogers' *Diffusion of Innovations* the focus is on the informal social group and the formally organized system rather than the individual as an innovator. Relates concepts of diffusion research to those of organizational change stating that "social change is an effect of communication."

Sarason, Seymour B.: *Creation of Settings and the Future Societies,* Jossey-Bass, San Francisco, 1972.

Examines the processes and problems common to the creation of settings ("any instance when two or more people come together in new and sustained relationships"). Draws upon personal participation in the creation of new settings in education and other fields to describe and analyze failures and successes. Social systems, socialization, and leadership are examined.

————: *The Culture of the School and the Problem of Change,* Allyn and Bacon, Boston, 1971.

The author uses the ecological approach to describe the school setting, revealing what everyday school life is like. He feels that the examination of "the regularities" of behavior and programs to determine patterns is more significant in trying to effect change than the imposition of an innovation. His two detailed case reports of the process of change reveal such patterns.

Saunders, Robert L., R. C. Phillips, and H. T. Johnson: *A Theory of Educational Leadership,* Merrill, Columbus, Ohio, 1966.

Delineate the role of the local school in decision making. Propose a design for implementing the theory described and evaluating cooperative programs of instructional improvement. Outline necessary conditions and anticipated outcomes of putting the theory into action.

Schein, Edgar H., and W. G. Bennis: *Personal and Organizational Change through Group Methods,* Wiley, New York, 1965.

Develop a three-stage temporal theory of change in which the T-group laboratory has an initial "unfreezing" effect on the individual, creating a need for change. A period of search and experimentation follows during which behavioral change actually takes place. This is followed by refreezing of behaviors due to counter forces generated within or external to the person who opposes the change.

Schmuck, Richard A., et al.: *Handbook of Organization Development in Schools.* Prepared at the Center for the Advanced Study of Educational Administration, University of Oregon, Eugene, 1972.

"This handbook is a guide to planned actions for facilitating human responsiveness and adaptability in school organizations."—Preface

Schmuck, Richard A., and Matthew Miles (eds.): *Organization Development in Schools,* National Press Books, Palo Alto, Calif., 1971.

Presents the rationale behind OD, the problems encountered in OD research, and the effects of OD on specific organizations where it has been employed.

Smith, Louis M., and Pat M. Keith: *Anatomy of Educational Innovation,* Wiley, New York, 1971.

An ecological study of attempted change in a single school with the process of change closely examined.

Tye, Kenneth A.: "Creating Impact." Unpublished paper. |I|D|E|A| Research Division, Los Angeles, 1967.

Examines much of the research and theory dealing with small groups. Relates findings to the process of dissemination of educational innovations.

University City, Mo. School District: *The Comprehensive Project for Improvement in Learning,* edited by Glenys G. Unruh, July 1966.

A report to the Ford Foundation based on a strategy of program change attacking three fronts simultaneously: restructuring organization, modernizing curriculum, and releasing human dynamics. Outlines an envisioned school system contrasted with present conditions. Discusses, briefly, problems of the change process.

Watson, Goodwin (ed.): *Change in School Systems,* NEA, Washington, 1967.
Papers published for the Cooperative Project for Educational Development by National Training Laboratories, NEA, which focus attention on processes of the schools and on strategies designed to test and develop the core ideas outlined in companion volume, *Concepts for Social Change.* Matthew Miles, "Some Properties of Schools as Social Systems"; Charles C. Jung, Robert Fox, and Ronald Lippitt, "An Orientation and Strategy for Working on Problems of Change in School Systems"; et al.

————: *Concepts for Social Change,* NEA, Washington, 1967.
Working papers which develop the core ideas about planned change to give direction to the Cooperative Project for Educational Development (COPED). Paul C. Buchanan, "The Concept of Organization Development, or Self-Renewal as a Form of Planned Change"; Goodwin Watson, "Resistance to Change"; Donald Klein, "Some Notes on the Dynamics of Resistance to Change: The Defender Role"; et al.

Wiles, Kimball: "Contrasts in Strategies of Change," *Strategy for Curriculum Change,* Association for Supervision and Curriculum Development, NEA, Washington, 1965, pp. 1–10.
Allocates such functions as basic research, field testing, and evaluation to agencies outside the school system and states that innovation occurs outside the school system. Diffusion and integration occur within the system.

Woods, Thomas E.: *The Administration of Educational Innovation,* Bureau of Educational Research, University of Oregon, Eugene, 1967.
A school superintendent reviews sophisticated behavioral science research for the school practitioner in concise and understandable fashion. Based on the assumption that before the administrator can develop skills to manage programs of change, he must have some knowledge of aspects of change and consequences ensuing from different change strategies. Embodied in this brief pamphlet are many of the ideas presented in Miles' book, *Innovations in Education.*

Yates, Alfred (ed.): *The Role of Research in Educational Change,* Pacific Books, Palo Alto, Calif., 1971.
Report of 1967 international meeting of experts from fourteen countries sponsored by UNESCO Institute for Education, Hamburg. Part I includes chapters on the process of change, methodology, and recommendations.

PART II. PERIODICALS AND FILMS

Periodicals

Abbott, Max G.: "The School as a Social System: Indicators for Change," *Socio-Economic Planning Science,* vol. 1, 1969, pp. 167–174, Pergamon, Great Britain.

Spells out some of the organizational properties that enable the school to assess accurately new demands and to adjust appropriately to them. Propositions and hypotheses suggested here are based on current organizational theory supported in part by empirical research conducted in nonschool organizations.

Bridges, Edwin M.: "A Model for Shared Decision-Making in the School Principalship," *Educational Administration Quarterly,* vol. 3, Winter 1967, pp. 49–61.

Discusses some crucial questions that principals should consider in sharing decisions with teaching staffs: conditions under which it seems appropriate, the steps of the decision-making process in which participation is possible, the ways to constitute the group, and the role of the principal to assure quality decisions.

Bridges, Edwin M., and L. B. Reynolds: "Teacher Receptivity to Change," *Administrator's Notebook,* vol. 16, February 1968.

Examine the effect of the "teacher's belief system" on receptivity to change and question the validity of the "experience equals inflexibility" judgment applied to more experienced teachers.

Chesler, Mark, Ronald Lippitt, and Richard Schmuck: "The Principal's Role in Facilitating Change," *Theory Into Practice,* vol. 2, December 1963, pp. 269–277.

Suggest need for the principal to secure information about staff relationships through discussion and to be sensitive to indications of his success in these relationships. Teachers need to feel new practice could help solve their problems and would be easily adaptable to their situation.

Cunningham, Luvern L.: "Viewing Change in School Organizations," *Administrator's Notebook,* vol. 11, September 1962.

Develops four major concepts instrumental in effecting change: social system, change agent, diagnosis, and intervention.

Dalin, Per: "Planning for Change in Education: Qualitative Aspects of Educational Planning," *International Review of Education,* vol. 16, 1970, pp. 436–449.

Describes briefly some major strategies for change (from Havelock);

discusses present concepts of planning for educational change; and specifes particular changes we need to plan for: curriculum and educational structures.

Downey, Lawrence W.: "Direction Amid Change," *Phi Delta Kappan*, vol. 42, February 1961, pp. 186–192.
Gives a model for the study of change in the educational setting. Offers criteria to examine, to evaluate, and to anticipate the consequences of change.

————: "Organizational Theory as a Guide to Educational Change," *Educational Theory*, vol. 11, January 1961, pp. 38–44.
Identifies a series of procedures for change in public schools along five dimensions: cultures, politicoeconomic environments, institutions, individuals, and informal groups. Uses the "organization equilibrium concept" in his theory of change. Useful to principal in developing awareness of the change process in his school.

Educational Leadership, vol. 25, no. 4, January 1968.
This issue focuses on change and examines some of the approaches that have been tried in innovation. Richard Foster's article, "The Search for Change," proposes that if a school system is open, the setting is then available for a variety of approaches. Egon Guba offers techniques for better diffusion of innovations. Ralph Purdy summarizes factors which appear to limit or facilitate innovational practice. Other articles deal with criteria for evaluation and impact of innovations.

————, vol. 27, no. 4, January 1970.
Theme articles on "Sharing in Change" include Luvern Cunningham's "Community Involvement in Change," Richard Miller's "Kinds of Change," and Samuel Mangione's "Bringing Perspective to the Change Situation."

Eicholz, Gerhard C.: "Why Do Teachers Reject Change?" *Theory Into Practice*, vol. 2, December 1963, pp. 264–268.
Presents a framework to help the change agent identify forms of rejection and select strategies to introduce change successfully. Delineates forms of rejection, causes of rejection, state of subject, and anticipated response.

Goodlad, John I.: "Educational Change: A Strategy for Study and Action," *The National Elementary Principal*, vol. 48, January 1969, pp. 6–13.
Describes the creation of the League of Cooperating Schools in Southern California as an effort by the |I|D|E|A| Research Division to study educational change and improve schools. He develops the rationale behind it and the research effort accompanying it.

Griffiths, Daniel E.: "The Elementary School Principal and Change in the School System," *Theory Into Practice*, vol. 2, December 1963, pp. 278–284.

Reports a study of administrative performance conducted in 1962 measuring 232 principals on the extent to which they introduced or considered the introduction of change as they dealt with a variety of simulated educational problems. Finding: elementary school principal seldom introduces a new idea into the school system. Shows that sanctions from board of education, superintendent, parents, and community are necessary corollary to innovation.

Hansen, Kenneth H.: "Design for Decision," *NASSP Bulletin*, vol. 51, November 1967, pp. 105–113.

Expresses disenchantment with global "models" of the change process. Selects four ideas which *do* merit attention: the concept of problem diagnosis, points of entry and leverage, temporary systems, and management of conflict. Advocates structuring for change, built-in evaluation, situational decision making, and administrative style in policy forming.

Howes, Virgil M.: "A Strategy for Research and Change: The League of Cooperating Schools," *Childhood Education*, vol. 44, September 1967, pp. 68–69.

Describes briefly the creation of an educational laboratory for experimentation and research with a network for communication and a facility for field testing and demonstrating innovations.

|I|D|E|A| *Reporter*, Fall Quarter, 1969.

This issue on "Change" contains articles by John Goodlad, "Studying and Effecting Educational Change"; Mary M. Bentzen, "Study of Educational Change and School Improvement"; and others from the |I|D|E|A| Research Division involved in the change program.

Kowitz, Gerald T.: "The Change and Improvement of School Practices," *Phi Delta Kappan*, vol. 42, February 1961, pp. 216–219.

Makes the point that improvement based upon the willingness of the administrator to examine his operations can result in a gradual, evolutionary improvement. Offers a model to assess educational change.

————: "Examining Educational Innovations—Part II," *American School Board Journal*, vol. 148, January 1964, pp. 17–19.

Knowledge of specific goals, as well as underlying assumptions, of the innovation and their possibility of fulfillment are essential before change takes place.

Lortie, Dan C.: "Change and Exchange: Reducing Resistance to Innovation," *Administrator's Notebook*, vol. 12, February 1964.

Argues that social scientific analysis, using the concepts of latent function and exchange, can help the administrator to anticipate and deal with resistance to change.

Miller, Richard I. (ed.): "A Multidisciplinary Focus on Educational Change," *Bulletin of the Bureau of School Services,* vol. 38, December 1965.

Reports the 1965 Midwest Regional Conference of Elementary Principals with Robert Chin's "Change and Human Relations," D. A. Booth's "Change and Political Realities," and C. M. Coughenour's "Change and Sociological Perspectives." The latter discusses the role of the principal in change, stressing the general problems of orientation to change and adaptability, as well as the problems of organization and implementation.

Myers, Donald A.: "The Principal as a Procedural Administrator," *National Elementary School Principal,* vol. 47, February 1968, pp. 25–29.

Suggests that the role of the principal is to assist teachers in their efforts to make rational decisions by following appropriate procedures and using criteria developed at the institutional level. The principal must also keep abreast of developments in the field, gather resource ideas, know available educational resources, and exercise good judgment when facing alternatives.

Novotney, Jerrold M.: "How to Manage Change," *American School Board Journal,* vol. 155, December 1967, pp. 25–26.

Suggests a model for implementing change based on assumptions that the principal can be the change agent and that he has recognized need for change. See also his "The Principal: The Key to Educational Change," *Catholic School Journal,* vol. 68, February 1968, pp. 68–73.

Rogers, Everett M.: "What Are Innovators Like?" *Theory Into Practice,* vol. 2, December 1963, pp. 252–256.

Innovators seek new ideas from impersonal sources such as university research and are cosmopolite in social relations, forming cliques including other innovators.

Thelen, Herbert A.: "New Practices on the Firing Line," *Administrator's Notebook,* vol. 12, January 1964.

Describes three major phases of change: enthusiasm, vulgarization and spread, and institutionalization. Discusses assessment of change briefly.

Theory Into Practice: vol. 5, no. 1, February 1966.

The issue opens with a discussion of need for planned change. Articles on the study of change as a concept are followed by several on the effect of planned change—on the classroom, on the local school, on national agencies, etc.

Walton, Richard E.: "Two Strategies of Social Change and Their Dilemmas," *Journal of Applied Behavioral Science*, vol. 1, Spring 1965, pp. 167–179.

Two strategies, involving power tactics on the one hand and attitude change activities on the other, are analyzed, showing that the methods of achieving and employing power are detrimental to the methods of achieving more friendliness and trust, and vice versa. Discusses ways group leaders attempt to cope with and sometimes integrate the two strategies into a broader strategy of social change.

Watson, Goodwin, and Edward M. Glaser: "What We Have Learned About Planning for Change," *Management Review Magazine*, vol. 54, November 1965, pp. 34–46.

An article in response to the question, "How can we implement change in ways that preserve and enhance human dignity?" Offers an outline of steps including the identification of problems, the generation of proposals to solve problems, the scheduling of resources needed and available, and the effecting and maintaining of change. Stresses knowledgeable leadership in planning and direction, the importance of staff involvement, organizational climate, desirability of pilot programs, and the need to be aware of side effects.

Willower, Donald J.: "Educational Change and Functional Equivalents," *Education and Urban Society*, vol. 2, August 1970, pp. 385–402.

"Approaches to innovation direct attention away from social system considerations." Contends that the school displays an array of structures that are functional for the organization and its adult personnel but dysfunctional or neutral for pupils. Functional equivalents or alternatives are suggested after analysis of social structures, roles, and social norms.

Films

Institute for Development of Educational Activities: *The League.* |I|D|E|A|, Melbourne, Fla., 1971.

Film reports on |I|D|E|A| Research Division's Study of Educational Change in cooperation with the League of Cooperating Schools in Southern California. Part I: The Strategy; Part II: A Matter of Trust; Part III: Try It Sometime; Part IV: I Just Wanted to Let You Know How Well Rhonda is Doing in School. Also, three excerpts: Case History of a Teaching Team; Staff Meeting; Why Visit Another School?

PART III. ADDITIONAL REFERENCES FROM THE TEXT

Books and Pamphlets

Accountability: Review of Literature and Recommendations for Implementation, North Carolina Department of Public Instruction, Divisions of Planning, Research and Development, May 1972.

Alkin, M. C., and J. E. Bruno: "Systems Approaches to Educational Planning," *Social and Technological Change: Implication for Education,* edited by Philip K. Piele and Terry Eidell, The Center for the Advanced Study of Education, Eugene, Ore., 1970, pp. 191–244.

Allen, Dwight: "Putting Teaching Talent to Work," *Educational Manpower: From Aides to Differentiated Staff Patterns,* edited by James L. Olivero and Edward G. Buffie, Bold New Venture, Indiana University Press, Bloomington, 1970, p. 17.

Amidon, Edmund J., and John B. Hough: *Interaction Analysis: Theory, Research, and Application,* Addison-Wesley, Reading, Mass., 1967.

Anderson, Robert H.: "Preparing Staffs for Working Together," Chapter 6, unpublished manuscript, Harvard University, 1970.

Bales, Robert F.: "The Equilibrium Problem in Small Groups," *Working Papers in the Theory of Action,* edited by Talcott Parsons, R. F. Bales, and A. Shils, The Free Press, Glencoe, Ill., 1953, pp. 111–161.

Bendiner, Robert: *The Politics of Schools,* Harper & Row, New York, 1969.

Bentzen, Mary M., and Associates: *Changing Schools: The Magic Feather Principle,* McGraw-Hill, New York, in press.

Bernabei, Raymond: "Instructional Accountability," paper presented to the Mid-Atlantic Interstate Project Conference on Educational Accountability, New York, Feb. 10, 1972.

Bidwell, Charles: "The School as a Formal Organization," *Handbook of Organizations,* edited by James March, Rand McNally, Chicago, 1965.

Blake, Robert R., Herbert A. Shephard, and Jane S. Mouton: *Managing Intergroup Conflict in Industry,* Gulf, Houston, 1964.

Borg, Walter R., et al.: *The Minicourse: A Microteaching Approach to Teacher Education,* Macmillan Educational Services, Beverly Hills, 1970.

Boyan, Norman J.: "The Emergent Role of the Teacher and the Authority Structure of the School," *Collective Negotiations and Educational Administration,* edited by Roy B. Allen and John Schmid, University of Arkansas Press, Fayetteville, 1966.

Browder, Leslie H., Jr.: *Emerging Patterns of Administrative Accountability,* McCutchan Publishing, Berkeley, Calif., 1971.

Browne, C. G., and Thomas Cohn: *The Study of Leadership*, The Interstate Printers & Publishers, Danville, Ill., 1958.

Campbell, D. T., and J. C. C. Stanley: *Experimental and Quasi-experimental Designs for Research*, Rand McNally, Chicago, 1967.

Center for the Study of Evaluation: *CSE Elementary School Test Evaluation*, University of California, Los Angeles Graduate School of Education, Los Angeles, 1970.

Christie, Samuel, Adrianne Bank, Carmen M. Culver, Gretchen McCann, and Roger Rasmussen: *The Problem Solving School*, Institute for Development of Educational Activities, Dayton, Ohio, 1973.

Cornell, Terry D.: *Performance and Process Objectives*, Educational Innovators Press, Tucson, Ariz., 1970.

Cuban, Larry: "Teaching the Children: Does the System Help or Hinder?", *Freedom, Bureaucracy and Schooling*, Association for Supervision and Curriculum Development, NEA, Washington, 1971, p. 160.

Dashiell, Dick: "Lessons from Detroit and Cleveland," *Collective Negotiations in Public Education*, edited by Stanley M. Elam, Myron Lieberman, and Michael H. Moskow, Rand McNally, Chicago, 1967.

Donovan, Bernard: "Speaking for Management," *Collective Negotiations in Public Education*, edited by Stanley M. Elam, Myron Lieberman, and Michael H. Moskow, Rand McNally, Chicago, 1967.

Elseroad, Homer O.: "Professional Negotiations in Montgomery County," *The Collective Dilemma: Negotiations in Education*, edited by Patrick W. Carlton and Harold I. Goodwin, Charles A. Jones, Worthington, Ohio, 1969.

Etzioni, Amitai: *A Comparative Analysis of Complex Organizations*, Free Press of Glencoe, New York, 1961.

Farquahar, Robin, et al.: *Educational Leadership and School Organization in the 1970's*. American Educational Research Association symposium papers, Minneapolis, Mar. 4, 1970.

Forsberg, James R.: *Accountability and Performance Contracting*, ERIC Clearinghouse on Educational Management, Eugene, Ore., 1971.

Frank, Lawrence K.: *How To Be a Modern Leader*, Association Press, New York, 1954.

Gans, Thomas G.: "Teacher Militancy, the Potential for It, and Perceptions of School Organizational Structure," paper presented at the Annual Meeting of the American Educational Research Association, Chicago, April 1972.

Gardner, John: *Self-Renewal*, Harper & Row, New York, 1964.

Goodlad, John I., and R. H. Anderson: *The Nongraded Elementary School*, Harcourt, Brace & World, New York, 1963.

Goodlad, John I., Renata von Steophasius, and M. Frances Klein: *The Changing School Curriculum,* Fund for the Advancement of Education, New York, 1966.

Goodlad, John I., M. Frances Klein, and Associates: *Behind the Classroom Door,* Charles A. Jones, Worthington, Ohio, 1970.

Goodlad, John I., M. Frances Klein, Jerrold M. Novotney, and Associates: *Early Schooling in the United States,* McGraw-Hill, New York, 1973.

Goldhammer, Robert: *Clinical Supervision: Special Methods for the Supervision of Teachers,* Holt, Rinehart & Winston, New York, 1969.

Golembrewski, R. J., and A. Blumberg (eds.): *Sensitivity Training and the Laboratory Approach,* F. E. Peacock, Itasca, Ill., 1970.

Gordon, C. Wayne, and Leta McKinney Adler: *Dimensions of Teacher Leadership in Classroom Social Systems,* University of California, Los Angeles, 1963.

Gow, J. Steele, B. Holzner, and W. Pendelton: "Economic, Social and Political Forces," *The Changing American School,* part II, Yearbook of the National Society for the Study of Education, 1966.

Griffiths, Daniel E.: "Board-Superintendent-Teacher Relations: Viable Alternatives to the Status Quo," *Struggle for Power in Education,* edited by Frank W. Lutz and Joseph Azzarelli, The Center for Applied Research in Education, New York, 1966.

Gross, Bertram M.: "The Scientific Approach to Administration," *Behavioral Science and Educational Administration,* Sixty-third Yearbook, National Society for the Study of Education, University of Chicago Press, Chicago, 1964.

Hall, D. M.: *Dynamics of Group Discussion,* Interstate Printers & Publishers, Danville, Ill., 1961.

Halpin, Andrew W., and Don B. Croft: *The Organizational Climate of Schools,* Midwest Administration Center, The University of Chicago Press, Chicago, 1963.

Hare, Paul, Edgar Borgatta, and Robert Bales: *Small Groups—Studies of Social Interaction,* Knopf, New York, 1955.

Heintz, Ray, and Malcolm Preston: "Effects of Participatory vs. Supervisory Leadership on Group Judgment," *Group Dynamics,* edited by Dorwin Cartwright and Alvin Zander, Harper & Row, New York, 1953.

Helmar, Olaf: *Social Technology,* Basic Books, New York, 1966.

Herndon, Terry: "The Future of Negotiations for Teachers," *The Collective Dilemma: Negotiations in Education,* edited by Patrick W. Carlton and Harold I. Goodwin, Charles A. Jones, Worthington, Ohio, 1969.

Isaac, S., and W. B. Michael: *Handbook in Research and Evaluation,* Robert R. Knath, San Diego, 1971.

Jackson, Philip W.: *Life in Classrooms,* Holt, Rinehart & Winston, New York, 1968.

Jaques, Elliott: *The Changing Culture of a Factory,* Redwood Press, London, 1970.

Johnson, Carmen M.: "The Effects of Analyzing Instruction on the Classroom Performance of Teachers," unpublished doctoral dissertation, University of California, Los Angeles, 1970.

Katz, Daniel, M. Maccoby, and N. C. Morse: *Productivity, Supervision and Morale in an Office Situation,* Survey Research Center, University of Michigan, Ann Arbor, 1950.

———, and Robert L. Kahn: "Leadership Practices in Relation to Productivity and Morale," *Group Dynamics,* edited by Dorwin Cartwright and Alvin Zander, Harper & Row, New York, 1953.

Katz, Michael: *Class, Bureaucracy and Schools, The Illusion of Change in America,* Praeger, New York, 1971.

Kelley, Harold H., and John W. Thibaut: "Group Problem-Solving," *Handbook of Social Psychology,* vol. 4, edited by Gardner Lindzey and Elliot Aronson, Addison-Wesley, Reading, Mass., 1969, pp. 1–101.

Knowles, Malcolm, and Hulda Knowles: *How To Develop Better Leaders,* Association Press, New York, 1955.

Lessinger, Leon M.: *Every Kid a Winner: Accountability in Education,* Simon & Schuster, New York, 1970.

Lewin, W. P., Ronald Lippitt, and Ralph White: "Leader Behavior and Member Reaction in Three Social Climates," *Group Dynamics,* edited by Dorwin Cartwright and Alvin Zander, Harper & Row, New York, 1968.

Lieberman, Myron: "Education and Accountability," paper presented to the Mid-Atlantic Interstate Project Conference on Educational Accountability, New York, February 1972.

———: "Implications of the Coming NEA-AFT Merger," *The Collective Dilemma: Negotiations in Education,* edited by Patrick W. Carlton and Harold I. Goodwin, Charles A. Jones, Worthington, Ohio, 1969.

———: *When School Districts Bargain,* part I, Public Personnel Association, Chicago, 1969.

Likert, Rensis: *The Human Organization,* McGraw-Hill, New York, 1967.

Lindgren, Henry: *Effective Leadership in Human Relations,* Hermitage House, New York, 1954.

Lippitt, Ronald, et al.: "The Teacher as Innovator, Seeker and Sharer of New Practices," *Perspectives on Educational Change,* edited by R. I. Miller, Appleton-Century-Crofts, New York, 1967

Lortie, Dan: "Teacher Socialization—The Robinson Crusoe Model," *The Real World of the Beginning Teacher*, report of the Nineteenth National Commission of Teacher Education and Professional Standards (NCTEPS), NEA, Washington, 1966.

Mager, Robert: *Preparing Instructional Objectives*, Fearon, Palo Alto, Calif., 1962.

McCloskey, Gordon: *Education and Public Understanding*, Harper & Row, New York, 1959.

McGregor, Douglas: *The Human Side of Enterprise*, McGraw-Hill, New York, 1961.

McNeil, John D.: *Toward Accountable Teachers: Their Appraisal and Improvement*, Holt, Rinehart & Winston, New York, 1971.

Miles, Matthew: *The Development of Innovative Climates in Educational Organizations*, research note, Stanford Research Institute, Menlo Park, Calif., April 1969.

————: "Some Properties of Schools as Social Systems," *Change in School Systems*, edited by Goodwin Watson, Cooperative Project for Educational Development (COPED), NEA, 1967.

Musgrove, Frank, and Philip H. Taylor: *Society and the Teacher's Role*, Routledge and Kegan Paul, London, 1969.

National Education Association: *The Elementary Principalship in 1968*, Department of Elementary School Principals, Washington, 1968, p. 25.

————: *Facts on File*, 1970.

National Training Laboratory: *Standards for the Use of Laboratory Methods*, Washington, 1969.

Oettinger, Anthony G.: *Run, Computer, Run, The Mythology of Educational Innovation*, Harvard, Cambridge, Mass., 1970.

Perry, Charles R., and Wesley A. Wildman: *The Impact of Negotiations in Public Education*, Charles A. Jones, Worthington, Ohio, 1970.

Peterson, O. F.: *Leadership in Action*, National Training Laboratory, Washington, 1961.

Petrullo, Luigi, and Bernard M. Bass: *Leadership and Interpersonal Behavior*, Holt, Rinehart & Winston, New York, 1961.

Plowman, Paul D.: *Behavioral Objectives*, Science Research Associates, Chicago, 1971.

Popham, W. James: *Criterion-Referenced Measurement*, Educational Technology Publications, Princeton, N.J., 1971.

Proceedings of the Conference on Educational Accountability, sponsored by Educational Testing Service, Chicago, June 1971.

Quinn, James: "Planning for Accountability in Education: Issues, Problems, Directions," unpublished paper, Insgroup, Inc., 5855 Naples Plaza, Long Beach, Calif. 90803.

Rasmussen, Roger: "Alternative Means of Analyzing the COPED Meetings Questionnaire to Measure Participants' Perceptions of School Faculty Meetings," unpublished paper, |I|D|E|A| Research Division, Los Angeles, 1972.

Schmuck, Richard A., and Philip J. Runkel: *Organizational Training for a School Faculty*, Center for the Advanced Study of Educational Administration, University of Oregon, Eugene, Ore., 1970.

Seldon, David: "Winning Collective Bargaining," *Collective Negotiations in Public Education*, edited by Stanley M. Elam, Myron Lieberman, and Michael H. Moskow, Rand McNally, Chicago, 1967.

Selvin, Hanan C.: *The Effects of Leadership*, Free Press of Glencoe, New York, 1960.

Shepard, R. N.: "On Subjectively Optimum Selections Among Multi-Attribute Alternatives," *Human Judgments and Optimality*, edited by Maynard W. Shelley and G. L. Bryan, Wiley, New York, 1964, pp. 257–281.

Stogdill, Ralph M., and Alvin E. Coons: *Leader Behavior: Its Description and Measurement*, research monograph, Ohio State University Press, 1957.

Stufflebeam, Daniel L.: "Evaluation as Enlightenment for Decision-Making," *Improving Educational Assessment and an Inventory of Measures of Affective Behavior*, edited by W. H. Beatty, NEA, Washington, 1969.

Thelen, Herbert, and Dorothy Stock: *Understanding How Groups Work*, Adult Education Association, Chicago, 1956.

Tye, Kenneth A.: "Educational Accountability in an Era of Change," paper presented to the White House Conference on Education, St. Louis, February 1970.

Waller, Willard: *The Sociology of Teaching*, Wiley, New York, 1965.

Walton, Richard E., and Robert B. McKersie: *A Behavioral Theory of Labor Negotiations*, McGraw-Hill, New York, 1965.

Webb, Eugene, et al.: *Unobtrusive Measures, Nonreactive Research in the Social Sciences*, Rand McNally, Chicago, 1966.

Webb, Harold: "The National School Boards Association and Collective Negotiations," *Collective Negotiations in Public Education*, edited by Stanley M. Elam, Myron Lieberman, and Michael H. Moskow, Rand McNally, Chicago, 1967.

Weick, Karl E.: *The Social Psychology of Organizing*, Addison-Wesley, Reading, Mass., 1969.

Williams, Richard C.: "Teacher Militancy: Implications for the School," *Social and Technological Change: Implications for Education,* edited by Philip K. Piele, Terry L. Eidell, and Stuart C. Smith, Center for Advanced Study of Educational Administration, Eugene, Ore., 1970.

Williams, Richard C., Charles C. Wall, W. Michael Martin, and Arthur Berchin: *Effecting Organizational Renewal in Schools,* McGraw-Hill, New York, 1973.

Young, Charles R.: "The Superintendent of Schools in a Collective Bargaining Milieu," *The Collective Dilemma: Negotiations in Education,* edited by Patrick W. Carlton and Harold I. Goodwin, Charles A. Jones, Worthington, Ohio, 1969.

Periodicals

Abelson, M., et al.: "Planning Education for the Future: Comments on a Pilot Study," *American Behavioral Scientist,* 1967, p. 10.

Bales, Robert F., and Fred L. Strodtbeck: "Phases in Group Problem-Solving," *Journal of Abnormal and Social Psychology,* vol. 46, 1951, pp. 485–495.

Becker, Howard S.: "The Teacher in the Authority System," *Journal of Educational Sociology,* vol. 27, 1953, pp. 128–141.

Blanchard, Kenneth, and Paul Hersey: "Change and the Use of Power," *Training and Development Journal,* vol. 26, no. 1, January 1972.

Bridges, Edwin M., J. Wayne and David J. Mahan: "Effects of Hierarchical Differentation of Group Productivity, Efficiency, and Risk Taking," *Administrative Science Quarterly,* vol. 13, no. 2, September 1968.

Briner, Conrad: "Administration and Accountability," *Theory into Practice,* vol. 8, October 1969.

Campbell, J. P., and M. Dunnette: "Effectiveness of T-Group Experiences in Managerial Training and Development," *Psychological Bulletin,* vol. 70, 1968, pp. 73–104.

Changing Schools, a publication of the League of Cooperating Schools, Institute for Development of Educational Activities, vols. I through V, edited by Carmen Johnson.

Coleman, Peter, and Herbert A. Wallin: "A Rationale for Differentiated Staffing," *Interchange,* vol. 2, no. 3, 1971, p. 29.

Cunningham, Luvern: "Hey Man, You Our Principal? Urban Education as I Saw It," *Phi Delta Kappan,* vol. 51, November 1969, pp. 123–128.

Dyer, Henry S.: "Guidelines for Drawing Accountability Boundaries," *Nation's Schools,* vol. 89, no. 5, May 1972.

Education Summary, vol. 23, no. 24, February 19, 1971. (Editorial note by Ben Brodinski.)

Elam, Stanley M.: "Prospects for an NEA-AFT Merger," *The Nation,* October 1965.

English, Fenwick, and James Zaharis: "Crisis in Middle Management," *NASSP Bulletin,* vol. 56, April 1972.

Etzioni, Amitai: "Human Beings Are Not Very Easy to Change After All," *Saturday Review,* June 3, 1972.

Evaluation Comment, vol. 2, no. 3, Center for the Study of Evaluation of Instructional Programs, University of California, Los Angeles, September 1970.

Fantini, Mario: "Options for Students, Parents, and Teachers: Public Schools of Choice," *Phi Delta Kappan,* May 1971, pp. 541–543.

Gag, D. "Judgment Analysis for Assessing Doctoral Admission Policies," *Journal of Experimental Education,* vol. 38, 1969, pp. 92–96.

Gibb, Cecil A.: "Principles and Traits of Leadership," *Journal of Abnormal and Social Psychology,* vol. 42, 1947, pp. 267–284.

Green, Thomas F.: "Schools and Communities: A Look Forward," *Harvard Educational Review,* Spring 1969, pp. 221–252.

Grobman, Hulda: "Accountability for What?: The Unanswered Question," *Nation's Schools,* vol. 89, no. 5, May 1972.

Harrison, Roger: "Choosing the Depth of Organizational Intervention," *Journal of Applied Behavioral Science,* vol. 6, 1970, pp. 181–202.

Hencley, Stephen P.: "Impediments to Accountability," *Administrator's Notebook,* vol. 20, no. 4, December 1971.

Hoffman, P. J., P. Slovic, and L. G. Rorer: "An Analysis of Variance Model for the Assessment of Configural Cue Utilization in Clinical Judgments," *Psychological Bulletin,* vol. 69, 1968, pp. 338–349.

Huff, R. J.: "Parochiaid: The Cry for Help Gets Louder," *Nation's Schools,* September 1969, pp. 16–24.

|I|D|E|A| *Reporter,* Winter Quarter, 1971.

Jacobsen, Stanley: "Principals Under Pressure," *National Elementary Principal,* vol. 47, no. 6, May 1968.

Janowitz, Morris: "Alternative Models of Institutional Change in the Slum School," *Phi Delta Kappan,* vol. 52, February 1971, pp. 334–337.

Jencks, Christopher: "Education Vouchers: Peril or Panacea," *Teachers College Record,* February 1971, pp. 327–404.

————: "Giving Parents Money for Schooling," *Phi Delta Kappan,* September 1970, pp. 49–54.

Killen, G. A.: "Federal Aid to Private and Parochial Schools: An Analysis," *NASSP Bulletin,* September 1970, pp. 88–100.

Klein, Stephen P.: "The Uses and Limitations of Standardized Tests in

Meeting the Demands for Accountability," *UCLA Evaluation Comment*, vol. 2, no. 4, January 1971.

Lennon, Roger T.: "To Perform and to Account," *Journal of Research and Development in Education*, vol. 5, no. 1, Fall 1971.

Lessinger, Leon M.: "Accountability in Public Education," *Today's Education*, vol. 59, no. 5, May 1970.

————: "A Historical Note on Accountability in Education," *Journal of Research and Development in Education*, vol. 5, no. 1, 1971.

————: "It's Time for Accountability in Education," *Nation's Business*, August 1971.

Lewin, Kurt: "Frontiers in Group Dynamics: Concept, Method and Reality in Social Science: Social Equilibria and Social Change," *Human Relations*, vol. I, no. 1, June 1947, pp. 5–41.

Lindblom, Charles: "The Science of Muddling Through," *Public Administration Review*, vol. 19, 1959, pp. 79–88.

Lipham, James M.: "Dynamics of the Principalship," *National Elementary Principal*, vol. 41, no. 4, January 1962.

Madden, George: "A Theoretical Basis for Differentiating Forms of Collective Bargaining in Education," *Educational Administration Quarterly*, vol. 10, no. 2, Spring 1969.

Martin, R., and C. Blasche: "Contracting for Educational Reform," *Phi Delta Kappan*, March 1971, pp. 403–6.

The National Elementary Principal, vol. 50, May 1971, "Sensitivity Training and the School Administrator: A Special Section," pp. 46–77.

Negotiations Research Digest, vol. 3, no. 5, January 1970.

————, vol. 5, no. 3, November 1971.

Novotney, Jerrold M.: "Training to Lead—A Rationale," *Journal of Business Education*, January 1967.

Phi Delta Kappan, "8 Articles on Accountability," December 1970.

Popham, W. James: "Found: A Practical Procedure to Appraise Teacher Achievement in the Classroom," *Nation's Schools*, vol. 89, no. 5, May 1972.

Rose, Gale W.: "Organizational Behavior and Its Concomitants in Schools," *Administrator's Notebook*, vol. 17, March 1967, p. 7.

Saretsky, Gary: "Every Kid a Hustler," *Phi Delta Kappan*, June 1971, pp. 595–596.

Schwartz, Ron: "Accountability, Special Report," *Nation's Schools*, vol. 85, no. 6, June 1970.

Seldon, David: "Productivity, Yes. Accountability, No.," *Nation's Schools*, vol. 89, no. 5, May 1972.

Slovic, P.: "Analyzing the Expert Judge: A Descriptive Study of a Stockbroker's Decision Process," *Journal of Applied Psychology,* vol. 53, 1969, pp. 255–263.

Stake, Robert E.: "The Countenance of Educational Evaluation," *Teachers College Record,* vol. 68, 1967.

Stenner, J.: "Four Approaches to Education Performance Contracts," *Educational Leadership,* April 1971, pp. 721–725.

Stogdill, R. M.: "Personal Factors Associated with Leadership: A Survey of the Literature," *Journal of Psychology,* vol. 25, 1948.

Tyler, Ralph W.: "General Statement on Evaluation," *Journal of Educational Research,* 1942.

APPENDIX A

Part 1 Teacher Questionnaire on Principal Leadership

Code Number _____

Grade Level _____

Number of Years in this School _____

All information contained in this questionnaire is confidential. Scores on these questions will be analyzed in terms of what the entire staff agrees upon.

We are concerned with how things get done in your school, who makes decisions, and *in general,* how you see your principal's role in regard to the functioning of the school.

INSTRUCTIONS: Below are some questions about how principals and teachers work in a school. Please choose the answer that describes the way things are *usually* done in this school.

1 Does the principal talk about administrative procedures or about educational problems at faculty meetings?

_____1 Talks mostly about administrative procedures.

_____2 Talks about administrative procedures, but sometimes about educational problems.

_____3 Talks mostly about educational problems.

2 Does the principal provide for and make use of a professional library which relates instruction to new ideas, practices, and procedures?

_____1 He rarely provides or makes use of a professional library.

_____2 He provides a professional library and occasionally makes use of new ideas, practices, and procedures.

_____3 He provides and makes specific use of the professional library for new ideas, practices and procedures.

3 Does the principal arrange times for you to meet with staff members on mutual problems?

_____1 He rarely arranges time.

_____2 He sometimes arranges time.

_____3 He almost always arranges time.

4   Does the principal take or send teachers to visit schools where they are practicing new methods and procedures?

_____1   He rarely takes or sends us.

_____2   He sometimes takes or sends us.

_____3   He almost always takes us, when possible.

5   Does the principal help provide the necessary resources you need to achieve your educational goals, or are you left to your own devices?

_____1   I hardly ever get any help.

_____2   I get some help, but not as much as I need.

_____3   I get all the help I need.

6   Does the principal interview new staff members and tell them they will be working in a school using ideas, methods, and practices in keeping with our changing society?

_____1   The principal rarely orients new teachers by telling them they are expected to try new approaches.

_____2   The principal sometimes orients new teachers by telling them they are expected to try new approaches.

_____3   The principal almost always orients new teachers by telling them they are expected to try new approaches.

7   Does the principal attend professional meetings and workshops and make use of information by initiating activities in the staff?

_____1   He rarely attends or makes use of the information received.

_____2   He attends and sometimes makes use of the information received.

_____3   He attends and almost always makes use of information received.

8   Does the principal show that he is knowledgeable about changes in educational practices by his participation in staff meetings, task groups, or individual conferences?

_____1   The principal lacks familiarity with changes in educational practices.

_____2   The principal occasionally shows familiarity with educational practices by references to new developments.

_____3   The principal almost always shows familiarity by references and application of new developments.

9 Does the principal show interest in new developments in education by his support for teachers' use of new ideas, methods, or procedures?

_____1 The principal rarely supports new ideas, methods, or procedures.

_____2 The principal sometimes supports new ideas, methods, or procedures.

_____3 The principal almost always supports new ideas, methods, or procedures.

10 Does the principal aid in the promotion of new ideas, methods, and procedures by using outside resource people or being a teacher of teachers himself?

_____1 The principal rarely uses outside resources or takes responsibility for teaching.

_____2 The principal sometimes uses outside resources and takes responsibility for teaching.

_____3 The principal almost always uses outside resources and takes responsibility by being a teacher of teachers.

11 When the principal has made up his mind about something, has he ever changed it when the teachers objected?

_____1 Hardly ever.

_____2 A few times when the teachers had good reasons.

_____3 Quite often, whether the teachers had good reasons or not.

_____4 Practically every time anyone objected.

12 How much direction does the principal give at faculty meetings?

_____1 The principal urges the faculty to accept his point of view.

_____2 The principal expresses his point of view but does not impose it on the faculty.

_____3 The principal lets a point of view emerge from the faculty.

13 When the principal asks teachers to do something they do not want to do, does he or does he not explain why they have to do it?

_____1 He almost always explains why.

_____2 He sometimes explains why.

_____3 He hardly ever explains why.

14 After the faculty has identified a problem area they want to work on, who usually decides who is to proceed?

_____1   The principal decides and tells us.

_____2   The principal listens to our ideas about it, and he decides.

_____3   The principal talks it over with us and helps us decide.

_____4   The principal lets us decide.

15   What kind of help does the principal give a team or group working on a particular problem?

_____1   The principal tells the group what to do and how to do it.

_____2   The principal tells the group what to do but lets the group decide how to do it.

_____3   The principal leaves it all up to the group.

16   Does the principal encourage orderly rooms and adherence to time schedules?

_____1   The principal cares very much about order and adherence to time schedules.

_____2   The principal sometimes cares about order and adherence to time schedules.

_____3   The principal rarely concerns himself about order and time schedules.

17   In a discussion about the use of new materials, new organizational plans, or new methods for teachers, who makes the decisions?

_____1   We usually do it the way the principal decides.

_____2   The principal and teachers decide together.

_____3   The principal expects the teachers to decide, but gives advice if we ask.

_____4   The teachers usually make the decision and tell the principal.

18   Does the principal make the school a place where you can not only teach effectively but also enjoy some personal satisfaction? (Such as faculty parties, a pleasant faculty lounge.)

_____1   Almost always tries to make the school enjoyable.

_____2   Sometimes tries to make the school enjoyable.

_____3   Practically never tries to make the school enjoyable.

19   Does the principal show that he dislikes teachers in the school or not?

_____1   Shows dislike for none of the teachers.

_____2   Shows dislike for a few teachers.

_____3   Shows dislike for some teachers.

_____4   Shows dislike for most teachers.

20 Does the principal make contacts with you in a way which makes you nervous and uncomfortable, or does he make contact in a helpful manner?

_____1   Just about always helpful.

_____2   Often helpful, but occasionally makes me uncomfortable.

_____3   Often makes me feel nervous and uncomfortable, but not always.

_____4   Just about always makes me nervous and uncomfortable.

21 Does the principal support promotion of the basic skills primarily, or does he also support teachers' ideas?

_____1   Supports primarily the basic skills.

_____2   Supports the basic skills, but sometimes teachers' ideas.

_____3   Supports teachers' ideas in all areas.

22 In this school, are you supposed to use the principal's ideas or your own ideas?

_____1   The principal makes available primarily his ideas as resources.

_____2   The principal makes available his ideas, but sometimes considers ideas of teachers.

_____3   The principal almost always considers teachers' ideas.

23 Does the principal show that he will help you with school work and other things you might want to talk to him about?

_____1   Neither with school work nor anything else.

_____2   With school work, but nothing else.

_____3   More with school work than other things.

_____4   About the same with school work and other things.

_____5   More with other things than school work.

24 Does the principal show that he likes teachers in this school or not?

_____1   Shows that he likes all teachers.

_____2   Shows he likes most teachers.

_____3   Shows he likes some teachers.

_____4   Shows he likes just a few teachers.

25 Is the principal usually fair or usually unfair when he decides things about teachers?

_____1 He is always fair.

_____2 He is usually fair.

_____3 He is fair to most teachers; a few are treated better, a few are treated worse.

_____4 He is unfair to most teachers.

26 Does the principal show evidence of more interest in your needs and satisfactions as a teacher, or is he more interested in your subject matter competence?

_____1 Shows little or no concern about subject matter or the needs and satisfactions of teachers.

_____2 Most interested in subject matter competence.

_____3 Most interested in subject matter competence, but sometimes in the needs and satisfactions of teachers.

_____4 More interested in the needs and satisfactions of teachers than in subject matter competence.

Part 2   Index of Teacher Morale and Professionalism

INSTRUCTIONS: Below is a list of some teacher activities and work methods. Please circle the answer that *most closely approximates* the way you feel these things occur amongst teachers in your school.

1   Almost always happens
2   Sometimes happens
3   Hardly ever happens
4   Never happens

Index of Morale

1	Teachers spend time before and after school planning with other teachers.	1	2	3	4
2	Teachers in this school feel a sense of pride in the school.	1	2	3	4
3	Teachers work cooperatively with their fellow teachers.	1	2	3	4
4	Teachers respect the judgment of the administrator of the school.	1	2	3	4
5	Even when official policy might be restrictive, teachers make arrangements to help each other.	1	2	3	4
6	Teachers share a common educational philosophy.	1	2	3	4
7	Teachers resent coming to extra meetings.	1	2	3	4

Index of Professionalism

1	Teachers give formal reports on meetings they have attended to other teachers.	1	2	3	4
2	Teachers in this school read educational journals and share these ideas with each other.	1	2	3	4
3	Teachers in this school attend summer workshops or institutes voluntarily.	1	2	3	4
4	Teachers in this school belong to teachers' professional organizations (other than CTA or AFT).	1	2	3	4

5	Teachers initiate meetings on educational problems.	1 2 3 4		
6	Research findings are used to help teachers in this school make decisions about the educational program.	1 2 3 4		
7	Teachers show their awareness of curricular changes by discussion and experimentation of new ideas.	1 2 3 4		

Part 3   Pupil Questionnaire on Teacher Leadership

School _____

Code Number _____

Grade Level _____

Age _____

Have you been in this class the whole semester?

Yes _____   No _____

INSTRUCTIONS: Below are some questions about how the teacher and pupils work in this class. Please try hard to choose the answer which describes best the way things are usually done in this class. Good classes are carried on in many different ways, and your answers will be different from the answers of pupils in other classes.

1   Are you given new work in arithmetic before you are able to get the right answers to the old work?

_____1   I am not given new kinds of arithmetic until I can do the old kind correctly.

_____2   I am sometimes given new kinds of arithmetic before I can do the old kind.

_____3   I am almost always given a new kind of arithmetic before I can do the old kind.

2   Does the teacher see to it that you complete all the written assignments or not?

_____1   Makes sure we complete practically all written assignments.

_____2   Sometimes makes sure we complete written assignments.

_____3   Hardly ever makes sure we complete written assignments.

3   Does this teacher go over a day's work with you again before going to the next lesson, or do you go on without reviewing?

_____1   Reviews every lesson (either at the end or the beginning).

_____2   Reviews most lessons.

_____3   Reviews some lessons but not regularly.

_____4   Hardly ever reviews lessons.

4   What does this teacher most often do when he is teaching the class something new and the pupils don't understand?

_____1   Tries to explain it again another way.

_____2   Gives the same explanation over again.

_____3   Moves on to something else even though we don't understand.

5   How often are you required to show the teacher (by writing or telling the answer to a question or a problem) that you understand what is being taught?

_____1   Several times every day.

_____2   Once every day.

_____3   Almost every day.

_____4   Several times a week.

_____5   Never.

6   When you have learned a certain kind of arithmetic, do you use it over again during the year or stop using it after you have taken up a different kind of problem?

_____1   Keep using a kind of arithmetic over and over again.

_____2   Keep using a kind of arithmetic sometimes after we have taken up a new kind.

_____3   Hardly ever use an old kind of arithmetic after we take up a new kind.

7   How are your papers usually corrected?

_____1   I don't know, papers aren't returned.

_____2   A grade or comment for the whole paper is given but all mistakes are not marked.

_____3   All mistakes are marked.

_____4   All mistakes are marked and we are shown how the work is wrong.

8   Do pupils have to get permission to leave their seats in this class or not?

_____1   We can never leave our seats without getting permission.

_____2   We can leave our seats without permission if we follow certain rules.

_____3   We can leave our seats without getting permission almost any time.

9   How much instruction does the teacher give a social studies committee?

———1   We never have social studies committees.

———2   The teacher tells the committee exactly *what* to do and *how* to do it.

———3   The teacher tells the committee *what* to do, but lets it decide *how* to do it.

———4   The teacher leaves almost everything up to the committee.

10   When the class starts a new social studies unit, who plans how you will do the work?

———1   We do it the way the teacher plans it.

———2   The teacher and the pupils plan it together.

———3   The teacher expects the pupils to work out a plan, but he gives advice if we ask him.

———4   The plan is entirely up to the pupils.

11   When the teacher has made up his mind about something, has he ever changed it when the pupils objected?

———1   Hardly ever.

———2   A few times when the pupils had good reasons.

———3   Quite often, whether the pupils had good reasons or not.

———4   Practically every time anyone objected.

12   What does the teacher do when he and the pupils disagree about some idea in social studies?

———1   Doesn't encourage pupils to express opinions.

———2   Lets pupils express their opinions but only sees his side.

———3   Lets pupils express their opinions and we look at both sides.

13   When the teacher asks pupils to do something they do not want to do, does he or does he not explain why they have to do it?

———1   He almost always explains why.

———2   He sometimes explains why.

———3   He hardly ever explains why.

14   How often would you say this teacher has changed assignments this year because the pupils objected to them?

———1   Hardly ever.

———2   A few times when the pupils had good reasons.

———3   Quite often, whether the pupils had good reasons or not.

———4   Practically every time anyone objected.

15   After you know *what* you are going to do in this class, who usually decides *how* you are going to do it?

_____1   The teacher decides and tells us.

_____2   The teacher listens to our ideas about it, but he decides.

_____3   The teacher talks it over with us, and helps us decide.

_____4   The teacher lets us decide.

16   How many committees have you been on this year in this class?

_____1   None.

_____2   One or two.

_____3   Three.

_____4   Four.

_____5   Five or more.

17   Does this teacher show that he wants to make the work interesting for the pupils or not?

_____1   Almost always interesting.

_____2   Sometimes interesting.

_____3   Not very interesting.

_____4   Practically never interesting.

18   Does the teacher ask you questions in a way which makes you nervous and uncomfortable about answering them, or does he ask you questions in a kind way?

_____1   Just about always kind.

_____2   Often kind, but occasionally makes me uncomfortable.

_____3   Often makes me feel nervous and uncomfortable, but not always.

_____4   Just about always makes me nervous and uncomfortable.

19   Does this teacher show that he dislikes pupils in the class or not?

_____1   Shows dislike for none of the pupils.

_____2   Shows dislike for a few pupils.

_____3   Shows dislike for some pupils.

_____4   Shows dislike for most pupils.

_____5   Shows dislike for everyone in the class.

20   Does this teacher try to make the class enjoyable for the pupils or not?

_____1 Almost always tries to make the class enjoyable.

_____2 Sometimes tries to make the class enjoyable.

_____3 Practically never tries to make the class enjoyable.

21 Does this teacher show that he likes pupils in this class or not?

_____1 Shows he likes all pupils.

_____2 Shows he likes most pupils.

_____3 Shows he likes some pupils.

_____4 Shows he likes just a few pupils.

_____5 Shows liking for none of the pupils.

22 Is this teacher usually fair or usually unfair when he decides things about pupils?

_____1 He is always fair.

_____2 He is usually fair.

_____3 He is fair to most pupils; a few are treated better, a few are treated worse.

_____4 He is unfair to most pupils.

23 Does this teacher help you with the work or let you get it for yourself?

_____1 I hardly get any help.

_____2 I get some help but not as much as I need.

_____3 I get all the help I need.

24 Does the teacher make sure you learn the facts, or is he more interested in how pupils feel about things?

_____1 Shows little or no concern about the facts or how we feel.

_____2 Just makes sure we learn the facts.

_____3 Makes sure we learn the facts but is sometimes interested in our feelings.

_____4 More interested in our feelings than in our learning the facts.

25 Does this teacher show that he will help you with school work and also help you with anything else you would like to talk to him about?

_____1 Neither with school work nor anything else.

_____2 With school work but nothing else.

_____3   More with school work than other things.

_____4   About the same with school work and other things.

26   Does this teacher give you credit for how well you do on your papers and tests or does he give you credit for trying and showing improvement?

_____1   Only for how well I do on papers and tests.

_____2   For how well I do on papers and tests and for trying and showing improvement.

_____3   For trying and improving whether I do well on papers and tests or not.

27   In this class are you supposed to use the teacher's ideas, the ideas in the book, or your own ideas?

_____1   We are supposed to use our own ideas *more* than the teacher's or those in the books.

_____2   We are supposed to use the teacher's ideas, the ideas in the books, and our own ideas.

_____3   We are only supposed to use the teacher's ideas and the ideas in the books.

The Criteria Instrument

INSTRUCTIONS This instrument contains a series of questions about various school practices. Read each statement and check the category (Never, Seldom, Sometimes, Frequently, Usually, or Always) which best describes the existence of this practice in your school. Check only one response for each statement. Please answer all questions, being certain to indicate *what actually exists in your school* rather than what you believe ought to exist. Your responses will be kept confidential.

In my school:

	Never	Seldom	Sometimes	Frequently	Usually	Always
1 Discussions include contributions by most of the members present.						
2 Staff meetings are generally reserved for matters concerned with curriculum, instruction, and school organization—not administrivia.						
3 Decisions are clearly communicated to all persons who are affected by the decision.						
4 Meetings are on time.						
5 The staff engages in discussions aimed at defining school goals.						
6 When a decision is made action is taken to implement it.						
7 Teachers make instructional decisions.						
8 The principal has the respect and good will of the students.						
9 Persons examine and/or experiment with several approaches before making a decision.						
10 Teachers visit other schools.						
11 Teachers read professional educational material.						
12 Anyone who is interested is encouraged to take the responsibility for implementing decisions.						

	Never	Seldom	Sometimes	Frequently	Usually	Always

In my school:

13 Teachers periodically visit other classrooms in the school.

14 The principal respects the teachers.

15 Meetings are such that members listen to each other.

16 Teachers can arrange to have their teaching critiqued by other teachers.

17 Each meeting is followed by a written memorandum that summarizes the proceedings of the meeting.

18 The principal knows his staff well.

19 Teachers attend conferences relative to their professional growth.

20 Many persons assume the leadership positions during group discussions, depending upon the function to be performed.

21 Both principal and teachers participate in making decisions which affect the school.

22 Meetings have an agenda composed of items that any member of the staff can suggest.

23 Teachers try to evaluate the extent to which school goals have been realized.

24 Issues and programs discussed by the staff are suggested by both teachers and principal.

25 Dialogue is appropriate to the problem confronted, for example, brainstorming when seeking new and imaginative ideas and task orientation when attempting to solve a particular problem.

26 Persons become familiar with the experiences of other schools before making a decision.

27 The principal encourages others to provide leadership.

	Never	Seldom	Sometimes	Frequently	Usually	Always

In my school:

28 Meetings involve only persons who need to be involved.

29 The principal encourages and assists the staff in developing goals for the school.

30 Actions can be modified to handle unanticipated situations.

31 Issues and programs discussed by the staff can be suggested by parents.

32 The principal communicates effectively with students.

33 Teachers work to implement the goals of the school.

34 Group decisions are reached by consensus.

35 Dialogue has a purpose.

36 Teachers critique each other's teaching.

37 Dialogue allows for in-depth discussion of issues that are pertinent to the education of children.

38 Decisions are made on the basis of school goals.

39 The principal utilizes resource persons from the district to help teachers.

40 The principal builds the status of his staff.

41 Issues and programs discussed by the staff can be suggested by the students.

42 Teachers attend courses at colleges and universities.

43 The principal shows that he appreciates his staff.

44 Responsibilities for carrying out actions are assumed by many different people on the staff.

45 Meetings are such that persons can engage in an open and frank discussion of issues.

In my school:

		Never	Seldom	Sometimes	Frequently	Usually	Always
46	Decisions are carried out with enthusiasm and good will.						
47	The principal communicates effectively with teachers.						
48	Actions are carried out with a high degree of organization and efficiency.						
49	When appropriate, the advice of district personnel is sought before a decision is made.						
50	Teachers experiment with new materials.						
51	The principal encourages the staff to visit other classrooms.						
52	The principal has the respect and good will of the teachers.						
53	Before a decision is made, the implications of alternative actions are thoroughly explored.						
54	There is a high degree of commitment on the part of people responsible for putting decisions into action.						
55	Group decisions are reached by voting.						
56	The principal respects the opinions and beliefs of teachers.						
57	Appropriate actions are taken based on the decisions made.						
58	Meetings are such that there is an interaction of teachers.						
59	The principal communicates effectively with the community.						
60	Persons read what scholars and informed practitioners have written on the subject and bring relevant ideas from their reading into the dialogue.						
61	The principal provides fair and equitable treatment for all.						

In my school:

		Never	Seldom	Sometimes	Frequently	Usually	Always
62	Teachers respect the opinions and beliefs of students.						
63	The principal promotes openness in his staff.						
64	Teachers evaluate their teaching in terms of achieving school goals.						
65	After an action has been taken, it is evaluated.						
66	Meetings can be called by both teachers and principal.						
67	The principal attends conferences relative to his professional growth.						
68	Teachers respect the opinions and beliefs of other teachers.